# Telling History

# Telling History

## A Manual for Performers and Presenters of First-Person Narratives

JOYCE M. THIERER

A Division of
ROWMAN & LITTLEFIELD PUBLISHERS, INC.
*Lanham • New York • Toronto • Plymouth, UK*

Published by AltaMira Press
A division of Rowman & Littlefield Publishers, Inc.
A wholly owned subsidary of The Rowman & Littlefield Publishing Group, Inc.
4501 Forbes Boulevard, Suite 200, Lanham, Maryland 20706
http://www.altamirapress.com

Estover Road, Plymouth PL6 7PY, United Kingdom

Copyright © 2010 by AltaMira Press

British Library Cataloguing in Publication Information Available

**Library of Congress Cataloging-in-Publication Data**
Thierer, Joyce M., 1949–
  Telling history : a manual for performers and presenters of first-person narratives / Joyce M. Thierer.
      p. cm. — (American Association for State and Local History book series)
   Includes bibliographical references and index.
   ISBN 978-0-7591-1306-0 (cloth : alk. paper) — ISBN 978-0-7591-1307-7 (pbk. : alk. paper) — ISBN 978-0-7591-1308-4 (electronic)
   1. Historical reenactments—United States—Handbooks, manuals, etc. 2. Historical reenactments—Handbooks, manuals, etc. 3. Historical drama, American—Handbooks, manuals, etc. 4. Historical drama—Handbooks, manuals, etc. 5. First person narrative—Handbooks, manuals, etc. 6. One-person shows (Performing arts)—Handbooks, manuals, etc. 7. Performing arts—Handbooks, manuals, etc. 8. United States—History—Methodology—Miscellanea. 9. United States—History, Local—Miscellanea. 10. History—Methodology—Miscellanea. I. Title.
   E175.7.T45 2010
   792.09—dc22

                                                                              2009023943

∞ ™ The paper used in this publication meets the minimum requirements of American National Standard for Information Sciences—Permanence of Paper for Printed Library Materials, ANSI/NISO Z39.48-1992.
Printed in the United States of America

# Contents

# Introduction, or, "Read before Dissembling and the Story of This Book"

I DID not label this section "Preface" because many people skip prefaces, and I really want to communicate briefly to as many as possible of my readers, or prospective readers. I thought about entitling it "Read before Assembling," but I am confident that a large number of you are hands-on learners, people like me who look at the instruction book only as a last resort. If you have even read this far perhaps it was because I found a title that intrigued you. More on dissembling later.

There are two things that I want to impart very quickly before getting on to the circumstances of the nascence of this book: first, that I am qualified to write it, and, secondly, that I anticipate a wide range of readers. I am an independent scholar-performer and entrepreneur as well as a university professor. I am the founder of Ride into History, a historical performance touring troupe that has performed from the Smithsonian to Saipan, and from Minnesota to Texas. I have been on juried rosters of state and regional humanities and arts organizations. I have given workshops to close to a thousand people aged eight to ninety. Those workshops were sponsored by museums, libraries, humanities councils, schools, art commissions, city and county governments, and regional and state tourism organizations. I have consulted with museums and historic sites. I have taught college history for over twenty years and public history for ten of those. I have presented academic papers and panel discussions at national public history conferences, national and state history conferences, and state and regional museum conferences. Having accomplished so much, I now look forward to sharing with you what I've learned along the trail. In fact, look for my trail stories along the way.

Secondly, I want to say quickly that I recognize that readers of this book will have differing goals. You will likely want to skip over parts of the book and focus on others. I want you to know that this will not hurt my feelings one bit. In fact, it is as I intended. With that in mind, the following is my advice on what parts to read, depending on what you want to get from it.

Public history and museum studies students will want to read the entire book. You will want to understand the methodologies and theories, the big picture. You will also want to know how historical performance can be used by history organizations, and how to create a historical performance yourself, to be as marketable as possible and have a hands-on understanding of historical performance.

Likewise, teachers of public historians and trainers of historical performers will want to read the entire book. Contact me at Ride into History (ridehist@ satelephone.com) for permission to make copies of worksheets—and just to network.

If you want to learn to create and perform a first-person narrative, or are already doing so and want some help bumping it up a level—you are a reenactor who wants to work solo, an actor who wants to contribute to history learning, a museum volunteer or staff member who wants to enhance the experience of visitors, or a teacher who wants to use historical performance to better teach students—if this feels like you, you will especially want to read chapters 1 through 5 in order to get an overview of historical performance and learn how to create a performance that is both accurate and entertaining. Teachers, check out the eighth chapter, too, because it has a lot of good material about youngsters. If you want to become a professional, an independent entrepreneur, and take one or more historic figures on the road and be paid to reach a wide range of audiences, then in addition to the first five chapters, the sixth chapter, which explores how to turn performance into a business, will interest you.

Staff members in charge of programming, people who want to enhance the experience of visitors to their museum, historic site, or community but do not anticipate actually doing the performances themselves will find chapter 1, with its explanations of the differences between types of costumed interpretation, and chapter 8, with a sense of the direction of historical performance, to be quite useful. Specifically for you, though, is chapter 7, "Enhancing Museums and Historic Sites with Historical Performance." Among other things, chapter 7 explains what you can (and should) expect from a professional historical performer. It speaks to organizations that want to put together a site-specific or traveling troupe, onetime or ongoing, such as a Chautauqua. I might not know your site, but I have enough experience with many different sites to offer something that will be of use to you. I hope that I spark in you the desire to apply historical performance to your own needs and desires to tell history's stories.

And, finally, there are those of you who have heard some of our "trail stories," the anecdotes that rise with the dust from the roads we have traveled and get shaken out during post-performance discussions, around campfires, or at gatherings of friends and family, and said that we should publish these tales. You might want me to autograph the title page before you skim chapter 1, read the trail stories we have inserted in boxes in all of the chapters, and skim chapter 8. And then, maybe you will decide that you would like to try your hand at creating a first-person narrative, after all, and go back to chapter 2, "How to Choose a Historic Figure to Portray."

That's the end of my how-to-use-this-book section, except to say, "No dissembling allowed, of course." That was just to get your attention (and maybe to have you blow the dust off your dictionary because you did not really believe that I said what I did). Historical performers must be as accurate as possible, and you can read more about that in the rest of this book. So now, a little about my commitment to telling history, and how this book came to be.

I am a very fortunate individual. I am an academic historian who loves classroom teaching while also, within that academic framework, being able to answer a calling to share history with the public. That calling to shout about history from the rooftops has led me to historic performance, and my passion for historic performance has led me to share my knowledge here.

My career as an academic historian began in the fall of 1984. That was the semester I discovered that I loved to teach. I was working on my master's degree in history at Emporia State University (ESU). ESU did not usually allow students to take full responsibility for classes. I had, however, been a tenured academic librarian at two other institutions, so I was not much of a risk. My intent was to return to libraries after completing this second master's degree (the first was an MLS). My intent changed radically, however, after I experienced an epiphany in the front of the classroom. I had a contribution to make—I had knowledge that my students needed, and even, in many cases, wanted. We had formed a community of learners with the luxury of forty-five hours in which to investigate the "Cultures of the Great Plains." Together we had explored the geography of the Plains. My identity as a teacher started with "Indians," and really hit me during the seventh class meeting as we tackled "Women on the Plains." My mantle of authority was of pure velvet; I knew everything, it seemed—or at least enough to answer every one of their questions. I went home and proclaimed, "I love to teach!" Thus it was that I became committed to earning a doctorate so that I could continue to share my knowledge in the college classroom.

Long before my classroom epiphany, however, I had experienced a similar mantle of authority on my family's farm. From the late 1960s until 1981, my parents invited the world to Molasses Days, their annual living history festival. Every fall for over twenty years, no matter where I lived, I went home to cut cane in the fields, dust artifacts in our museum, harness my horse to the cane press, direct traffic in the parking lot, and answer questions asked by thousands of visitors. I gained a sense of mission, but not one of vocation. Molasses Days ended with the illness and death of my mother.

The year after my mother's death I discovered the potential link between my parents' passion for educating the public and my declared passion for teaching history. The second epiphany came during my Museum/Archives Internship at Little Bighorn Battlefield National Monument during July of 1985. My first battle talk was outside the visitor's center overlooking a portion of the battlefield in 102 degree heat. I was to describe the entire battle in twenty minutes and then take "any and all questions and treat them with respect." The questions seemed to go on forever, which I interpreted as a sign that I had not been clear and concise in my message. I was a Great Plains farm girl who never sweated, not even throwing hay in the loft in August. But I was sweating. Soon I realized, though, as audience members uncrossed their arms and leaned forward, that I had rapport with them. They trusted me because I knew what I was talking about. Of course, it helped my confidence that my park ranger mentor was smiling and nodding on the sidelines. One audience member was an academic historian with an expertise in the Indian Wars. I would not have known this had he not come up and talked with me about the role of mustangs and American horses in the battle, and the role of horse fatigue. As an agricultural historian and horse owner I was well qualified to help him with his research. I had the respect of a professional historian. According to the written visitor evaluations, though, most of my audience had been families on vacation. For a few it was their primary destination, but for most it was one of several stops. I learned that there was a wide audience for good, sound historical research delivered in an engaging manner. I took slides of the battlefield, and when I was back in Kansas I gave a talk for our fledgling Phi Alpha Theta history honorary. I took that talk to various local groups. I never knew when there would be serious Custer historians in the audience, or what other deep knowledge existed within audience members, so I always treated my audiences with respect.

Sometime around then I discovered that my major professor, Tom Isern, was not only teaching history in the classroom and mentoring graduate students through the research and writing of theses but also taking history out to the public, primarily through Kansas Humanities Council programs. I had not fully appreciated that the first class I taught was funded as part of a National Endowment for the Humanities grant, but it soon became evident that much of the synergy in our department in the 1980s came from grant-funded opportunities, opportunities that brought the academy and the broader community together.

Having been raised on a farm near a rural town of about two thousand, Tom was an ardent proponent of taking history to the people whose families had made history. He helped them appreciate that like their ancestors they, too, were making the decisions that are the stuff of history. He found in me a kindred soul, one who knew that the knowledge of rural people was deep. Like Tom, what I was able to do was to put that knowledge into historical context, to talk about aurochs to people familiar with modern and recent breeds of cattle. He tapped me to work on several projects funded by the National Endowment for the Humanities (NEH) and the Kansas Humanities Council (KHC, then Kansas Council of the Humanities), which sends scholars with advanced degrees in the humanities as consultants for the public on local projects, including preserving and sharing their stories.

In the spring of 1989, Tom, then chair of social sciences, tapped me to deliver a lecture to a KHC-funded Secondary School Teacher Seminar the next summer. When it was discovered that the other lecturer would not be available, I was asked to deliver another lecture. (That was the summer, and the audience for which, my interpretation of Calamity Jane was born—but more on that later.)

KHC also provided primary funding for the Kansas Chautauqua. Two years later, while I was working on my doctorate and teaching at Kansas State University, I took over for Tom as the "stand-up historian" for the Kansas Chautauqua. Every week for four weeks we educated and entertained a different small-town Kansas audience. My job was to prepare the audience by putting the upcoming historic figure into historical context, to tie past, present, and future together, and to repeat questions raised by the public and rephrase them in a manner that, say, Dwight Eisenhower, having no knowledge of 1990 events, could interpret.

In many ways I was becoming my mentor, which was not a bad thing at all.

Historians refer to their "methodologies." To a large extent that has meant the methodologies of research. Sometimes methodologies have been controversial. For instance, material culture historians, who study such artifacts as photographs, quilts, and ledger art, have debated traditionalists who insist that the written word is the only valid historical source. But methodology also refers to the means by which historical research is shared, and with whom. Traditionalists prefer the printed word, preferably in publications—journals and weighty tomes—read only by other historians. Many of these same academic historians harbor deep within their breasts a desire to be the talking head on a PBS documentary, to be recognized by not only their peers but also the public as THE expert in their subject area. To become a Household Name. To be Famous. But not to have to deal directly with the public.

On the other hand, I, and many other academics, glory in the public. We love their challenging questions, their insistence that we make our knowledge relevant to their lives. We love it when a new student introduces himself by saying that his grandmother who lives two hundred miles away in Garden City (or Jetmore or Oakley) says to tell me hello, and how much she learned from my lecture on fences, and that she is sure he will enjoy my class.

For two decades the author of this book has been known to a wide variety of audiences as Calamity Jane. The first decade went along well enough with the formation of Ride into History, a peak year average of two performances a week, and being inducted onto the Kansas Humanities Council's rigorously juried History Alive! roster. Then, about the time that people were telling Ride into History that we were not only scholars but also theater, and Ride into History was selected for the Kansas Arts Commission's Kansas Touring Program, I began to fret.

Calamity Jane was being booked into many outdoor festivals. Those festivals were the source of much of my fretting. I fretted because Western-themed festivals had one role for women: that of saloon floozy. While my interpretation of Calamity Jane refuted that stereotype, it was uncomfortable to be the only exception. I fretted because I saw people dressed in gorgeous, historically correct clothing who were unable to discuss the historic context of that clothing. I fretted because I saw reenactors who refused to step out of their role to answer audience questions.

The straw that broke the camel's back was an event at historic Fort Hays in Kansas. Having arrived early for a Calamity Jane performance, I eagerly looked forward to learning some local history. Buses were arriving with school children who were to go from station to station. I found a former student, now teacher, and asked if I could make the rounds with some of her fourth graders; she agreed to my request. The teacher had cleverly set the children up to be reporters. Before they set out, she had them all salute her with their stenographer tablets and pencils, to make sure they were prepared to ask and record questions at each station. The children eagerly scattered with their assigned small groups, heading toward various stations to see costumed interpreters.

My group's first station was a man in full cowboy regalia with a saddle at his feet. He told the children, "I'm a cowboy. I have a gun. And I shoot it." It was much too short an account, and the children did not know what to do with so little information. They could not even ask follow-up questions because they did not know enough to be able to follow up. They looked at each other, at him, then at the parent with them. Should they move on? The whistle had not yet blown to signal a shift to the next location. They looked at their notepads and again at him. Everyone was uncomfortable. I asked the cowboy to tell the youngsters about his saddle. He replied, "It's a saddle." Unable to resist a teachable moment, I crouched down and showed the children how it was an A-frame saddle, characteristic of a day when horses had high, narrow withers, and how one could look for the maker's mark on the saddle, just as cars had maker's names. I also called attention to the cowboy's bandana and explained how many uses it had, everything from keeping trail dust out of one's respiratory system to being a potholder when taking a skillet off the fire. We dissected all of his garb and gear. I was pleased when, after the whistle blew and we moved on, I heard the "cowboy" share some of this information with his next group.

I remember feeling relief because our next station was a soldier. After all, we were at a fort, and the young man should have good stories about daily life. Instead, this performance was a mirror of the first: "I am a soldier. I have a gun, and I shoot it." If he knew more, he was not able to share it with the young reporters. Again I helped the youngsters by describing his accoutrements, from the kepi on his head to his McClellan saddle.

The third station was a gorgeously attired "Young Buffalo Bill Cody" who, I knew, had won prizes as a look-alike. In addition to his rifle, he had real buffalo parts (a hide and bones) and convincing reproductions of meat hanging on a drying rack. He bragged in first person about his hunting acumen and talked in third person about buffalo hunting, moving back and forth in a manner I found confusing. He did not encourage questions, and few were asked. As the students were leaving, however, one hung back to ask a special question, "What about your son Kit? Were you sad when he died?" "Cody" brusquely replied, "I don't have any children," and walked briskly away from him. The child tried to tell him that he had read a book about Buffalo Bill, and it said he had a son named Kit who died, but "Cody" would not respond. I realized that "Cody" was refusing to step out of his selected time period, when Kit was not even on the horizon, but what he was doing was not fair when only one player in the performer-audience dyad knew the rules to the game. I was able to explain this problem of chronology to the child, but I could not explain why "Cody" had not been generous enough to his young audience to step out of character and explain it himself. If he had done so he might have learned as I did that the answer was important to the youngster because his own name was Kit, and his father had recently died. His teacher had told him that he would have the opportunity to have his questions about another Kit's relationship with his father answered on that day in that place. He had hoped to find a father who might understand a son's grief. I was beyond fretting; I was furious.

That evening when, still angry, I recounted that story over the telephone to my partner, Ann Birney (aka Amelia Earhart), it clicked into place with other costumed historical interpretations that had failed to live up to my expectations. After considerable ranting and raving on my part, I conceded that the only ethical response was to try to make historical performance better. Okay, the truth: at first I balked, "Train the competition??" Ride into History, while mission driven, is a for-profit partnership. I did not have a tenure-track position, and so financial success was important. It would seem that the fewer people who were doing well what I did well, the better business would be. Ann, however, helped me understand that anyone's bad performance would decrease the likelihood that presenters would risk sponsoring another historical performance, for fear that it, too, would not deliver. And I have had many opportunities since then to say that she was right. It was a big task we had ahead of us, but we formed a not-for-profit organization, the Ride into History Cultural and Educational Project, Inc., and looked for opportunities to improve historical performance. A dandy soon presented itself.

Before that straw broke the back of the camel, Mary Lou McPhail of the Kansas Department of Commerce's Travel and Tourism Division had encouraged us to write an Attraction Development Grant. We had protested that we were not an attraction, per se, but she seemed confident that we had a contribution to make once we figured out what it was and how to articulate it. With our new calling to train historical performers we finally understood what we had to offer. We promised that we would not only do training but also raise museum and historic site awareness of the availability of historical performers, and help museums and historic sites understand the potential of historical performance.[1] We even wrote into the grant a carrot that would entice Young Buffalo Bill Cody to the workshop.[2] The grant provided a trajectory that continues today as twice a year we provide workshops for the general public in our studio, and for museums and historic sites at their homes.

The grant funded the creation of http://www.historicperformance.com, the website that has become the home of the Kansas Alliance of Professional Historical Performers, an organization that evolved when attendees of the first workshop kept showing up at subsequent workshops, wanting to develop and market their work with other historical performers. And the synergy even inspired the creation of Emporia State University's public history courses.

Following my presentation on "A Family Farm Diversifies: An Early Model of Living History" at the National Council on Public History in Ottawa, Canada, in 2001, I exchanged cards with an AltaMira Press representative at her booth. The next year she approached me at the Organization of American Historians conference in Washington, D.C., where I had talked on "Teaching Undergraduates" in a panel on Pedagogy and Praxis. It might have been the title of Ann Birney's paper on that same panel ("Jesus Had a Rhinestone in Her Nose") that caught her attention, but she asked if I had considered writing a book. At that time I was far too busy, but I began tossing ideas into a box labeled "AltaMira Press Book," and had Ann do the same.

This book is the work of a very fortunate academic historian who teaches and practices public history. Much of my good fortune is the result of collaborations with and support from many, many individuals and organizations, some of whom I have mentioned above. In addition, I would like to thank the generous board of the Ride into History Cultural and Educational Project, Inc., for providing workshop support, and my academic home, Emporia State University, for a summer Research and Creativity grant to visit museums and historic sites that use costumed interpretation. Along the way, Wendy Jones, head of Museum and Education Programs for the Minnesota History Center; Ken Bubp, chief operations officers of Conner Prairie; and Jan Milroy, volunteer coordinator at Iowa's Living History Farms, were especially generous with their time and explanations.

As is probably the case with most such focused endeavors as this book, friends and relatives have patiently listened to me apologize for giving my attention to the book instead of to them. My brother's birthday celebration will be delayed. The café in Admire has not seen me for weeks, and the Admire PRIDE organization has had to muddle along without me.

Several friends and professionals were particularly generous with their time. Librarian, friend, and former colleague Jean Hatfield spent most of one night brainstorming the book's prospectus revision. Park University Library director Gail Ann Schultis, there for me from the beginning of it all, volunteered to take her red pencil to this manuscript. Grady Atwater, site director for Kansas State Historical Society's John Brown Museum and Historic Site, read and commented on the manuscript. Loren Pennington (aka Dwight Eisenhower and Governor Alfred Landon), a major force in Emporia State University's creation

xvi                                                       INTRODUCTION

of the Kansas Chautauqua as well as numerous other public history endeavors, shared generously his memory and archives, as did Nancy Kelley, who managed and was the drama coach for the Kansas Chautauqua for its first four years. Fred Krebs, still a Chautauquan and a man of such aliases as journalist William Allen White, writer L. Frank Baum, and politician/Chautauqua perennial William Jennings Bryan, has also been most generous, as have other Kansas Humanities Council History Alive! scholar-performers as they make the transition away from that organization to a new structure for reaching the public. The Kansas Humanities Council has funded many of our workshops through grants to communities, allowing us to experiment with various publics and formats. I must acknowledge Marci Penner and the Kansas Sampler Foundation for enthusiasm and encouragement, but especially for providing nurturing space for those first workshops. Several members of the Kansas Alliance for Professional Historic Performers answered our questions, read drafts, and offered suggestions. Emporia State University graduate student Dana Carter converted the Venn diagram to black and white.

And, of course, Ann Birney, who read almost every word of almost every revision and, if truth be told, no doubt wrote a few of the words, too—if that should be the case, then this is my apology for not crediting those specific contributions.

As I began writing this book, I had to determine whether it would be solely descriptive of existing practice, or also prescriptive, recommending possibilities. The attentive reader will find it both.

## NOTES

1. Ride into History Cultural and Educational Project, Inc., "Tourism Attraction Development Grant Program, Fiscal Year 2002 Application—Round 1," Kansas Department of Commerce and Housing.

2. Eric Sorg, well known for his portrayal of Buffalo Bill, and author of *Buffalo Bill: Myth and Reality* (Santa Fe, N.Mex.: Ancient City Press, 1998), came out of his recent medical retirement to lead the workshop with us and critique performances.

# 1

# The Significance of Historical Performance

THIS guide was created to help museum staff members, festival planners, and program directors determine what they want in the way of performed interpretation. It is for those who want to *be*, for example, Amelia Earhart or George Washington; *bring*, for example, Amelia or George to their venue; or, for example, *create* a troupe of individuals who tell the stories of the history of aviation or the American Revolutionary War era. It will also help them decide whether to develop their own troupe of historical performers or hire freelance professionals. The book tells those who want to develop a historical performance how to select a character, research primary and secondary sources, create a script, craft a look, and, finally, tell history to diverse audiences.

This book will help individuals determine which tradition of history sharing they want to make their own, and how to do historical performance if that is where they belong. It will help those training historical performers as they answer the questions that I have been struggling with over the years: What do you call what we do? How do I begin? Whom should I portray? What do I include and what do I leave out? How important is my appearance? Do I need to be an actor? How much do I need to know? What if I get nervous? Who will my audience be? Do I really need to do this by myself?

And, to facilitate discussion between and among performers and presenting organizations,[1] in this chapter I propose a taxonomy of modes and traditions for sharing history through performance, after which I focus most of the rest of the book on the most complete tradition, that of historical performance. If you are a staff member or volunteer for a historic site or museum, hopefully this information will enhance your experience in enhancing the learning experience of your visitors, whether they are local or tourists.

This manual also includes marketing and business advice for independent interpreters or small troupes, and advice for museums, historic sites, and community organizations who want to develop their own historical performance troupes, take Chautauquas on the road, or hire independent scholars/performers. In addition, it provides concrete examples of programming involving young people as performers and a guide to using historical performance. It is designed to be used by institutions and individuals as they move from the "thinking about it" stage to "This is something we/I want to do," and on to "Okay, we have the performances, how do we develop audiences?" and "How do I evaluate such programs?"

What does the book *not* cover? This book will not provide guidance for managing a touring group. For instance, although it will discuss Chautauqua programming, and why an individual performer might want to sign onto a Chautauqua, if you are going to manage a touring historical performance troupe you will want to look elsewhere for the nitty-gritty on providing payroll on the road, arranging lodging in small towns, and providing food after a show when no eateries are open.[2] Also, this book will not be a how-to for living history, reenactments, or museum theater, because other works do a fine job with those.[3] On the other hand, although this book is focused on the performed history-interpretation tradition of historical performance, living history interpreters and others charged with interacting informally with individuals or small groups will find that preparation for longer, formal narratives, especially those in which questions will be taken, is excellent preparation for informal visiting in character, so I advocate preparing for both at once.

Why historical performance? Dramatic historical interpretation can be an effective teaching tool for adults and children both. A four-year study of adult museum programming found that museums use dramatic presentations because they have an "emotional impact" that is conducive to "long-lasting learning." And, "excellent museum programs," the study found, "can change people's lives."[4] Wendy Jones, museum manager of the Minnesota History Center, told author Tessa Bridal that dramatic interpretations help "the museum 'provide a place where people actively participate in finding personal meaning from things of the past.'"[5] Conner Prairie's training DVD describes a mutual respect between interpreter and guest: "Guests meet us at a distinct and spontaneous moment of time" to which, it says, they bring their past, and interpreters bring the past that they are interpreting.[6]

The result is active participation because an entertaining performance, a well-told story, inspires audience members to focus by appealing to diverse learning styles. Individuals who learn best by hearing information delight in hearing words instead of having to read labels or accounts of an event. Kinesthetic learners imagine wearing the clothes and carrying out the activities described in the stories. Kinesthetic learners also delight in interacting with the past through discussion or the handling of objects. Interpersonal learners identify with aspects of the speaker's experience and personality. Visual learners create and retain images based on the performers' descriptions, remembering gestures and clothing. Logical learners place the performer into historical context, linking this narrative to other information.[7] Dramatic interpretation can also provide what Barbara Clark calls "safe spaces" for the "new, creative insights" that are characteristic of the "intuitive function" of the brain.[8]

The problem is that while museum, historic site, and school professionals who have experienced an excellent dramatic historical interpretation want such programming for their clientele, excellent costumed historical interpretation is rare. This is in part because some decision makers believe that one must be a trained actor to carry off a convincing performance, resulting in performers who memorize scripts and are not able to discuss historical context. On the other hand, other professionals are convinced that acting and story crafting should be secondary to historical accuracy—they convince a scholar to lecture while in costume, too often resulting in really boring interpretation—or really confusing interpretation that moves back and forth between then and now, and between first and third person, instead of establishing a setting and sticking to it until the appropriate time to become the scholar again.

Who should do historical performance? The author believes that it is possible—and crucial—for historical performers to have both extensive knowledge of their subject matter, including historic context, and the ability to perform a convincing portrayal. I also believe that these two things are possible without having earned a graduate degree and without acting training or experience. Storytelling and acting skills in particular can be taught to those with aptitude and commitment. This belief is based on experience in learning and teaching first-person historical narratives: direct-address monologues followed by audience interaction in character and then as the scholar. The two current members of my historical performance touring troupe have been performing for a total of thirty-four years. Both of us hold doctorates in appropriate fields, but neither of us had acting training or experience. After being convinced to apply for the Kansas Arts Commission's Touring Program roster (which is when we started using the term "sneaky history" to describe what we do), we sought and received advice from theater faculty members, but beyond that our improvement was from critiquing each other and observing our audiences. It can be done, and we have taught hundreds of people to do it, including well-read and passionate reenactors who were not satisfied with weekends on battlefields or playing fast-draw against "the Marshall."

I am also passionate about involving young people as historical performers. Museum programming literature refers to youngsters as audiences for historical performance, or participants in living history demonstrations, not as historians in their own right. Involving youngsters as researchers and interpreters of history brings new audiences to historic sites and museums, illuminates the participation of children in creating history throughout time, and inspires a sense of museum (and history!) ownership among the youth. Involving youth in a deep way also provides opportunities to learn new skills and inspires increased interest in classroom history. This book will discuss, in the final chapter, four such models for nine- through fifteen-year-olds: weeklong Youth Chautauqua Camps held in conjunction with Kansas, Kansas-Nebraska, and Great Plains Chautauquas; two-month school residencies; a weeklong summer arts program; and a five-day program culminating in artifact-based "Night at the Museum" tours in which exhibits "come to life." And it will also describe a cross-generational museum program.

This book was also created to help individuals determine which tradition of history sharing they want to make their own (for an overview see figure 1.1), and, in chapters 2 through 5, how to do historical performance if that is where they belong.

## MY STORY

My own foray into historical performance began due to my fear of teachers. It was late spring 1989. I had writer's block big time. I was to deliver a lecture to high school teachers as part of a secondary school teachers' seminar. Never mind that I had the credentials, currently completing my doctorate in American history. Never mind that I had been lecturing on this topic, the history of rural women, for several years. Never mind that I was so highly thought of that I had also been asked to give two additional lectures for this National Endowment for the Humanities project when my major professor was unable to fulfill his commitment. Never mind that I had been teaching prospective teachers in college classrooms for five years. Never mind any of that. I was terrified. I knew that those teachers, the seminar attendees, just like my teachers thirty years earlier, were going to question the validity of everything I said, and I would find myself once more in the principal's office, a kid with dyslexia (not diagnosed back then) who, because she had trouble reading (those letters danced around on the page something ferocious, especially under fluorescent lights), was discounted as a nonlearner and a smart aleck.

As I anguished over my dilemma, my sidekick, Ann, who was quite successful academically, thank you very much, and just hadn't a clue, tired of my whining and sniveling. (She would also tell you that the rending of garments was getting to be a bit much.) She challenged me, saying that if I wasn't going to write, then I might as well be riding. It is common knowledge that the world looks better from horseback. And it was a beautiful day. There's something about centering yourself on a horse that centers you with the world. And it is much easier to solve problems when you are centered.

I explained again about teachers past and future, and Ann finally got it, saying something like, "So, maybe you need help from someone who's bigger and badder than those teachers," and asked about my childhood hero.

I told Ann about Calamity Jane, and how much strength I drew from this very real person, who was close to people and animals, but also very independent, a survivor. I told her that I had always wanted to share Calamity Jane's story.

A strategy was born. What if I first met the teachers as Calamity Jane? How might that be arranged? Sending Calamity Jane to the university to talk to the teachers would be much less scary than having to do the talk as Joyce, but Calamity's talk might not meet grant requirements. A compromise was created. The teachers would meet Calamity one evening early on in their weeklong seminar. They would sit in lawn chairs around the fire ring in the backyard and be visited by Calamity Jane, on horseback (my equine buddy Spirit becoming a security blanket disguised as a snowflake-dappled buckskin).

It worked. A few weeks later the dozen or so teachers watched with delight as I galloped up out of the pasture atop Spirit and my grandfather's 1900 stock saddle, whooping and hollering, then coming to an abrupt halt in front of the group. "Why, this ain't no town. It's just a little ol' farmstead. And you all look like Easterners. But you've heard of ol' Calamity Jane, ain'tcha?" And I launched into a first-person narrative based on Calamity Jane's letters to her daughter and her autobiography.[9] The whole thing (and my lectures) had been created in a matter of weeks, so I had not memorized all of my script. The last portion, therefore, was stapled to plywood boards at my feet, which I had to put on my glasses to read. In spite of the primitive nature of the performance, the audience loved it. They laughed. They cried. My storytelling talents shone, and Spirit, it turned out, was a ham, yawning appropriately and drinking from my cup. I was brave and the teachers were friendly. I obviously knew a great deal, to be able to answer questions in character and explain Calamity Jane's role in the mythic west and in women's history. There was no question that the teachers would respect me the next day as a lecturer, and a historical performer was born in one who had no theater background and to that point had not particularly enjoyed being in the limelight.

Suddenly part of my identity was this "thing" that I was doing for which I had no name other than "becoming Calamity Jane" and, in time, "becoming" other historic figures. As an academic, it bothered me that it was so difficult to articulate the nature of my performances.

## TAXONOMY

Historical performance is just now coming into its own. Historic sites are recognizing and capitalizing on historical performance as a means to compete for the attention of various publics while also educating. The language of performed history interpretation, however, is not well defined. Hence, communication problems sometimes occur between program planners and those they might want to bring in to entertain and educate their public. Museum staff members might not know whether a reenactor and a historical performer are the same thing. How do I know if this person who calls herself a historical performer is really a historical performer and not a reenactor? And what is a Chautauquan? A living history demonstrator? Does what they call themselves make a difference in what they charge us? What will we get in return?

There are so many descriptors for performed history interpretation that it is very confusing. I created a taxonomy (see figure 1.1 and table 1.1) to differentiate between forms of history sharing in order to help both performers and presenting organizations determine what will work best in a given setting and situation. And, of course, I will also provide narrative to explain the ideas represented by the figure and table.

Personally, I love the three-part format of the Chautauqua-style first-person narrative (lower right region in figure 1.1), a monologue followed by questions in character and then as the scholar out of character, for reasons that I will get into later. I can, however, sympathize with Everett Albers's characterizations of Chautauqua programs as ranging from "very good" to "horrible."[10] My goal since 1977 has been to rid the world of "horrible" historical performance while also differentiating between historical performance and such other contemporary traditions as that of the Chautauquan, the historical interpreter, museum theater, the storyteller, and the reenactor. These and other modes of sharing history should be respected for the contributions they make, as well as understood for their priorities. Look-alikes, for example, are all about appearance

**Figure 1.1.    Best Practice Priorities of Performed History Interpretation: A Taxonomy**

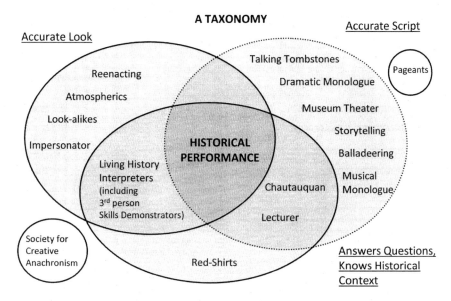

and should not be expected to talk. Chautauqua is all about the talk, and the look is often barely representational. We need to be able to differentiate between them, to codify our own jargon for the good of us all. For one thing, it will enhance social interactions:

It's embarrassing. For all parties. Someone is really excited about introducing me to a colleague or friend: "This is Joyce Thierer. Dr Thierer does . . . is. . . . What do you call what you do?" "I am," I tell them, "a historian/researcher/scriptwriter/historical performer. My signature performance is a first-person narrative of Calamity Jane." And then I usually go into character for a sentence or two. I have to go beyond telling to showing for them to really understand the nature of a first-person narrative.

I actually prefer the above open-ended stumble to having someone introduce me as a reenactor, which is what happens most often. This is because I am not a reenactor, and I have to explain that I am not, and how I'm not, instead of just describing what I am, a historical performer. Or sometimes I am introduced as an impersonator, which makes the snobby scholar in me shudder. "Why?" you ask. Good question, which I will answer by describing and classifying other performed history-sharing traditions. I'm sure periodontists have the same problem of people not knowing what they do, but what do dental professionals have that we do not? A taxonomy![11]

**Table 1.1. First-Person Narrative Forms: A Guide for Organizations Presenting Programs**

| Form | Product | Do NOT Expect* | Sample Fees (in 2007 money) |
|---|---|---|---|
| Atmospheric | Stroll in costume— visual only | Accurate clothing or knowledgeable interaction with public | Free food (more for corporate events and if clothing is accurate) |
| Look-alike | Stroll in look— visual only | Knowledgeable interaction with public; completely era-appropriate props | A meal, to $300 for corporate events |
| Impersonator | The look, and small talk appropriate to the period | Extensive knowledge about the historic figure being impersonated | $50 to $400 for corporate events |
| Reenactor | 1) Accurate garb<br>2) Encampment, gear<br>3) Informal interaction with the public<br>4) Sometimes reenactment of an event | Knowledge beyond the very specific event, group; also do not expect reenactors to know significance of events | Travel honorarium paid to the group |
| Costumed Interpreter | Informal interaction with the public, references to those with other/more expertise | Knowledge of historical significance or historical context | Usually staff member or volunteer at historic site |
| Talking Tombstone | Brief memorized script | Answer questions | Volunteer |
| Dramatic Monologue | Stage performance of at least an hour | Historical knowledge unless the performer researched the script | $1,000, up |
| Chautauquan | 30–40 min. monologue followed by audience discussion with historic figure and then by discussion with scholar | Accurate clothing and props | $500, up |
| Historical Performance | 30–40 min. monologue followed by audience discussion with historic figure and then by discussion with scholar | | $500, up |

*Source:* Copyright 2009, Ride into History, ridehist@satelephone.com.
\* While individuals within each performance form may be exceptional and able to produce the services in this column, get references and make sure that it is in the contract. Also, be sure that someone who describes themselves as, for instance, a historical performer is not really a reenactor or impersonator.

As can be seen in the Venn diagram (see figure 1.1), "Best Practice Priorities of Performed History Interpretation: A Taxonomy," historical performers alone use a script, have the contextual knowledge to address audience questions, and present an accurate period look. While individuals within other traditions may migrate into the central region with historical performance, such as people who identify as Chautauquans who are sticklers about having an authentic look, the excluded characteristic is not currently a requirement of their chosen tradition—that is, Chautauquans who wear polyester while representing pre-twentieth-century figures are in general not frowned on by other Chautauquans.

My first step, therefore, toward improving the traditions of performed history interpretation is to define terms. Several other valiant people have done this with varying degrees of success, and I will acknowledge their influence as I proceed, but my perspective is, I believe, a bit broader, and therefore somewhat privileged among public history scholars, so I am offering my own list of terms as a contribution to practitioners and scholars alike.

Performed history traditions can be characterized as having at least one of three general characteristics: if there is an expectation for a period "look," the look will be accurate; there is a scripted text; the public can interact informally, asking questions of the performer. As you can see from the diagram, there is no hierarchy for the three characteristics or the individual traditions within them—each is useful in various situations, but each is also different from the others.

I have been working on the language of history performance for almost ten years. In fact, we asked attendees at our very first adult workshop to describe what it is that we do. I well remember the flip chart page going into a second page as we listed everything that we might be called, generically. We continued this over two more workshops until we finally came up with the term "historical performer." I was then, however, left with the task of differentiating between "historical performer" and all of those other terms from the flip chart tablet. I decided that it was best approached by looking at the priorities of each history-sharing tradition. I determined that each tradition or mode was characterized by one to three basic priorities: an accurate look, a researched script, and answering questions from the public. The resulting clusters helped me understand what the expectations should be for each type of performance (see figure 1.1).

### Accurate Look

The first priority of the group in the far left region of the "Accurate Look" circle is just that, their appearance. For people participating in this category, the look must be accurate to the era, place, and class being represented.

History-sharing traditions that prioritize an "accurate look" include atmospherics, look-alikes, impersonators, and reenactors. Those who require an accurate look but also prioritize the knowledge that lets them answer the public's questions are living history, costumed interpreters, and simulated or living-skills demonstrators. Historical performers are in the central region of the diagram because they demand of themselves an accurate look, enough knowledge to be able to answer the public's questions, and a scripted performance. I am going to address the first two regions of the Accurate Look circle in the next several pages, leaving historical performance until after I have addressed the other traditions in the "Answers Questions" and "Accurate Script" circles.

### Atmospherics

Atmospherics and look-alikes are the most basic. "Atmospherics" is, I believe, my own term. These are the people in representational or era-accurate clothing that lend atmosphere to an event, suggesting with their look that attendees are entering a different era. They are usually en masse. Think about centennial events, with men in beards sporting era-ambiguous black suits, and women donning not-quite-accurate "prairie dresses" and sunbonnets. Or, on a higher, best practices plain, there are individuals in accurate clothing: ladies with parasols and gents in ties and tails strolling the grounds of a nineteenth-century mansion—rarely a woman in skirt and waist with her sleeves rolled up, washing clothes at a tub behind the house. Atmospherics sometimes hire on as movie extras. Civil War reenactors have a delightful word for people who wear the uniform for a reenactment but behave anachronistically: mannequins.[12]

If they have another income and are hobbyists passionate about era clothing, they might provide their services free. The only downside is that, as can be seen from the chart, atmospherics cannot be expected to impart knowledge—or information—to visitors. Unless they are historic site staff members or volunteers who have already been trained, there needs to be an agreement on how they will respond to questions from visitors. Will they receive orientation so they can identify directional questions ("Where is the bathroom?" "Where can I buy food?" "Do you have any animals here?") and answer them? What should they do if they are asked questions for which they do not have answers (e.g., there are no animals in their area, so they do not know for sure if the site has animals—or where handicapped accessible bathrooms are located). Do they pull an anachronistic cell phone out of their costume and ask for help? Or is there a contemporary-garbed staff member, a "red-shirt" stationed nearby, to whom they will refer the visitor?

*Look-alikes*

Look-alikes have the body shape and facial features of a famous person. They dress in the most iconic image of that individual. There are Abraham Lincolns, Buffalo Bill Codys, John Waynes, and Lone Rangers—you name the movie star or historic figure, and there are look-alikes and contests to determine who looks most like that person. Do not, however, expect look-alikes to either sound like the person they are representing (see trail story 1.1) or know much about that person. And most definitely do not expect them to be able to place their individual in historical context. They just need to strike a pose and hold it; when being judged, they are like live wax figures, evaluated only on how well they match an iconic photo image. They do not speak.

### A Trail Story

#### 1.1. JOHN WAYNE SHOULDA KEPT HIS MOUTH SHUT

Once upon a time I was invited to a weekend Western festival where I was to present Calamity Jane in the evening. At the noon meal I found myself at a table of "look-alikes." Paladin, the Lone Ranger, Gene Autry, Zorro, and John Wayne were there, all with women whom I assumed were their significant others. Only the women talked, which felt awkward. Finally, I asked the woman sitting next to me where they were from. She started to tell me when her husband, the "John Wayne" of the group, chimed in. I was shocked, not that they were from Virginia, although this was surprising, but rather at his voice, which was very high and whiney, an extreme contrast to "the Duke's" low, slow-paced voice. It completely ruined his image for me. Every time I looked at him I heard that voice and simply could not suspend my disbelief. The effect was totally ruined when he opened his mouth.

In the Buffalo Bill Cody contests, as an example, there are categories for the younger Buffalo Bill, the middle-aged look, and the older look. The real prize is not the certificate or the small amount of cash that might accompany it— the real prize is bragging rights. Prize-winning look-alikes can transition from being hobbyists to being paid impersonators.

*Impersonators*

Impersonators are look-alikes who have broadened their knowledge so they can greet the public in character with era-appropriate phrases and gestures. Often they can make small talk and introduce themselves. Do not expect them to have extensive knowledge about the person they are representing. Also, do not expect them to be willing to step out of character to answer an anachronistic question or admit a lack of knowledge. They just might be rude rather than break character, as I described in the story of a young Buffalo Bill in the introduction.

Museums and historic sites should look at their goals for a particular event and decide what kind of experience they want for their public. We know the public expects authenticity, and that, "to them, authentic museum experiences are grounded in thorough, well-documented research."[13] If you bring in costumed atmospherics, look-alikes, and impersonators, do not expect research-based knowledge. They will lend ambience and, in the case of impersonators, schmooze with your visitors, and that should be the extent of your expectations of them. And, of course, everything you expect should be spelled out in a contract.

On the other hand, if your staff members or volunteers are dressing up only to create ambience, or you let your staff members get away with being impersonators when they could do so much more, you are missing opportunities for significant public interaction, and thus, you are shortchanging your guests and, probably, boring your staff. One of the problems that museums have repeatedly expressed is that staff members do not want to "dress up" because they feel "silly" and that they are not doing "real" history. This is because dressing in period costume has come to be associated with atmospherics, look-alikes, impersonators, and reenactors who typically have no interest in history beyond their very narrow niche—clothing of a particular era, or a particular battle. It is this image that must change to encourage the best possible people to provide the most authentic possible experience for visitors to museums and historic sites. In other words, staff members and volunteers who are in costume MUST know more than a narrow script. They must be knowledgeable and they must be learners, and learners who can dialogue with guests, including being willing and able to admit when they do not have an answer. This is the situation that Conner Prairie found themselves in, and why they trained their staff members to become costumed interpreters and also created museum theater. More on those forms later in this chapter.

## A Trail Story

### 1.2. HOW I BECAME A CHAMPION STRIPPER

From 1961 to 1981 my parents diversified the family farm by inviting city folks to see how sorghum was made into molasses in the "old days." Three Sundays each fall people came from all over to our Mill Creek Museum. Authenticity was my parents' byword. The press and pan were set up at the site where my grandparents had used them. Open-pollinated sorghum seed was gathered and planted, and we also harvested all of the cane the "old way." My horses provided power for the press. My mother learned to spin and weave. She demonstrated soap making, and found that the lye soap sold.

One Sunday, in the late 1970s, we had three thousand visitors, and we ran out of cane. There was another Sunday of Molasses Days to go, so we needed to strip and cut enough cane to both make molasses during the week so we could sell it on the weekend and have enough cane to demonstrate the process of pressing and cooking all day. Each day that week my cane knife and I had to strip and cut enough cane to fill a twelve-foot hay wagon two to three feet high. And that is how the author of this book became one of the two top sorghum cane strippers in Wabaunsee County, Kansas. Of course, the other champion stripper was seventy-five years old and I was fifty years shy of that, but he had been my teacher, and had held the record for decades, so I am still proud. It nearly killed me, but it was necessary for the family economy. Accurate look? No, we just wore our farm work clothes.

*Reenactors*

Jenny Thompson, reenactor and author of *War Games: Inside the World of 20th-Century War Reenactors*, states that "Contemporary reenacting most clearly traces its roots [to] the historical pageant."[14] In 1961, with the centennial of the Civil War, any representation or look would do. As people continued their interest in celebrating the war, however, they went from pageants to passion, and accuracy of look became the focus of that passion.

Reenactors are the best-known group in the "accurate look" category, so theirs is the term that is often applied to other performers, both because reenactors are almost ubiquitous and because other terminology has been lacking. I have known impersonators to adopt the term to increase their status, the word "impersonator" having a bit of stigma attached to it as implying fakery. True reenactors are always members of an organization, be it loose-knit or strict. There are many, many genres of reenactors. Civil War reenactors probably have the highest profile because they have the highest membership, but it seems that there are reenactment groups for every war or conflict, including an increasing number of World Wars I and II and Vietnam reenactors.[15] Also highly visible are black-powder or buckskinner or muzzle-loading rifle groups. Buckaroos, Old West gunfighter, and action "shootist" groups are now all over the nation, and even Europe, not just west of the Mississippi. Members of all of these groups tend to portray stereotypical males dressed to match their firearms. When women are involved they are either in disguise as men[16] or likewise stereotypical (think saloon floozies).

Members of reenactment groups are almost always hobbyists. Reenactors have done an excellent marketing and branding of "the look." They reenact events such as battles but are more often involved in demonstrating gear at a festival, or adding ambience at an event.

Historic sites and museums that are not interpreting a battlefield want reenactors to come because they add visual texture for the public. They add color and drama to events. Perhaps your museum or historic site has challenges keeping your volunteers on track. When you add reenactors it is stirring in another layer: someone else's volunteers. A common Kansas scenario is as follows: one member of the group volunteers the whole; you are assured that you will have ten to fifteen, maybe all twenty-five Civil War reenactors on your grounds for your special day. You advertise that the public will be able to visit with soldiers in authentic gear. There will be a reproduction cannon fired and reproduction flags fluttering. It begins raining Thursday before your Saturday event. You get a call. The forecast is for rain continuing throughout the weekend. Only a few of the fellows now want to camp out, but they might all still come. Saturday, the day of your event, you have no cannon and no flags; you have only the one person with whom you talked. He is in uniform, and he has a gun, but his powder is wet. Some of the public have braved the weather because you have done a terrific job of promoting the event, and there you are with one lone soldier. One soldier does not an army make. And, of course, you have no contract because you were not going to pay them anything. If, on the other hand, that soldier was trained as a historical performer, he or she could save the day, and you would have a contract. More on that later.

Reenactor groups constantly recruit "newbies," thus increasing their visibility not only through increasing numbers but also with the families and friends of their members. They started as small clusters of like-minded enthusiasts, kept informed with mimeographed newsletters. Now, for just about any era or topic in which you are interested, you can find cyberspace representation of multiple groups. Search "Vikings" to see what I mean, or wade through seemingly endless listings of Civil War groups. Whatever era interests a prospective reenactor there are many opportunities for participation.

Reenactors will usually create a persona, or "impression," from their era. They may or may not have done extensive research into that person and his or her immediate context. Some reenactors are treasure troves of trivia on their battle. It is, however, the rare reenactor who knows enough history to be able to place the events they are reenacting into the larger historical context.[17]

Reenactors dress up because they enjoy dressing up and because they enjoy having a good time with their buddies. They would do their schtick whether or not someone was watching. In fact, many reenactment events are private, and people who are not invited or who arrive not in correct period dress are barred from the area. Some reenactors tolerate the public view because if they get paid they can justify their hobby expenses as income producing or, perhaps (I am not an accountant), as required for educational volunteering. Many mentally spar with spectators who try to trick the reenactor into stepping out of character. Ask a dyed-in-the-wool reenactor where the bathroom is, and, depending on the era, you will probably be subjected to questions about what that room is, and why you would want to take a bath there. Woe to the visitor who really, really needs to find the bathroom! Some visitors enjoy trying to fool reenactors into slipping out of character or out of their time. All trained interpreters deal with the concept of my time/your time, whether or not it is called that at their site.[18] The public assumes that reenactors are trained interpreters and they are NOT.

Reenactors sometimes involve the public in their activities, including mock combat (shooting competitions, gunfights, and sword fights), period clothing competitions and style shows, cookouts, dances, encampments, rendezvous, or gatherings, where they meet friends and "shoot the breeze." As more than one of my historical performer friends who is also involved with mountain man reenactment says, "Who does not love things than go bang?"[19] The American Frontier Reenactment Guild and some cowboy action shooting associations offer group insurance (always a good idea when firearms and the public are combined).[20]

Historical performers who were reenactors have told me that they have observed two basic categories among their reenacting buddies. Powder burners are those who participate because they get to shoot cool guns with a group; most do not want to get dirty. "Pretty boys" participate because of "the look"— they enjoy wearing the uniform, and, like powder burners, shun dirt. Many reenactors, I am told, want to relive their childhoods—buds, guns, camping, grunge, and a no-girls-club mentality. All of this is frivolous to "hardcores," a term applied "to reenactors who are intently focused on authenticity, put a lot of effort into the hobby, and are generally 'serious.'"[21]

The first two groups, the "powder burners" and "pretty boys," disrupt one of the stated rules of engagement used in battle reenactments. The "ghost" rule is that while no one ever really dies, if you draw a number that is supposed to declare you wounded or dead then you are to fall to the ground and stay down until time is called. Many powder burners, however, not wanting to miss the fun, and pretty boys not wanting to lie in the mud, seemingly never die. Another departure from the reality of battle is that when horses are involved none are supposed to go down. The artillery is to stop firing when reenactors cross a predetermined line. A narrator explains departures from history and the rules of engagement to the public so they know what is happening. Of course, this is very much pseudo-history, but it does get people thinking about history who might not otherwise do so. In fact, they just might have questions to ask, and it is crucial that the historic site or museum decide who is going to answer those questions. That "who" should not be a reenactor, unless they have training beyond that required for reenacting. For one thing, your audience is likely to include a few sincerely interested, but skeptical, academics. Historical performers can meet the needs of the widest range of publics. A series of historical performers before and after the battle can provide various intimate perspectives of the event.

Hardcore reenactors are the most knowledgeable but also the least likely to participate in public events. In eighteen years I have rarely seen one at an event or historic site. They do not speak to the public or appear before an audience. "Hardcores" live to reenact with like-minded individuals away from the public's prying eyes, participating in private, by-invitation events.

The narrator of the battle is generally a local celebrity with a well-modulated voice who reads a script. This script is the extent of the reenactment group's concession to the educational role that the museum expects of them. Following the battle enactment, if there is an encampment, reenactors return to camp and sit around, talking to their buds. Some will talk to guests; most will ignore the public, pretending there is an invisible wall between them and the public. They want to stay in "my time," and the public cannot cross over, thinking that the reenactors are rude. The public has not been given the rules of engagement for reenactors in camp! Someone has been assigned to talk, just as someone is assigned to die. Chances are that someone is an enthusiastic newbie who is willing to go on forever because they have no friends in camp yet.

When reenactors do engage the public, they are more likely to pay attention to men, then boys, with women and girls ignored. In one interaction that I observed, a reenactor asked an adolescent boy if he wanted to handle a pistol. When he hesitated, the younger girl in the group reached out for the gun. The reenactor's response was "Girls don't handle guns!" She knew otherwise. In fact, she told him that six hundred women that we know of fought disguised as men in the same war he was reenacting. How sad that a girl of about ten had to correct the person expected to educate her! He was seemingly embalmed in gender stereotypes and aware of little beyond his gun.

A few reenactors, when they do talk to a visitor, may go into a bit of first-person narrative to give name and unit information and then switch into third person to talk to the audience about their cool stuff. Reenactors have "the look," but they are not historical performers.

My hope is that more reenactors of all stripes and eras will adopt some of the suggestions in the later chapters. They already have the cool stuff, the look, and have begun some research. I really encourage reenactors to transition by researching their era and its context and creating a scripted talk. Several in Kansas have bitten the bullet and now do well-presented performances. Norman Joy, aka Robert E. Lee, told me during a workshop break that by doing historical performance he could have his cake and eat it too—he had the incentive to dig ever deeper into Robert E. Lee's life and times, but he can still go off with his reenactor buds.

Here is one last incentive for reenactors who want to do more character development and more research, and are willing to go out on their own: Want to buy more cool toys and stuff? As a historical performer you can form your own business, and if you are serious about your endeavor, those "toys" will probably be tax deductible (although I am neither accountant nor tax attorney, so consult yours—and see chapter 6).

### Society for Creative Anachronism

See that small bubble in the lower left of the taxonomy diagram (see figure 1.1)? The Society for Creative Anachronism (SCA) was founded in 1966 at

Berkeley, California, and has since spread across the nation and beyond with the increased popularity of Renaissance festivals. Almost as numerous as reenactors, the SCA is, as Jay Anderson states, "highly organized along feudal lines into shires, baronies and kingdoms,"[22] and to be commended for having been comparatively gender equitable "from the start."[23] They do not, however, do "real" history, being unfettered from the constraints of historical accuracy. They celebrate the aesthetic, rather than reenact specific events, and are a joyous representation of the diversity of the past, as well as that of the present. For this group, history is about fun: eat, drink, and be merry. Their jousts thrill with thundering horses, armored knights, clashing arms, and colorful banners, but it is never any particular joust being reenacted, and, like reenactments, no one really dies. Ann Fletchall says of the Arizona Renaissance Festival, "It is a simulacrum which appeals to the masses by mixing time periods and fact and fantasy under the guise of 'recreating' a Renaissance era marketplace."[24]

Unlike reenactors, they dress representationally and are not concerned with historical accuracy in their look—or anything else. Helmets, for instance, are often padded for protection with foam rubber. From the outside they may look era correct, but under their gowns and robes they wear today's clothing, and they are likely to use synthetic fabrics. Their response to blending the eras is quite logical and matter-of-fact: if folks in the Renaissance era would have had access to such things as safety pads and machine-washable clothing, they, too, would have used them. SCA members and groups have a Web presence and are often available for events on a contract basis.

### Answers Questions, Knows Historical Context

To be able to answer the public's questions you must know a great deal, about both the setting or subject immediately at hand and its historical context, including how it relates to us today.

#### Red-Shirts

There is only one tradition in the Answers Questions, Knows Historical Context circle that does not overlap with either of the other two circles. The red-shirt tradition has been articulated only recently but is crucial to maintaining good relations with visitors and a meaningful experience for everyone.

"Red-Shirt" is shorthand for uniformed historical site staff members who do third-person interpretation from the perspective of the visitor's era. Conner Prairie red-shirt staff members wear blue shirts with their logo, and the National Park Service, of course, has uniformed rangers. The important thing is that the individuals be readily identified by the public as knowledgeable and available to answer questions from a modern perspective. Red-shirts are crucial when other interpreters are expected to stay in a different era.

Andrew Robertshaw, of the History Re-enactment Workshop, who takes credit for the term and concept of "Red T-Shirting," says,

> One potential problem of live interpretation is that a visitor who is unprepared for meeting role-playing "performers" who are unable to speak about events after the period they are portraying, may feel confused or even intimidated. . . . [The red T-shirt's] role is to meet every visitor as they arrive, explain how the interpretation works and offer them a variety of ways of approaching it. . . . Many visitors like the idea of . . . following and observing without [being] drawn into the activities. To prevent the experience [from] becoming completely passive, the Red T-Shirters can also act as a catalyst for interaction between interpreters and visitors, provide a running commentary in certain situations, drawing parallels between historical and modern processes.[25]

Ken Bubp, chief operating officer at Conner Prairie, notes the irony of their pre-2003 interpretation policy and practices: they were the first to extensively use costumed first-person interpreters, but "no one answered, where's the bathroom?"[26]

There are three alternatives to red-shirts: risking considerable visitor frustration ("where's the bathroom"), not having first-person interpreters, and allowing first-person interpreters to slip out of character to impart particular information. Stacy Roth, author of *Past into Present: Effective Techniques for First-Person Historical Interpretation*, credits Tom Sanders of Fort Snelling in St. Paul, Minnesota, with the concept of "my time/your time," in which the costumed interpreter approaches anachronistic questions by saying, "in your time you do this, in our time we do this parallel activity."[27] Personally, I feel uneasy in the presence of such "ghost interpreters," who are in the present as shades of the past. I much prefer that intelligent, well-trained interpreters (and aren't they all intelligent and well trained?) be encouraged to slip out of character as necessary, as described by Laura Peers, author of *Playing Ourselves: Interpreting Native Histories at Historic Reconstructions*, who tells us that, for instance, all visitors to the Northwest Company Fur Post are guided by staff members who "use first-person interpretation . . . but also switch into third-person (informal discussion) as needed." "Every visitor," she says, "is . . . given a customized tour."[28] A skilled interpreter can signal the change to the public with voice, words, and stance.

**Accurate Look/Answers Questions**

This region of the taxonomy diagram (see figure 1.1) is the land of Jay Anderson's "time machines," "vehicle[s] that enable people to re-enter another period of time, vicariously, and to simulate life there if only for a short period."[29]

*Living History Interpreters*

This region is a great challenge in creating a taxonomy because so very many terms have been used for those time-travel facilitators: interpreter, costumed interpreter, living skills demonstrator, living historian, first-person living history interpreter, living history demonstrator, third-person interpreter, history simulator, interactive interpreter, and so on. My original intent was to use the "standard sources": the venerable Tilden,[30] Anderson, and Roth, and the National Association for Interpretation (NAI)–sponsored Definitions Project. They all use different phrases, however, and the latter even contradicts itself within four definitions (hopefully, that will be changed by the time this book goes to press).

I am going to have to jettison most of those sources for definitions and, because the NAI has done so much work already, adopt a term suggested in their term "living history": *living history interpreter*. NAI has defined "living history" as "the use of a physical environment and the sights, sounds, and smells of the period being represented," and says that "the two major types of interactive *living history interpretation* are first-person and third-person." That works. On the other hand, what NAI calls "first-person living history interpretation" in a separate definition is, in fact, historical performance:

> The act of portraying a person from the past (real or composite). The intent of this style is to present the attitudes, briefs, view points, language, and mannerisms of another period in history in a way that is immediate, entertaining, and thought-provoking. Through the portrayal of a character, they create for the visitor the illusion that their historic personage has returned to life. Also known as "character interpretation" or "first-person interpretation."[31]

"First-person living history interpretation" as they had defined it—that is, without involving an actual "physical environment"—would, therefore, have been either redundant or contradictory. (More on historical performance below.)

Laura Peers, in her study of telling native peoples' stories at historic sites, "chose the term 'interpreter' to describe those who work at historic sites, wear period clothing, and interact with visitors on site." She describes them as paid staff members, trained by the organization, as opposed to "hobbyists and volunteers who are reenactors . . . dress[ing] up at weekends in period clothing largely for their own purposes of entertainment."[32]

The living history interpreters tradition is more likely to be made up of paid staff members than is any other except the red-shirt. There are, however, many freelance skills demonstrators who augment museum staffs or interpretations for which the staff would find it difficult to prepare.

The word "interpreter" was coined—and its concept triumphantly celebrated—by Freeman Tilden a half century ago. We now take for granted the use in public history of the term "interpreter," but in 1957 when Tilden wrote *Interpreting Our Heritage*, Cold War–era parents were taking their youngsters to national parks to learn survival skills and experience a sense of their country's majesty, and Tilden cautioned National Park Service staff members that "the word interpretation as used in this book refers to a public service that has so recently come into our cultural world that a resort to the dictionary for a competent definition is fruitless."[33] He went on to define and describe this new concept:

> I am prepared to define the function of Interpretation by the National Park Service, by state and municipal parks, by museums and similar cultural institutions as follows: An educational activity which aims to reveal meanings and relationships though the use of original objects, by first hand experience, and by illustrative media, rather than simply to communicate factual information.

He continues, "Interpretation is the revelation of a larger truth that lies behind any statement of fact," and "interpretation should capitalize mere curiosity for the enrichment of the human mind and spirit." Since then, the concept of interpretation has been adopted by not only the National Park Service (NPS) but also non-NPS museums and sites. The function of translating for the public what they are seeing, whether it is in a forest or a tenement home, is almost invariably done by an interpreter.[34] (Our guests, however, will think first of "interpreter" as someone who translates between languages, and it might be best to remember that until our jargon enters common language it is just that— ours and only ours.)

Setting is crucial for living history interpreters because setting determines their activities. If you are in a farmhouse or a farm garden it is going to be different than if you are in a blacksmith shop. Thus, the setting is going to determine the skills that you demonstrate and interpret. Living history interpreters need information specific to the daily activities they are interpreting at their site. They also, however, need knowledge of the historical context of the place, the era, and the people. Living History Farms (LHF) in Urbandale, Iowa (gotta love that oxymoron—farms/urban), provides training materials for interpreters that include extensive primary materials. Interpretations are primarily if not totally first person, placing a responsibility on interpreters and costumed historians to be authentic. The site manual for the LHF 1900 Farm includes brief analyses of the significance of an item, activity, or event and lists of such frequently asked questions as "What kind of horses do [you] have?" "How much do they weigh?" "How much can they eat?" "What is the green thing in the pantry?" "Would they really have a telephone?" "Why would they wear such hot clothing in the summer?"[35] That "hot clothing" for living history interpreters tends to be owned by the museum or site, to ensure accuracy, as is the case at LHF. Especially at museums and historic sites where the essence of the experience is "stuff," authenticity is owed the visitor.

While doing fieldwork in the spring and summer of 2007, visiting Midwest museums and historic sites that use various forms of performed interpretation, I found that, while Conner Prairie in Indiana used red-shirts very effectively, the interpreters at Living History Farms were also effective in that they smoothly left first person when I asked if they would mind talking about their experience as interpreters. Of course, this was a special favor, and when a group approached, I stepped back and the gracious interpreters switched back to their earlier time period. Of course, an organization's interpretive mission will shape its interpretive practices.

At Connor Prairie my favorite area was the 1836 village, which had enough people, all in costume, to feel really alive, even toward the end of a very hot summer workday. In fact, there were even a half dozen or so YOUNG PEOPLE in evidence. And they were doing young people things—not only tending gardens and running errands but also throwing water on each other, and talking about who liked whom. The interpreters had assumed carefully developed composite characters. I talked to a physician, who told me in answer to a question that his wife had swathed the hall mirror in Osage orange-dyed, loosely woven muslin to keep flies from specking the gold on the mirror frame. It was an excellent way to say subtly, "Look! We have no screens over our windows and doors, which leads to illnesses that the doctor was treating as well as inconveniences such as fly manure on pretty objects." In the same household was a very cheerful young woman. She was living and working at the doctor's to pay off a public debt. Her husband had disappeared some months ago, and she expected him to show at any time, but from other things I had seen and heard in the town I was skeptical that he would reappear. I talked to a spinner as she spun and to a carpenter in his shop. I talked to a potter's sister who was only watching the shop "until my brother gets back." I visited with the daughter-in-law of an innkeeper who was looking forward to the day when she and her husband would be able to afford a little farm of their own. There was one blue-shirted staff member sitting on a bench in the center of town in case people wanted to ask questions that the 1836 denizens could not interpret.

Also in 2007 I visited Fort Snelling in St. Paul, Minnesota, because of its reputation for first-person interpretation. Ironically, however, the administration had just mandated a universal change to third person. The result was interesting. The interpreters were all in period clothing, which always leads me to expect first person. One interpreter kept catching herself switching to first person accidentally (after all, she had been doing first person for years), and voiced aloud the hope that she would eventually get used to third. Another longtime interpreter rebelled by giving a sub voce first-person account, indicating to us that his was an act of rebellion based on a conviction that first person was much more effective than third.[36] I informally queried an administrator about the change and was told that some visitors were uncomfortable with first person. Perhaps their guests would have been more comfortable if red-shirts had been available or if the interpreters had been allowed to step out of their roles, not as ghosts (my time/your time), but rather as knowledgeable (as they indeed were!) staff members.

Roth describes "costumed interpreters" in a setting in which "visitors roam at will and encounter interpreters in realistic situations and activities. Visitors engage them on a personal level, letting conversation flow where it may and perhaps participating with a chore or assuming a role themselves."[37] Ideally, living history interpreters are representing a particular person or composite of real people who would have been in the location in which she or he is now meeting the public. They have to know a great deal about their particular setting, both place and time (and not stray beyond the day and time being represented). Historic site policy will determine whether they have the freedom to determine if a question is best answered by firmly stepping out of character or if they need to have a red-shirt intervene.

Blacksmith Pete Bleskie at Fort Larned in Kansas is a fine example of a living history interpreter who does a skills demonstration while also describing his historical context. As he works in his shop, he also discusses the roles of others at the fort, giving a carefully nuanced take on his role as a civilian working there. Then he breaks character to discuss not only what he has made but also why and then takes questions with infinite patience. Skilled demonstrators are almost always a hit with guests as they are using real tools doing something often as costumed interpreters. Although it is not a living history site by any

---

**A Trail Story**

### 1.3. TENT IDENTITY CONFUSION

Last year I performed Calamity Jane for a historical society near Kansas City in the lodge of a gated community that had once been a lake resort. The lodge had been lovingly restored, and a member noted that, on the site, even before the lodge came to be there had been tent Chautauquas. After the event a member who had figured prominently in the restoration took Ann around the building. As they paused in front of a photograph of a group activity from the very early part of the twentieth century, Ann remembered what I had been told and remarked favorably about their Chautauqua tradition. Her guide vehemently denied that there had ever been a religious tent revival on the grounds. He had clearly conflated revivals and Chautauquas and felt so strongly about it that Ann knew it was not a teachable moment! The two are definitely very different. Often we speak of the Chautauqua revival, but it is about reviving Chautauqua, not about a religious revival. It is another case of the need to consider terminology, no matter how fond we are of certain words.

---

means, Silver Dollar City in Branson, Missouri, is replete with skilled demonstrators who sell their wares. Festivals contract for many of these same skill demonstrators, such as rope-makers and spinners.

### Scripted

Three groups make up the scripted region of the diagram: the group whose task it is to present only a script (and therefore can be actors), those who present a script and also have the responsibility for answering questions (and therefore must have contextual knowledge), and historical performers, who have a script, answer questions, and have an accurate look.

#### Script Only

*Talking Tombstones*   Talking tombstones is also known as "graveside conversations." These take place in a cemetery, weather permitting, and feature local history. Very short scripts are read or recited, often by the local theater group or forensic students in clothing borrowed from the local theater costume shop. Script includes birth date, and, unlike other forms, they get to talk about their own death, the more gruesome the better. At Fort Hays, Kansas, there was a sergeant who was "shot by a disgruntled trooper, four buffalo hunters who froze in a freak snowstorm, a young girl who died of typhoid, and a soldier who contracted hydrophobia from the bite of a rabid wolf."[38] Generally, their characters are not well known to the audience, so talking tombstone participants have literary license to take their dramatics over the top. This form can also be used at historic sites with lantern or flashlight tours—it's a good way to getting people into the site at an "off" time. History and haunts—it doesn't get any better. Unless, of course, it's historical performance, which carries the concept on and beyond!

*Dramatic Monologues*   What is a historical performance without a question-and-answer session, without care about accuracy of clothing, and, often, without direct address? A dramatic monologue. A dramatic monologue is a solo performance. Two wonderful historical dramatic monologues are Kaiulani Lee's one-woman show *A Sense of Wonder* and, best known of all, Hal Holbrook's *Mark Twain Tonight*. Both plays were written by the actors, but there is a major difference. Lee portrays Rachel Carson musing to herself in her home. Carson is oblivious to the audience. The traditional fourth wall of theater is intact. Holbrook, on the other hand, employs direct address, as do historical performances. Roth nails this difference between a historical performance and many monologues when she describes Holbrook's portrait of Samuel Clemens as "creat[ing] a situation that place[s] theatergoers in a comfortable role as an audience rather than as voyeurs intruding on a private scene."[39]

Randy Smith wrote "The Historical Dramatic Monologue: Creating the One-Character Reenactment Presentation," for the *Muzzleloader*, one of the most-read periodicals of the black powder organizations. Smith uses the term dramatic monologue to include "historical journal reading, representative character portrayals or dramatic performances of real historical characters," and "first-person dramatic narratives."[40] (In the interest of transparency I will tell you that Smith comments favorably on performances by Ann, saying, "During a recent presentation of Santa Fe Trail life in Trinidad, Colorado, Ann Birney presents a dramatic narrative of the life of Julia Archibald Holmes. By allowing the audience to ask questions during the presentation, specific issues can be addressed as they occur. This is a challenging yet very rewarding format," and by me, "Joyce Thierer's dramatic narrative of Calamity Jane not only entertains the audience about the life of a historical character, but also provides some insight into the circumstances of women of the time period."[41]) I am convinced that after Smith reads this book he will narrow his definition of dramatic monologues while continuing to admire how performance can inspire interest in history.

*Museum Theater*     Science museums are in the forefront of organizations that use performance to explain complex concepts, as evidenced by books by Tessa Bridal and Catherine Hughes that are especially useful for large organizations creating theater departments.[42] The Minnesota History Center, however, also presumes performance when they design exhibits. Wendy Jones notes that their use of theater for interpretation is "rooted in research"; while they are concerned with delivering information, they can better engage audiences when they use a story. Performance interpretation staff members are on the exhibit team. Exhibit development includes a line item for performance interpretation, including not only staff members, clothing, and teaching artifacts but also the costs of writing and printing training manuals. In addition to site-based programming, the Minnesota History Center has a fee-based History Players program that delivers engaging first-person narratives of early Minnesotans to up to sixty students at a time in kindergarten through eighth grade.[43]

At the other end of the spectrum in terms of funding and formality, Lecompton Players at the Lecompton, Kansas, historical site combines staff members and volunteers who "own" their historic figures, which they present in a range of performances as situation and availability suggest, everything from a full-troupe performance to individual historical performances to atmospherics at a festival.

*Storytelling*     Historical storytelling, according to Dale Jones, is an art that involves using "vibrant, descriptive language" to create a "historically plausible" interpretation based on valid historical sources. Much of what he describes is in the domain of historical performers.[44] Most storytellers work solo and not in costume—their words carry the story. A good historical performance is made up of a series of stories, as we will discuss in chapters 4 and 5.

*Balladeering*     Humans have always had music and songs. These vary with cultures; for example, Indian tribal music is very different from German music. Balladeers add flavor to an interpretation because music is a device to provide information about who, why, what, where, and when. Balladeers appear anywhere and everywhere, usually in third person and sometimes in costume.

Balladeers play or sing songs from the past and work with or without instrumentation. Best practice is that the music is played on era-correct instruments. Accuracy of tone, of sound, is more important than the look—the music is the script, and accuracy is important. Bones aren't bones; bison bones sound different than bovine bones. Civil War–era songs and "Home on the Range" are often played on bones. Song words can be interpreted as much as any other artifact. Balladeers are often found on arts commission rosters and will often have CDs to sell after a concert.

*Musical Monologue*   Musical monologues are solo first-person dramatic narrative interspersed with songs that carry the story forward. They may be done a capella or with recorded accompaniment. Usually they will be attired in a representational look. Independent performer Judy Coder becomes Patsy Montana, interspersing Montanan songs with text to tell the story of a Western singer and radio celebrity who insisted on being paid the same as the male cowboy singers. Anyatika Timmons-Lee, now deceased, performed a monologue about the underground railroad in which she "followed the drinking gourd," using songs as she talked of her journey.

*Pageants*   Like the Society for Creative Anachronism, pageantry has its own bubble because it is a widely practiced tradition, but in general pageants cannot be trusted for historical accuracy of script or clothing. In fact, Ralph Davol wrote in 1914 that "Pocahontas may be shod in high-heeled shoes [and] a glimpse of blue jeans may appear beneath King Philip's blanket." Of course, in the same sentence he also said, "But the community pageant, on the whole, was never a complete regret, and never failed to inspire finer fellowship or make for life more abundant."[45]

The Medicine Lodge *Indian Peace Treaty Pageant*, when I saw it in the 1950s, was replete with "Indians" in oversized wigs and dark body makeup wearing fringed brown cotton faux buckskins. My students tell me that it has changed little. This is likely because it is difficult to recruit new directors, and costumes are expensive. So, rather than have a tourist attraction die, or local youngsters not hear the stories, the same people produce the pageant for decades. Like all pageants it is outdoors to emphasize the "larger than life" scope of their history and to allow the involvement of animals. There is also at least one narrator, sometimes several.

*Voices of the Wind People* is a relatively new pageant, performed biennially in Council Grove, Kansas, which exemplifies the "free use of mystic symbolism . . . expressed in visible form."[46] Organizers involve members of the Kaw Nation now of Oklahoma to narrate a portion of the pageant, the theme of which is how whites got the land from "the Indians." Manifest destiny, the belief that Americans were destined by God to occupy the continent from sea to sea, is supported by the mystic symbolism of the pageant.

The organization Wild Women of the Frontier has a new take on pageantry. Based in Topeka, Kansas, they ride around the arena, or down the parade route, on horseback, whooping and hollering, sometimes shooting, with Clint

Eastwood movie music blaring and a narrator giving a brief description of each historic figure they portray. Like reenactors they participate for their own enjoyment. Unlike hardcore reenactors, part of that pleasure comes from not having to worry about accuracy in clothing, horse tack, or the script that each has supplied to the narrator. The audience (or presenter) pays to watch them have a good time. A girl, her horse, and her girlfriends. It doesn't get any better than this. The past is as they wish it was. Nineteenth-century temperance leader Carrie Nation might be riding astride on a 1980s saddle, her yellow dress up around her thighs, but I will admit that I like the fact that the pageantry threatens the worldview of those who think that only men populated the Old West, or that all women in the West wore sunbonnets.

### Scripted/Answers Questions, Knows Historical Context

*Lecturers*  Museums and historic sites often contract for a speaker on a specific topic expecting an academic-style presentation, heavy on data. Lecturers are scholars with historical knowledge beyond their lecture, a paper that they usually read at a podium. This year, the Bicentennial of Abraham Lincoln's birth, for instance, Doris Kearns Goodwin, having recently published *Team of Rivals: The Political Genius of Abraham Lincoln*,[47] is very popular on the lecture circuit, as are other Lincoln scholars. They are paid a fee. They are dressed formally, as scholars. They are almost invariably expected to take questions. Speakers bureaus such as those created by humanities councils and professional organizations endorse and sometimes supplement the fees paid to lecturers.

*Chautauquans*  Chautauquans are first and foremost scholars. They deliver a first-person monologue of about thirty minutes as a historic figure, then take questions in character, followed by discussion in their scholar role with the audience. Chautauquans are usually university professors who are freelancing. Often they do programs on their own, but post-1976 a Chautauqua movement, inspired by the 1886–1935 Circuit Chautauquas, swept the Great Plains. Contemporary Chautauquas, like their predecessors,[48] usually tour, providing four to six days of education and entertainment (with an emphasis on the former) under a large tent in a single community.

Chautauquans do their own research, write their own scripts, and will expound forever should an audience keep asking questions. The tradition differs from that of historical performers largely because they are not as concerned about their physical appearance. Their tradition has been to raid their university's costume shop, and if polyester was what was available, so be it. We were pleasantly surprised, therefore, when Patrick McGinnis, portraying Franklin D. Roosevelt for the Kansas-Nebraska Chautauqua 2008–2010, had leg braces con-

---

**A Trail Story**

### 1.4. JUST A PAYCHECK

Commitment is key to providing a significant experience for visitors. Right there in front of a mythic Old West saloon about twenty people waiting for a gunfight witnessed a teenaged gunfighter who, as he pulled out his cell phone to text message his friends working at the local burger joint, told his co-workers in our hearing that he wished he was flipping burgers with his buds. He talked as he texted words to the effect of, "I hate this job; nothing ever happens! Oops, got to go do the gunfight." The script played out was something along the lines of "Get out of town or . . ." There were shots. Everyone fell down. Then everyone got up and walked away. A crowd had gathered, some waiting for almost ten minutes to see a show that was over in less than two minutes. How sad for the audience. No passion. No narrative. No real interpretation. And, this happened again in two hours. Aargh! The audience had more passion than the gunfight had. They had traveled to this community with mythic images of *Gunsmoke* in their minds. This site was definitely in need of a historical performance troupe, or at least some passionate reenactors.

---

structed and shoes modified to fit the braces. The Chautauquan's fast and loose approach to clothing makes "the look" group cringe, while the loose approach to history of the "looks only" people makes the Chautauquans cringe. Great Plains Chautauquan Clay Jenkinson is nationally known, having taken his portrayal of Thomas Jefferson nationwide, including the *Thomas Jefferson Hour*, syndicated through High Plains Radio.[49] On that show one can hear "Jefferson" expounding on contemporary—twenty-first-century—events, in the tradition of the "ghost" portrayals. It would, I believe, be more effective were he to step out of character and talk as the scholar. He plays fast and loose with setting, but that was often the case with early Chautauqua revivalists; he is not to be blamed because, after all, he is not a historical performer but rather a Chautauquan, and if he wants to play a bit of the ghost (historical performers' characters can never talk about their own death in a concrete, past-tense manner), well, so be it.

### Historical Performance

Historical performance is direct-address first-person narrative that includes a scripted monologue followed by taking questions in character and as the scholar. Historical performance is at the center of the taxonomy (see figure 1.1) because its best practices include accuracy in both script and look, as well as enough knowledge to be able to answer specific questions and discuss historical context with audiences. Its practitioners have two responsibilities: accuracy, as reflected in the diagram, and also entertainment, so that people will stay and learn.

---

**AND FURTHERMORE . . .**

Jon Lipski: "Ten Commandments of Museum Theater"

1. Thou shalt not be boring.
2. Thou shalt not be boring.
3. Thou shalt not be boring.
4. Thou shalt not be boring.
5. Thou shalt not be boring.
6. Thou shalt not be boring.
7. Thou shalt not be boring.
8. Thou shalt not be boring.
9. Thou shalt not be boring.
10. Thou shalt always deliver the information.

*Source:* Jon Lipski (playwright for the Museum of Science, Boston), quoted by Dale Jones, "Theater 101 for Historical Interpretation," *AASLH Technical Leaflet,* no. 227, 7.

---

Performers allow the audience to enjoy the myths while challenging the stereotypes. We know it is all about the audience. Historical performers create a product, a performance, that is designed to move and educate an audience, a text that we deliver verbally and visually. Historical performance is done by staff members and by independent contractors or historical troupes. It should not be done by actors who have little knowledge of or passion for history. Wherever it is performed, indoors or out, onstage or on horseback, historical performance can be thought of as oral biography or memoir. Historical performers are "keepers of the stories." We honor the person when we choose to tell their story, whether we become one historic figure or a composite of several figures. Preparing the performance is a process that requires substantial investment of time and energy (described in chapters 2 through 5).

History is the story of the decisions we have made over time and how we have explained those decisions. Historical performance represents the viewpoints of individuals who have made decisions that affect us today. It then encourages discussion, which in turn helps audience members consider their own efficacy, their own roles in the process that we call history. Historical performance combines the best practices of three traditions: the reenactor's concern with accurate clothing, the dramatic monologist's care to tell a compelling narrative, and the Chautauquan's focus on accurate information.

## NOTES

1. I will occasionally use the term "presenter" as it is used in the arts: the organization that brings in the performer.

2. Thanks to Anna Marie Thatcher of Periaktos Productions (e-mail to author, August 9, 2008), I can recommend two fine works that deal with tour management: Rena Shagan, *Booking and Tour Management for the Performing Arts* (New York: Allworth Press, 1996); and Jeri Goldstein, *How to Be Your Own Booking Agent*, rev. 2nd ed. (Charlottesville, Va.: New Music Times, 2006). The authors deal with stages and not Chautauqua tents, but the philosophy and most of the basics apply.

3. For skills simulators and demonstrators, the classic is Jay Anderson, *Time Machines: The World of Living History* (Nashville: American Association for State and Local History, 1984). He covers Stone Age to World War II events. This book and *A Living History Reader: Museums*, vols. 1 and 2 (Nashville: American Association for State and Local History, 1991), are readily available at libraries and to be purchased used. On reenacting, see R. Lee Hadden, *Reliving the Civil War: A Reenactor's Handbook* (Mechanicsburg, Pa.: Stackpole Books, 1996); Tony Horwitz, *Confederates in the Attic: Dispatches from the Unfinished Civil War* (New York: Pantheon Books, 1998); and Jenny Thompson, *War Games: Inside the World of 20th-Century War Reenactors* (Washington, D.C.: Smithsonian Books, 2004). Stacy F. Roth, *Past into Present: Effective Techniques for First-Person Historical Interpretation* (Chapel Hill: University of North Carolina Press, 1998), writes for historic sites using costumed interpreters. Tessa Bridal, *Exploring Museum Theatre* (Walnut Creek, Calif.: AltaMira Press, 2004), and Catherine Hughes, *Museum Theatre: Communicating with Visitors through Drama* (Portsmouth, N.H.: Heinemann, 1998), offer assistance for creating programs.

4. Bonnie Sachatello-Sawyer et al., *Adult Museum Programs: Designing Meaningful Experiences* (Walnut Creek, Calif.: AltaMira Press, 2002), xvii, 56–67.

5. Bridal, *Exploring Museum Theatre*, 152.

6. *Opening Doors to Great Guest Experiences*, DVD/CD (Fishers, Ind.: Conner Prairie, [n.d.]).

7. Howard Gardner, *Multiple Intelligences: New Horizons*, rev. ed. (New York: Basic Books, 2006).

8. Barbara Clark, *Optimizing Learning: The Integrative Education Model in the Classroom* (Columbus, Ohio: Merrill, 1986), 26–29.

9. Jane Cannary Hickok, *Calamity Jane's Letters to Her Daughter* (San Lorenzo, Calif.: Shameless Hussy Press, 1976); Duncan Aikman, "Life and Adventures of Calamity Jane, by Herself," in *Calamity Jane and the Lady Wildcats* (Lincoln: University of Nebraska Press, 1987), 351–62.

10. Everett Albers, "Reflections on Doing Chautauqua," received at Kansas Humanities Council History Alive! scholar training session, 1993.

11. American Dental Association, "Provider Taxonomy Codes," at http://www.ada.org/prof/resources/topics/topics_npi_taxonomy.pdf (accessed January 23, 2009).

12. Thompson, *War Games*, 208.

13. Susie Wilkening and Erica Donnis, "Authenticity? It Means Everything," *History News* 63, no. 4 (Autumn 2008): 19.

14. Thompson, *War Games*, 34.

15. Thompson, *War Games*, xii–xxv.

16. Eugene L. Meyer, "The Soldier Left a Portrait and Her Eyewitness Account," *Smithsonian* 24, no. 10 (January 1994): 96–104.

17. Thompson, *War Games*, 293.

18. Roth, *Past into Present*, 184.

19. Mike Adams, informal conversation with the author, Concordia, Kans., May 3, 2008.

20. American Frontier Reenactment Guild, at http://www.wheelerjobin.com/clients/afrg (accessed January 31, 2009).

21. Thompson, *War Games*, 292.

22. Anderson, *Time Machines*, 167–72.

23. Anderson, *Time Machines*, 207.

24. Ann Fletchall, "The Spectacle of the Festival," unpublished paper in author's possession, acquired January 26, 2009, 1.

25. Andrew Robertshaw, "From Houses into Homes: One Approach to Live Interpretation," *Social History in Museums* 19 (1992): 14–20, at http://www.hrw.ndo.co.uk/index1.htm (accessed January 31, 2009).

26. Ken Bubp, interview at Conner Prairie, August 9, 2007, notes in author's possession.

27. Roth, *Past into Present*, 17–18.

28. Laura Peers, *Playing Ourselves: Interpreting Native Histories at Historic Reconstructions* (Lanham, Md.: AltaMira Press, 2004), 18.

29. Anderson, *Time Machines*, 12.

30. Freeman Tilden, *Interpreting Our Heritage*, 3rd ed. (Chapel Hill: University of North Carolina Press, 1977). Tilden's book appears in just about every bibliography on interpretation.

31. National Association for Interpretation, "Definitions Project," at http://www.definitionsproject.com/definitions/index.cfm (accessed February 9, 2009).

32. Peers, *Playing Ourselves*, xxix.

33. Tilden, *Interpreting Our Heritage*, 3.

34. Tilden, *Interpreting Our Heritage*, 7–8.

35. Living History Farms, *Site Manual 1900 Farm* (Urbandale, Iowa [n.d., unpaginated], donated by LHF, in author's possession.

36. Informal discussions with interpreters, Fort Snelling, Minn., notes in author's possession.

37. Roth, *Past into Present*, 3.

38. Bob Wilhelm, "Fort Hays: Graveside Conversations," [news release], October 27, 2007.

39. Roth, *Past into Present*, 34.

40. Randy D. Smith, "The Historical Dramatic Monologue: Creating the One-Character Reenactment Presentation," *Muzzleloader* (May/June 2002): 71.

41. Smith, "Historical Dramatic Monologue," 73, 74 (captions to photographs).

42. Bridal, *Exploring Museum Theatre*; Hughes, *Museum Theatre*.

43. Wendy Jones, interview at the Minnesota Historical Society, May 4, 2007, notes in author's possession.

44. Dale Jones, "Theater 101 for Historical Interpretation," *AASLH Technical Leaflet*, no. 227, 2.

45. Ralph Davol, *A Handbook of American Pageantry* (Taunton, Mass.: Davol Publishing, 1914), 28.

46. Davol, *Handbook of American Pageantry*, 15.

47. Doris Kearns Goodwin, *Team of Rivals: The Political Genius of Abraham Lincoln* (New York: Simon & Schuster, 2005).

48. Before the circuit Chautauquas, there was the "mother Chautauqua," which began at Chautauqua Lake in far western New York State in 1874 as continuing education for Methodist Sunday School teachers, and continues as the Chautauqua Institution learning resort, at http://www.ciweb.org/ (accessed January 31, 2009).

49. Clay Jenkinson, *The Thomas Jefferson Hour*, at http://www.jeffersonhour.org/ (accessed January 26, 2009).

# How to Choose a Historic Figure to Portray

NOW that I have inspired you by describing why historical performance is important to museums and historic sites, as well as other educational organizations, it is only fair to explain how to go about creating a first-person narrative. Even if you plan to participate primarily in informal interactions in character for small groups of visitors to historic sites, the process of developing and performing a formal program can help you focus on all aspects of your character and be better able to convince the audience that they have travelled through time.

The staged performance is a series of stories. The performer should always have more stories than can be told in a single performance. Having a bag of stories or a hatful of stories will enable you to tailor the performance to the audience (a thought occurring to "Amelia Earhart"/Ann Birney onstage: "Omigosh, this is North Newton so chances are there are Mennonites here and they will be really interested in Amelia Earhart's pacifism so I would be shortchanging them if I waited to see if I had the opportunity to bring it up during discussion"). It will also help you relate in the one-on-one discussion with visitors to your site (Amelia again: "You're from Indianapolis? I was there two years ago, refereeing the Indy 500, the first woman to do so").

The process of developing a first-person narrative in which a costumed historian/performer takes the audience back in time requires attention to two responsibilities: solid research that leads to an accurate performance and careful shaping of the script to create an entertaining performance. Having said that, one of the most interesting—and challenging—aspects of creating a first-person narrative is, like all art and every scholarly activity, subjective. It will reflect your own interests and experiences. You are in control—you decide what limits to put on your research, what questions to ask now, and what to investigate later. You decide what you want the audience to take away with them about your historic figure and her or his era. Each individual will approach these questions differently. The goal, however, is to gain as much information as possible, to look at your person and that person's time from as many angles as you reasonably can, to expand your own awareness of both how other people have perceived the person and era over time and how that individual interpreted her or his own world and being. No matter what you may have learned in high school (hopefully not in college), history is no more objective than is life itself, so use your own interests and experiences to your best advantage in this process.[1]

## HOW DO YOU DECIDE WHOM TO PORTRAY?

Your choice of whom to portray is just that—yours. Unless, of course, you are helping an organization meet a specific need: "We want Juliet Gordon Low to visit our Girl Scouts." "We MUST have an in-house Abraham Lincoln."

Your first decision should be whether or not you want to make the commitment that is required to create a historical performance. If you are asked to do a very short performance as part of a larger program, with no time to take questions, you can learn one or two stories, create your look, and practice delivering the stories in character. What a shame, though, if you have gone to that much work and do not have, or make, the opportunity to expand your performance to include more stories and discussion. Things to consider and discuss with the sponsor or presenter follow:

- Will I be delivering my monologue with minimal if any audience interaction?
- Will I be expected to take questions in character?
- Will I be expected to step out of character and take questions as the expert behind the character?
- Is it a onetime event?
- Do I have time to do the necessary research before the event to create a script that will provide an accurate representation of the historic figure's thoughts and experience?
- Do I have time and money to create accurate clothing for that person at that time?

The first consideration of whom you should portray should be your interests or those of your organization, if you are affiliated with one. If you work or volunteer for a county museum, the person you perform should have a local tie. Lincoln, Kansas, for instance, by virtue of having been named for Abraham Lincoln, invites Lincoln performers to its annual festival. Also in Lincoln, county agricultural extension agent Kathy Lupfer-Nielsen wanted local people and those across the state to know that her rural town was once on the forefront of progressive politics. She developed a fine performance of local nineteenth-century newspaper editor/publisher and ardent suffragist Anna C. Waite for the seventy-fifth anniversary of American women getting the vote, and continues to make subsequent appearances as Waite.

One reason that Lupfer-Nielsen was able to perform Waite for several years was that she knew and enjoyed her character. As a newspaper editorial writer (and, in fact, the author of most of the paper's text), many of Waite's thoughts and beliefs were literally an open book. She was a public person with a recorded text. And Lupfer-Nielsen could take clues about her personality and develop those into an interesting character. Many specific details of Waite's daily life were not recorded, but some of those could be extrapolated by other contemporary sources—she would have shopped at stores that advertised in her newspaper, for instance, and those stores would carry the same goods that other plains mercantiles carried.

Waite operated outside the prescribed sphere for women in her day, which is one of the characteristics that makes her interesting, her conflict with society. Young people in particular are often drawn to outlaws. We challenge them to place the individual's aberrant behavior within historical context. For instance, Jesse James has been interpreted as a sympathetic figure, a Robin Hood reacting to social injustice and difficult economic conditions. On the other hand, we worked with one youngster whose family name was that of one of Adolph Hitler's closest staff members. She wanted to explore that person as a famous relative. We worked with her to understand that her audience would be disinclined to like her in character. She would have to carefully frame the performance in such a way that her audience was made up of sympathizers.

Enjoyment is also one reason you might want to choose someone who in some ways is not like you. Shy people should choose someone bold, someone confident. Then, when they are on stage they are that person, not their shy selves. One such very confident historic figure is James Lane, known for his vigorous support of whichever side he took during Kansas Territory's "Bleeding Kansas" era, when the fight over free versus slave state was central to life in eastern Kansas. Tim Rues, Kansas State Historical Society site director for Constitution Hall in Lecompton, portrays Lane for visitors as part of a play with several Lecompton Reenactors, or as an individual. As part of his preparation he adjusts his hair to reflect portraits of Lane that show him with his hair blowing wildly in the winds of change. Such a dynamic character could only be played with great energy.

Major anniversaries inspire interest in particular characters. For instance, just in time for the fiftieth anniversary of World War II, Teresa Bachman, a member of the Kansas Association of Professional Historical Performers who lives near Wichita, "Air Capital of the World," created a Rosie the Riveter–like character inspired by her aunt Gladys who worked in the Boeing airplane manufacturing plant during the war. Although Bachman focuses on the home front, the war theme is one that has wide appeal, and her performance has expanded the commemoration—that is, providing gender balance. In a similar mode, several years before the Lewis and Clark Corps of Discovery Bicentennial, I created a composite character of an earth lodge woman named Grower, based on the stories of many such people. By interpreting women's roles in the meta-stories of World War II and Westward Expansion and resistance, Bachman and I fill an important niche.

But back to Anna C. Waite. Had Kathy Lupfer-Nielsen wanted to earn her living as a historical performer, or put a new roof on the barn or even the chicken coop, she should have chosen someone better known to a wider circle of people. And by wide, we must face squarely the gender issue. Sad but true, a public performance of a woman speaking on "women's issues" will not attract many men. Even if Lupfer-Nielsen is interpreting nationally and still-renowned women's rights activist Elizabeth Cady Stanton, or her friend and colleague Susan B. Anthony, her audience would be limited. More on that when I talk of marketing in the next chapter, but for now, believe me when I say that to attract men, and women who only attend public events with their menfolk, Anna C. Waite would need to be framed first as an early Kansas newspaper editor or town settler talking about pioneer hardships, and only in the very fine print or on stage would she come out as a suffragist.

What characters work for a wide range of audiences? Generally, readily recognizable ones, such as historic figures featured in children's biography series. Preferably also people who dealt with concrete objects in addition to ideas. George Washington Carver was an agricultural researcher whose work with farmers helped the environment, but we know him primarily for his work with peanuts. Would Rosa Parks have become as famous without her bus? Amelia Earhart wrote passionately about social justice and world peace, but she would not have had her bully pulpit had she not been a record-setting pilot. Earhart's husband when he first met her recognized her publicity potential before she became the first woman to cross the Atlantic by air. Ann Birney is just building on what George Palmer Putnam did to build Earhart's career in building her own, performing as Amelia. Of course, once she is given the stage, like Amelia she uses it to speak about those passions. But it is aviation and the mystery of her disappearance that gets both Amelia and Ann on the contract, in the door, and on stage. Likewise, "my" Calamity Jane is identified with a masculine time and place, with horses and guns, the Old West. Even after a certain television series came along, people are not quite sure what Jane did in the Old West. That's a frequent question of people who have not seen my performance: "I have heard of her, but, what did she *do*?"

Margaret Sanger is a wonderful character. But try talking passionately about birth control in the tenements and slums to Great Plains farmers. It won't sell. It might sell conceptually to the American Association of University Women or Philanthropic Educational Organization (PEO) chapters, or Extension Home and Community Units, but they are not accustomed to paying more than travel expenses and a meal for programs. On the other hand, in larger cities there are audiences for women who portray Sanger. Likewise with socialist Mother Jones. Interpret these great, dynamic women if you live in a metropolitan area or like to travel to reach those venues.

Martin Luther King is going to be welcomed across rural Kansas because of white guilt if nothing else. And besides, we are vaguely aware that he is less threatening than Malcolm X. The Nebraska Humanities Council's 2007 Chautauqua included Charles Pace as Omaha-born Malcolm X. The Chautauqua was held in Kearney in south central Nebraska. Anything west of Lincoln in southeast Nebraska is sometimes characterized by those who live in the more populous area as "outstate," where no one lives and nothing of note happens. There is, however, a state university in Kearney—and a sense of humor, for their Museum of Nebraska Art is affectionately called "The MONA," a play on the slightly more famous New York MOMA, Museum of Modern Art. The theme for the Nebraska Chautauqua was Nebraska reformers and included William Jennings Bryan, who had traveled extensively with Chautauquas. As part of a series and in a university town, Malcolm X was welcome.

In general, one should look for opportunities to portray individuals with whom you share a passion, be it for baseball, medicine, or fashion design, and then create a script and performance that will help the audience understand the decisions that the individual made, and why that person is significant to us today. Take on characters who fit your interests and those of your organization, if you are working in an organization, and who would be of interest to your potential audiences. Use "famous" people to create an audience for less-famous people you would like to introduce to the public. Audiences who have seen Ann

Birney portray Amelia Earhart trust Ann to bring them high-quality programs, so the fact that they have never heard of Julia Archibald Holmes does not deter them from asking her to do Holmes.

### What Is a Composite Character and Why Would I Want to Use One?

In general, composite characters are best used to represent groups of ordinary people who did not individually leave enough primary resources from which to fashion an interesting narrative. This includes peoples who have no written record, such as the Kanza, Mandan, and Hidatsa of the eighteenth century on whom my Grower is based. It also allows me to bring home to Kansas the experience of the at least six hundred women who are known to have fought in the Civil War disguised as men.[2] Five of the women soldiers were connected to Kansas at some point in their lives, but they left few records. By combining what my research found about these five with what we know of other women soldiers, and the experiences of Civil War soldiers in general, I was able to create a compelling narrative with accurate historical context.

Ann Birney was motivated by another valid reason to create a composite character. In 1993, I needed one more performance to provide the four that Cottonwood Falls, Kansas, wanted for their community festival, which was about two months away. I recruited Birney into her very first historical performance by telling her that she could do anyone she wanted to do as long as she rode in on sidesaddle. (At that time, all of Ride into History's performances involved horses—and my vintage saddle collection.) With very little time to prepare and much to do, Birney wisely realized that if she was going to know more than any member of her audience about her character, it would behoove her to manufacture that character. She had recently been reading letters from Susan B. Anthony and other suffragists who were stumping for the vote for Kansas women during the 1860s and 1890s. She had also been researching women's rights newspapers. It was an era that was not familiar to most end-of-the-twentieth-century Kansans. Creating a composite character did not allow her to play fast and loose with history, but it did have the benefit of allowing her to craft her story to take into account her own lack of skill in riding sidesaddle. If, for instance, she had fallen off while riding onto the "stage," it would have been her character, Elizabeth, doing so, not Ann, and the explanation as to why she, a seemingly proper woman, was not adept at sidesaddle was not only in the script but also led to a discussion of contemporary concern over women losing virginity by riding astride, and then to medical theories of the time as to why women should not receive a higher education. Birney's success led to her eventual integration into Ride into History's historical performance touring troupe.

### What If You Don't Look Like the Person You Want to Portray?

Poet and critic Samuel Taylor Coleridge strove to inspire in his readers a "willing suspension of disbelief for the moment."[3] This is what we want our audiences to experience—we want to do everything we can to let them believe we are who we say we are and they are part of our setting. Part of our responsibility, then, is having a sense of how much our audience knows about our subject—what is likely to distract them from a willing suspension of disbelief. Clothing plays a role, but so does general personal appearance, some of which can be easily manipulated—wear contact lenses instead of glasses. Wear *colored* contact lenses if eye color is well known. If, on the other hand, the physical difference will be great, do not perform if the person is an icon—if their picture is used, for instance, in television and billboard advertising for sleep medication. Some things can be worked around—if you have a passion for Abraham Lincoln and have the right facial characteristics and coloring but are only five and a half feet tall, you can perform Lincoln, but you should work from a stage or riser—and make an entry after audience members are seated—so that you are higher than the audience. You will, of course, also want Lincoln's tall stovepipe hat to achieve his iconic look (and add to your height). It can be done.

---

**A Trail Story**

#### 2.1. AMELIA NOT FOUND

Just after a performance in Oklahoma City, an audience member honored Ann Birney with a poster advertising an upcoming USO dance. He told her they were entering the poster in a contest—last year's had won an award. He called her attention to various historic aviation figures, including Jimmy Doolittle, and there, he pointed out, was Amelia Earhart. Only it wasn't Earhart. It was Birney. What to do? She had to tell him. He made a quick phone call: sure enough, the designer had gotten the picture from the Internet.

---

If the person is not as well known as you would wish them to be, take advantage of that. Pilot Bonnie Johnson does an excellent portrayal of Louise Thaden, a contemporary of Amelia Earhart. Thaden is not well known outside of women's aviation history circles, and we rarely see her picture. So credibility is not a problem when Johnson tells us she is Thaden, even though she is considerably shorter than Thaden. On the other hand, the tall, slender Amelia Earhart is an icon, used in advertising everything from computers to Internet services. A short, plump Earhart I saw once had no credibility with the audience from the get-go.

There is an advantage to portraying someone who lived before photography was common. Calamity Jane was much photographed because she created a public persona. Biblical characters have some latitude because the history is ancient. On the other hand, the image of a blue-eyed, blonde Mary, mother of Jesus, has been discredited, so don't try it.

Or, portray someone who knew the individual if it is a story you really want to tell (see trail story 2.2). A light-skinned individual should not portray baseball great Jackie Robinson or one of the Tuskegee airmen. On the other hand, then–Topeka High School student John Freeman's portrayals telling the stories

## A Trail Story

### 2.2. HONORING ORDINARY PEOPLE, REMEMBERING FAMOUS ONES

Here's an example of an associate to a famous person that as far as I know has not been used, so feel free to do so: a December 26, 2006, article by Jan Biles in the *Topeka Capital-Journal* (http://www.cjonline.com/stories/122606/kan_burger.shtml), "Going with Life's Flips and Turns: Auburn Woman Nannied for Builder of Lindbergh's The Spirit of St. Louis." Biles interviewed Helen Burger, who was "nanny, cook and housekeeper for T. Claude Ryan, founder of Ryan Aeronautical Co. and builder of The Spirit of St. Louis." That article was a reminder of the many perspectives in history, the many stories that overlap each other. One could, of course, portray pilot Charles Lindbergh—or Anne Morrow Lindbergh, an author, pilot, and Charles's wife. But one could also portray one of the men who built Lindbergh's fascinating plane or the nanny, who, like Ryan, grew up in Kansas but found herself working in San Diego—seven days a week for $1 a day plus room and board. Either a Ryan or a Burger could talk about the more famous man, as well as give perspective on lives less well documented.

of African Americans in racist America took him to Washington, D.C., for National History Day competitions for three years (1996–1998). John is white. He portrayed white people who had intimate knowledge of his subjects.[4]

Chautauquan Clay Jenkinson, in discussing the decision of the 2008 Nevada Chautauqua to include John Hay, President Lincoln's secretary, instead of Abraham Lincoln himself, calls Hay his "Abraham Lincoln window." He says, "We decided to explore and celebrate and challenge and come to terms with Lincoln by way of people around him, and by concentrating on what he wrote and said rather than how he looked. We believe that in doing so—in letting Lincoln's absence speak more eloquently than any presence could achieve—we will get closer to the heart of his achievement and his greatness."[5] It could be, too, that because Jenkinson is not very tall, he is choosing to portray someone he could do more convincingly.

Age is another consideration. Again, it depends in part on audience knowledge of the individual. A sixty-year-old could portray an individual who died at forty if the age of death is not commonly known, and if the performer appears younger than the average sixty-year-old. One common mistake is that of an older person attempting to portray an individual at the time of the most significant event in her life instead of at an older age, looking back. Julia Archibald Holmes gained fame for becoming the first woman known to have climbed to the top of Pikes Peak in the Rocky Mountains. She did this in 1858 at age twenty. She lived to be forty-eight. A person could portray Holmes at any point between twenty and forty-eight, but the younger the portrayal the more limiting the text. At twenty, for instance, Holmes could talk about Bleeding Kansas and the Santa Fe Trail. But she could not talk about going with her husband to Washington, D.C., in 1861 after Abraham Lincoln's inauguration to ask for a federal appointment, which James Henry Holmes did receive. Nor could she talk about getting booted out of New Mexico for abolitionist activities. Or about living in Washington and working for the federal government.

Ann Birney laments that Amelia Earhart, her signature character, disappeared when flying around the world at the age of forty. Birney knows she will grieve when she has to "give up" Amelia but is thinking about whom she might portray that would be closer in age—perhaps Amelia's sister so many years after the disappearance, or the hairdresser who gave Amelia her famous curls and just might have had access to information not generally available to the public. Or any of the many women who were members of the Ninety-Nines, the international organization of women pilots that she helped found.

Anyone who does historical performances invests in research and authentic clothing, but the most expensive cost of all is time. Do consider carefully your choice of who you intend to be, and choose either someone you can be for years or someone who knew them. We integrate them into our identity, and we come to love them as we would a close family member, a significant "other" in our lives, in some cases like a twin, or an alter ego. You'd better believe that I will mourn when I have to "hang up" Calamity Jane's duds. I have yet to find a historical performer who can talk comfortably what is in most cases an inevitability.

Physical disability can also be an issue, but one that can be dealt with. Eric Sorg, of Laramie, Wyoming, when I knew him, was a professional actor who had done musical theater across the country and beyond. He was diagnosed with multiple sclerosis, a gradually crippling disease. He could no longer be trusted to deliver predictable lines that would serve as cues to other actors. He might or might not be able to stand or to walk onstage. Eric hated the idea of never being able to perform again. Instead of giving up theater, he chose to continue his career as Buffalo Bill. He created a monologue in which he was an elderly Buffalo Bill Cody reflecting back on his life. Over seven hundred times all over the world and in a wide variety of venues, he delivered his lines from a chair using his expressive visage and powerful voice to reach out to the audience, rising to his feet when and if he was able. He converted his master's thesis on Buffalo Bill Cody into a book that he sold in and around his performance, along with audio tapes of his performance.[6]

I was at Sorg's last performance, which was for the 1998 Boulder City, Nevada, Chautauqua, "Shaping American Myths." Eric and I were to perform the same night, just in case he could not make it through his full performance. "Cody" spent the afternoon sitting on the porch of the hotel, chatting and swapping "old stories" with "Calamity Jane," our feet up on the rail and him in a "regular" chair. We went into character when people stopped to talk. This was a tradition of his that is not part of my pre-Chautauqua warm-up. When the public was not in evidence we mostly talked shop but sometimes slipped into character, just for fun.

That evening Eric wheeled himself onto the stage. The audience did not know this was to be his last performance. He made it through in fine form. As he waved his hat and grinned broadly at their standing ovation, tears ran down his cheek. I watched his brilliant last public performance, knowing how much it had taxed him physically, and I worried about his future. My performance followed Eric's, and I was inspired, too, by a very appreciative audience. We took questions in character and, finally, took off our hats and became scholars to discuss Cody and Jane, as is typical with Chautauquas. The questions kept coming, and they were good questions. We were moving in and out of character to answer them. Of course, this made his evening long. His face and responses reflected his exhaustion. As we had agreed, he ended the performance when he had to, and I wheeled him off stage. We changed out of our costumes and into our "civvies," and went to the very raucous end-of-Chautauqua party, where he bragged he was negotiating to sell his copyrighted script to movie actor Peter Coyote. Eric chose the perfect historic figure with whom to end his days as a performer.

### HOW WILL YOU KNOW WHEN TO BOOK YOUR FIRST PERFORMANCE?

Book it now. That first performance is the motivation for you to commit to a character, do the research, create your script, practice telling your history, and refine the look of your historic figure. Based on over twenty years of doing historical performance, and over ten years of helping new historical performers, I have the authority to say that if you wait to perform until you feel you are fully ready you will never have a first performance. It is a process. Each time you will do better, improving your script and your delivery.

I am never "ready." I am always learning more and using it to fine tune my text. That is one of the advantages of a performance over a written text or a memorized script. That said, deadlines are useful. You will be as ready as you are, when the date and time of the first performance arrives. The audience is seated, and you are backstage wishing . . . wishing you had looked at one more source to answer that question you forgot about until now. Wishing you had gone through your script one more time. Wishing you had practiced with the wireless microphone while you were in costume. Wishing you could ask the audience for a little more time . . . but you can't. You go on. And you know you could do better. But the audience is appreciative, and they ask good questions, many or most of which you can answer on the spot, and you offer to follow up on the others. As things wind up you kick yourself because you totally left out the story about ———, and you are sure you said "uh" too many times. But your friend rushes forward and says, "That was great! I learned a lot and I even forgot it was you up there." And you think, "I can do this." And you start planning how the next performance will be even better. That is why I advise that you find a venue and get a date set up before you are "ready."

### WHO SHOULD HAVE THE HONOR OF BEING YOUR FIRST AUDIENCE?

Choose an audience that will be interested in your topic, but not experts, perhaps a community service group such as Kiwanis or Rotary, or a study club. A group like PEO that meets weekly or monthly appreciates free programs and provides a guaranteed and generally receptive audience. Offer them a thirty-minute performance followed by questions in character and then as the historian/performer, so the total program will be about forty-five minutes.

Public libraries are another source of audiences, including young people. If your program will fit into the summer reading theme, the librarian will probably welcome your contribution. Assisted-living centers are fine, but do not choose a nursing home for your first performance. You will want an alert and engaged audience.

Even before your first public performance, you will probably want to hold a house performance. Get a group of friends and their friends together for a potluck meal (or you buy the pizza), and share your performance with them. Afterward, ask them to make suggestions. And don't worry about following all of the suggestions—you will probably want to weigh the suggestions very closely.

But here we are planning a performance party, and you have nothing to say and nothing to wear. So we'd best do some research. On to chapter 3!

## NOTES

1. The ability to examine the world through a lens that does not include the viewer's own experience and preferences has been discredited by many historians, including Joan Wallach Scott, *Gender and the Politics of History* (New York: Columbia University Press, 1988); Eve Kornfeld, "History and the Humanities: The Politics of Objectivity and the Promise of Subjectivity," *New England Journal of History* 51, no. 3 (Winter 1995): 44–55; and Peter Novick, *That Noble Dream: The "Objectivity Question" and the American Historical Profession* (Cambridge: Cambridge University Press, 1988). Even science is infused with subjectivity, as demonstrated by Donna Haraway, "The Biological Enterprise: Sex, Mind, and Profit from Human Engineering to Sociobiology," *Radical History Review* 20 (1979): 206–37; Evelyn Fox Keller, *Reflections on Gender and Society* (New Haven, Conn.: Yale University Press, 1985); Ruth Hubbard, "Some Thoughts about the Masculinity of the Natural Sciences," in *Feminist Thought and the Structure of Knowledge*, ed. Mary McCanney Gergen (New York: New York University Press, 1988), 1–15; and Sandra Harding, *The Science Question in Feminism* (Ithaca, N.Y.: Cornell University Press, 1986).

2. De Anne Blanton and Lauren M. Cook, *They Fought Like Demons: Women Soldiers in the Civil War* (Baton Rouge: Louisiana State University Press, 2002).

3. "Samuel Taylor Coleridge: Biographia Literaria (1817)," chapter XIV, at http://www.english.upenn.edu/~mgamer/Extexts/biographia.html (accessed February 8, 2009).

4. Steve Fry, "Topeka Teens Chalk Up Wins at History Contest," *Topeka Capital-Journal*, June 15, 2001, at http://www.cjonline.com/stories/061501.com_history.shtml (accessed February 9, 2009).

5. Clay Jenkinson, "Making Hay while the Sun Shines in Reno," at http://nevadahumanities.org/programs/chautauqua/clay-jenkinson-article (accessed February 8, 2009).

6. Eric Sorg, *Buffalo Bill: Myth and Reality* (Santa Fe, N.Mex.: Ancient City Press, 1998).

# 3

# Researching for a First-Person Narrative

WHY must you do research to be a historical performer? Because your audience trusts you. You have an obligation to them to be as accurate as you can be. If they know very little about your historic figures, they will believe what you tell them. If they share with others their new knowledge and they are told they are wrong, your audience will feel betrayed, and rightly so. On the other hand, if an audience member has some knowledge of the historic figure and era and hears you misspeak, very likely they will question everything else that you say. If you are an old hand at doing historical research, scan this chapter and after you do your research go on to chapter 4 on creating the script. Whether or not you know how to research, you will probably find that some if not all of the worksheets at http://www.historic performance.com/worksheets.pdf will help you focus your research in a way that will be useful to you when you begin converting your research findings to scripted stories.

If you are concerned because it has been years since you had to do "real research," and then it was to meet a course requirement and to be honest you were less than enthusiastic because you *had* to do it, . . . pause . . . breathe. Easy now! This time, it is *your* quest and *you* are in charge. Yours is a worthwhile mission, and you have an exciting array of research tools available to you, so let's go get those facts! Let me assure you right here and now that the steps below are designed to work novices through the phases of research. Here, as in other parts of this manual, those of you with more expertise may glance over the following and use parts of it as a reminder of where you might go for data and information.

It is important to remember that you are researching not only for your script but also to be able to answer questions posed by audience members *and* to help audience members continue their own research. Therefore, it is important for you to collect lists of sources and what you found in each. In fact, one of the kindest things you can do for audiences is to give them a list of resources such as books, museums, films, and websites that were useful to you, and to note which ones were useful for what. In a written biography, most authors indicate where they found their information by using footnotes and a bibliography. As a historical performer you are presenting an oral biography, so you will need to be able to quickly respond when asked the name of a book, article, museum, authority, library, or archive. The ability to do so not only enhances the experience for audience members but also increases your credibility with the occasional skeptic. If someone challenges the validity of something you say, you can tell them where you found the information and why your source should be believed. On the other hand, a little humility is very appropriate because it could very well be that your audience member has access to better information, so, in general, be ready to listen when people offer new information, but you need also to be ready to weigh in with why you believe they are right or wrong. Dialogue and interpretation are important tools for exploring historical events.

Research is research—whether the outcome is a historical performance, a museum exhibit, an article for a refereed journal, or a family genealogy. Lest you think that history has some grand mystique about it and you are not sure of your place as a prospective researcher, Carl Becker defines history as "the memory of things said and done" and as "essential to the performance of the simplest acts of daily life." He calls our attention to the fact that every human conducts research, if only to see if we paid last month's utility bill.[1]

As I said in chapter 2, when I indicated you should choose a character and era you enjoy, research will be more pleasurable if you choose a topic or era that interests you. Plan to invest significant time on this portion of your project.

It is useful when researching to understand the difference between primary and secondary sources. Primary sources are those created at the time of an event such as diaries, newspapers, and photographs. Secondary sources, on the other hand, are written after the fact. The first authors of secondary sources pull together multiple primary sources. Subsequent secondary sources are created using earlier secondary sources and, hopefully, additional primary sources to create new interpretations. Usually you will start with secondary sources if they are available, and then go back to primary sources to confirm and expand on what the secondary sources say. If, say, you are creating a performance based on an ancestor, you might have a family history, but unless the individual you are interpreting wrote a memoir or is famous, most of your work will involve reading what primary material is available, including that of other people who shared that era and geographical area with them.

In this manual I repeatedly suggest that you write things down. I will say it again because it is so important: document, document, document. Keep a paper trail of your research, inedible bread crumbs that will lead you back through the forest of facts to the ones you need later.[2]

The list below will help you get started and keep your research moving along as you seek answers. This list will also help you start thinking about where you might go to find the answers to these questions and the many questions you will come up with as you begin the process of researching your character and his or her era. Yes, it is a long list. And, no, not all of the following items will be of use to everyone. This list is, however, based on many years of teaching individuals how to research.

- Familiarize yourself with the worksheets at http://www.historicperform ance.com/worksheets.pdf.
- Write and post where you will be reminded often the following: "I am researching [the name of your person] in order to perform a first-person narrative." Practice saying it. Not only will this remind you of your goal, but it will also help you articulate to others what you are doing. Putting your thoughts concisely on paper and perhaps posting this sign in several places will help you stay on the trail.
- Plan your project by asking questions. The old middle school list of the "5 w's and h" is very valuable to recall at the beginning and periodically throughout your research: who, what, when, where, why, how, and, of course, the historian's favorite question, "What is the significance of the person and events?"
- Brainstorm. Where might I find the answers to my questions?
- Plan to learn in general about your topic, but also plan to learn specialized knowledge and technological terms.
- Find out what your local library has on your historic figure and era.
- But even before looking at these reference tools, look at a few children's or young adult books to learn the basics. Also use college textbooks to learn what the person-on-the-street knows about your era and historical context.

- If your library is large enough to have a professional reference librarian, make an appointment to research. If your library is not that large, plan to go to one. Librarians and archivists are the historical performer's friend. They are experts. They can help you find data more quickly and easily. They know the collections. They know the keywords to aid research in their collections. Beyond biographies, there might be reference books, indexes, newspapers on microfilm, and other material that could be helpful. Libraries have many useful research indexes, online databases, electronic search systems, and CD-ROM systems to aid researchers. And, best of all, they will explain how these tools work and answer many questions about other research needs that you may have.

- A call and talk with a librarian or an archivist might save a costly research trip that may or may not end in meeting your hoped-for outcome. When you call have your query carefully thought out so they can really help you determine if they have what you might need. A too-general question of a research library (e.g., "Do you have anything on the West?") will be given less respect than a concisely phrased query: "I want to learn as much as I can about seamstresses in Laramie from 1870 to 1920, their work and personal lives. I have already checked city directories and have some names, dates, and locations."

- If your library does not have a specific book, article, or other material you need, ask to use Interlibrary Loan. Most materials can be borrowed from another library for your use, saving you time and travel money. You will, however, need to request them several weeks before you actually need them.

- If you find very little about the individual, your research will focus more on her or his historical context—the exciting times in which the individual was living.

- Check the Internet for museums dedicated to your individual, such as the Amelia Earhart Birthplace Museum in Atchison, Kansas. In this instance you might also want to visit aviation museums to look at aircraft similar to ones she might have flown. I found out that Calamity Jane's clothing was at the Buffalo Bill Cody Museum in Cody, Wyoming, from an article that I read.

- If you use a biography, look at the list of sources in the back. If it is a scholarly publication it will list not only books and articles but also archives and collections, such as those we used for Calamity Jane at the Deadwood Public Library and Adams House and Museum, Earhart collections at Purdue University and the Schlesinger Library at Radcliffe, and files on Julia Archibald Holmes at the Denver Public Library. At the Kansas State Historical Society Research Center, I found newspaper clippings quoting letters from female Civil War soldiers.

- Never look only on the Internet. One quick trail story here: I once typed in the search phrase "Calamity Jane" to see if anything was new on the net. To my surprise I found a middle school student's report. While it was well done considering her age, it was not truly a scholarly product.

- Consider keeping a research "work diary" in which as you research you document not only your findings but also your thoughts and your questions. This will help you do follow-up (in case you need additional help or information). Write things down as you go. Take copious notes. Be disciplined. Notes are the only way to find the material again. Make photocopies or photograph your sources. Write clearly. Write full citations in your notes: author, title, journal or publisher, date, pages, *and* where you found the work. As you research, keep a list of depositories and archives you access, as well as books, articles, and any of the many other access points of information that you may use. Note places where you know there is more material and begin to plan when and how you will get there. Write down the names, titles, organizations, addresses, phone numbers, and e-mail addresses of people who helped you in your research. Be disciplined and always write down full citations for the research when you have your hands on the material. This step is often seen by performers as a "time-consuming hassle." Perhaps, but do remember that you are doing real historical research when you can create an accurate historical performance. You are, indeed, doing research as a historian or author. Never assume that you will be able to find data again when you need it, so write the citation when you are looking at the information.

- Pick a citation style and be consistent. Most historians use the *Chicago Manual of Style*. It is rather daunting, but you can just emulate the style that I use in the endnotes and bibliography in this book—another reason to be glad that you bought it! Or, invest in a software product such as EndNote.

- Use quotation marks around anything that you use that is in the exact words of the author, whether it is a short phrase or long sentences. In your script you will be expected to use the actual words of the person you are portraying as much as possible (see chapter 4 on scriptwriting), but it is usually impossible to acknowledge a secondary source in a spoken script, so you will be synthesizing and rephrasing, not quoting, those concepts, but you still want to know what the original said.

- File your material where you can access it again. Of course, everyone has their own system, but I suggest file folders and storage boxes for your papers and a bookshelf for your books. Piles created for later access may not be found again.

- The post-performance scholarly dialogue will give you the opportunity to discuss where you collected data, including acknowledging help from librarians and archivists. And, yes, people will ask about your research—well, they will if you give them half a chance to dialogue. People in the audience are downright curious. They have learned something, and now they want to process their conclusions with you and perhaps even to read more. This, for a historical performer, is called the "EHAA!!" moment—the audience cares; they want to stay and talk. From the audience perspective it is as one person stated, "C-o-o-l! You mean you will talk to me about your research? And, you can even tell me a book that I can read. Let me borrow a piece of paper and pencil. I will be right back. Oh, you have a book list at the back of the room. W-a-a-y C-o-o-o-l!" Or words to that effect.

- Set parameters and adjust them as you research. If you are developing a performance based on the life of a Civil War soldier, you do not have time to read everything that has been written about that war. Instead, you will focus on that individual and the battles and places where he or she was posted. After you have developed your script you can dig further, creating more stories that can be told during the discussion, should the right question be asked, such as a question about Reconstruction. Focus, focus, focus.

- Break your research into smaller chunks so it does not become overwhelming. Plan a strategy for the whole project. Review your questions looking for small chunks. Jump in and start looking for the answers. Saying that, do remember that as you are looking for one answer, the answer to another question may be presented to you. Think about research as putting together a jigsaw puzzle—one piece at a time leads to a grand picture emerging out of those small irregular segments.

- Recognize that hands-on experience, if accurate, can enhance your ability to picture an event or process (see trail story 3.1). You get insights that you might not get out of books. Living history practitioners are one source of information. They test, acquire, and, sometimes, demonstrate skill sets that help other historians better interpret the documents and artifacts they come across in their research. Historical performers need to simulate skills of life in "their" era as well as the documented data they have been researching. A historical performer needs to know, ideally, what "their" person knew. Some of you will try out what you read with your own hands, and others will learn vicariously through others' research. Both are valid, as long as you have the knowledge. Learning the life skills of a person of your era, whether through books, weekend intensive skill training workshops, or by really watching someone do it or taking a more hands-on approach and learning from your more skilled friends, is a boon. Acquire skills like you acquire information from other forms of research.

## A Trail Story

### 3.1. THE HOE STORY

*Buffalo Bird Woman's Garden,* the result of the 1914 interview of Hidatsan Buffalo Bird Woman by anthropologist Gilbert Wilson, inspired this agricultural historian to attempt a garden like hers. I was seized by a burning desire to see if I could simulate in one corner of my horse corral a small part of what Hidatsa women had created. I used the Internet to order heritage corn, beans, and squash seeds. I assembled my tools: a small ash tree cut with an ax from the pasture became a digging stick, and another became the handle of my hoe. I already had rawhide. I got a beef scapula from a processing plant, knowing from Buffalo Bird Woman's account that the Hidatsa would have used buffalo bones. A gourd became my seed bowl. I was given a three-tine deer antler. I planted the seeds in hills, together, as she had. I learned that the scapula hoe was a scraper, not a chopper. I did not irrigate. As I was planting, and later as I was weeding, I found myself asking the women who had done this before, how they would have done it. The answers I heard inspired me to create my portrayal of Grower, a composite earth lodge woman almost a century older than Buffalo Bird Woman, who looks back on her grandmothers' lives, when to be a woman was to be a farmer, and forward to a future harbingered by iron hoes brought by whites. Experiential research augmented my book larnin' and made me more confident in my portrayal—that and having been vetted by several tribal elders.

- Leave yourself open to serendipity. In retrospect it may seem odd how answers seem to come out of nowhere. Researchers have stories about how, just as they were ready to give up, the Universe stepped in:
  - I had about given up on finding the answer! Then the next person I happened to talk to said, "Have you talked to _____?" And lo and behold, their friend had the answer I had been looking for high and low and was just about to give up on!
  - A shaft of light fell on a book on the shelf. Odd, I thought as I picked it up, and it fell open to the page I needed. Yep! There was the answer I had been looking for. Spooky!
  - A book fell off the shelf in the stacks right at my feet. So I looked around. No one was there, but the answer I needed was right there in that book. Odd, don't you think?
  - I fell asleep, thinking about my research. During a dream I traveled through time, gaining insight, and in the morning I was ready to tackle the problem again, but this time I knew what questions to ask.

So with luck and keeping all doors open, the "Aha!" moment happens. Such moments are really hard to footnote, but researchers are grateful for them nonetheless!

## AS YOU RESEARCH

- Skimming may help you acquire an overview of the topic, but that is not a real substitute for reading deeply and absorbing the facts you will need in order to write and perform a carefully nuanced historical performance.
- Evaluate your sources for quality and content. Determine their usefulness for your current topic. Keep the good and do not waste time on the not-so-useful material.
- As you research you will be discovering different interpretations of the same information. This is good as you are in the discovery phase of the project. Later you will decide which, if any, interpretation is the one you will choose to use.
- What do you do if your sources contradict each other (see trail story 3.2)? If you have two sources, check a third. But a simple vote doesn't solve the dilemma. Also check to see where the authors got their information. Did they use primary sources? Which author has the best credentials? Which work is most recent?

**A Trail Story**

### 3.2. "FIRST WOMAN TO CLIMB TO THE TOP OF PIKE'S PEAK?"

Ann portrays Julia Archibald Holmes, who climbed to the top of Pikes Peak in 1858. She also portrays Amelia Earhart. Imagine her surprise when she found an otherwise-scholarly work that said Earhart's mother was the first woman to climb Pike's Peak. If that was the case it would certainly be a fine contribution to the explanation of Amelia's adventuresome nature. Amelia "Amy" Otis, however, was not born until eleven years after Julia Holmes climbed the mountain. Ann says that she is probably one of three people who know of this discrepancy, and care. Her hypothesis is that Amy's family had not read Holmes's account of climbing the mountain in the nearby Lawrence newspaper, and their guide, also not knowing of a predecessor, bestowed the title on her, and the story continued in family lore. Will she work to solve this mystery? Probably not.

- Historians want to find three sources for any fact. Of course, it does not count if two of those sources are just citing the first source!
- The research process is rather like a spiderweb. It is not linear. Each item may be presented to you in a linear manner because the other writer has organized her or his own finding in a linear style. But the next item you find, read, and use may have a different twist on the data. Somehow, though, you will make sense of the disparate data, and, in the next step, scriptwriting, weave the bits and pieces together into a single story web.
- The reality of research is that you will have to consider multiple items at the same time. The writing of the script is where you will start organizing your data, factoids, and the many stories you are finding.

### WATCH FOR THEMES AND GOOD STORIES
- Think of how you will use the material now and as you convert it into your historical performance.
- Look for the "wow" factor. As you gain familiarity with the material do not lose that excitement—the audience will love it.

- As you research you will gain familiarity with the material and start to see repetition and patterns. This is good as it will help you note parts you may wish to keep in your script and perhaps parts you may want to place into your story bag or the "out-take" files.
- Write more questions to answer. And, yes, you will always be questing for more "cool data."
- As you review your material, pay particular attention to changes in interpretations, how historians have changed over the years, and how they think and write about historical events. Historians are influenced by their own historical context and personal experience as well as the thinking of their colleagues. The study of change in approaches to history is called "historiography." An example: historians writing in the first decades after the Civil War had very different interpretations than those of historians writing a century later.

My task in this book is to give you information that should be especially helpful for researching for a first-person narrative. If you want to turn your performance research into a publication, I recommend you use W. H. Mc-Dowell's *Historical Research: A Guide for Writers of Dissertations, Theses, Articles, and Books* (Upper Saddle River, N.J.: Longman, 2002).

Now that you have gathered your material, the next step is to determine what part of it you will use for your script and to organize it all into a first-person narrative of less than an hour. Onward!

**NOTES**

1. Carl Becker, "Everyman His Own Historian," *American Historical Review* 37, no. 2 (January 1932): 221–36.

2. For a cautionary tale as to why you should be very careful about note taking so that you do not plagiarize, using the words of others without saying that you are doing so, read online David Plotz, "The Plagiarist: Why Stephen Ambrose Is a Vampire," Slate, January 11, 2002, at http://www.slate.com/toolbar.aspx?action=print&id=2060618 (accessed January 23, 2009); or listen to "Plagiarism," *All Things Considered*, National Public Radio, January 10, 2002, at http://www.npr.org/templates/story/story.php?storyId=1136141 (accessed February 9, 2009).

# Creating Your Script

The way to make a movie is to understand that you're speaking to one person at a time. . . . You're telling them a story, gauging their reaction, watching in your mind's eye as they lean forward, making it as personal a telling as you possibly can.

—*Edward Zwick, director*[1]

Once you start doing historical performance you see inspiration everywhere, even in *Architectural Digest* advertisements.

—*Joyce Thierer, scholar-performer*

CONGRATULATIONS! You have done the foundation work. You have done the digging and assembled the materials. Now it is time to build the script, starting with the framework and then the finish work. You will find useful tools on pdf files at http://www.historicperformance.com/workshops .htm. You will want these tools to sort and prioritize your research material, determine a setting, convert the information into stories, and organize the stories, creating transitions between them and after your introduction and before your ending. I have written this all out, with examples, but first here's a brief list of the steps:

- Appendix A is a one-page list of the steps in creating a first-person narrative. You might want to preview them.

- One of those steps is to wear an article of your character's clothing while you work. My bias is toward hats. It is much easier for me to write a first-person narrative if I am wearing the hat that I will be wearing onstage—or a similar hat. Some people might wear a shawl. Or have a picture of the person or their childhood home, or family, in front of them as they work. Maybe a model of Clyde Cessna's plane. There is more on creating your "look" as your historic figure in the next chapter.
- Revisit your research questions (the five w's, one h, and "significance of"). You will use them so you clearly know what you want to say to create a more tightly scripted performance.
- An overview of what you want to accomplish in your performance will help you organize your ideas. What do you want the audience members to know when they leave?
- Think of what you are writing as a memoir rather than an autobiography—you will be focusing on themes, on aspects of your character's life, and do not need to tell everything.
- Decide what stories will lead the audience to what you want them to know. Use the worksheet on page 10 in the pdf file at http://www.historic performance.com/worksheets.pdf or on your computer to describe each with a few words and note where you found each story.
- What will your setting be? (page 18 in the pdf file at http://www.historic performance.com/worksheets.pdf)
- How will you get onstage? Look for a story that will do that. That is your introduction. Write down a few key words that describe that story (see appendix B, on script structure).
- Determine how you will end the program and find that story.
- The information that does not go into your script might be used during discussion, or maybe for a program for a special audience, like very young children or nurses or engineers. You always have more information than you can use during a single performance.

Remember that the bottom line in a historical performance is not about you—it is all about the audience enjoying and learning about your person and this life.[2] There are three factors in any performance: the performer, the script, and the audience. The audience must be foremost in our minds in everything we do. We research not only because we are curious but also because our audience is curious. We ask questions of our sources with our potential audiences in mind. We follow leads and explore topics not always because they interest us but also because they will be of interest to someone in a future audience. Likewise, we craft the stories in our performance with imaginary audiences in mind.

Respect is the most important thing you can give an audience, no matter what their age and experience. Chances are most adults in your audiences will know something about your person or era from experience or reading. They will want to refresh their knowledge, learn more, or affirm the value of their personal memories by putting their memories in historical context. They look forward to making an excursion into history with someone who is knowledgeable, someone they can trust to know more than they know. This is why it is crucial *not* that you know everything there is to be known about your topic but rather that you have budgeted enough time to learn more than most people know, including and especially where to find that nugget of information that you do not know but can help a seeker find. Research, as I said in the previous chapter, is ongoing. But you must also, of course, schedule time to write and practice because you want to honor your historic figure, your audience, and yourself by doing the best you can. Adult and younger audiences both like a good story. They will not hear the story in the same ways, but do not be afraid to take well-crafted stories to young audiences. Take away distractions, tell the right stories, tell them well, and they will listen for forty minutes . . . and learn. And you will make a difference in a good many lives— including the fact that you did not talk down to kids.

In this chapter you will go through the process of creating a script from your research. I suggest the following order:

1. Sort and prioritize your information;
2. Determine the setting for your performance;
3. Convert information into stories;
4. Organize the stories and create transitions; and . . .
5. Voilà, you have a script!

### SORT AND PRIORITIZE YOUR INFORMATION: WHAT WILL YOU INCLUDE IN YOUR SCRIPT?

After you have collected enough detailed data by doing field and library research to cover almost all aspects of your historic figure's life, it is time to convert those facts into a script. What will you include and what will you exclude? The easy answer is that, sadly, you must include very little and exclude most of what you have learned. The good news is that everything you exclude will still be available to you to use during the discussion, the question-and-answer portion of the program.

What will constitute that "very little" that you will include? First, events and decisions for which your historic figure is best known; second, events that explain your figure's character, personality, and motivation; and, as you prepare to go out to each venue, events that will speak to each particular audience.

What does the audience know about your person? Even with iconic historic figures, surprisingly (and this may be a relief) little. Where do most people go for information about famous people? An encyclopedia, online or in print. Therefore, compare a few encyclopedia articles and note the most-often-mentioned facts. Then see what biographies aimed at youngsters include. For this purpose avoid fictionalized biographies for really young folks and focus on those for middle school youngsters, maybe the easiest biographies in the Young Adult section, or the most sophisticated biographies in the Junior section of the library. Make a list of the stories told in these biographies. The worksheet that is page 10 at http://www.historicperformance.com/worksheets.pdf, or your own version of this form, would be a good place to record these stories.

Then make a list of difficult decisions that your person made and which events tell the stories of those decisions. Was there a turning point in your person's life? What conflicts with others, with nature, with her- or himself did the person resolve? (See pages 15 and 16 at http://www.historicperformance.com/worksheets.pdf.)

In forty minutes you can do onstage an introduction, five stories, transitions, and an exit. If you still have far more stories than can be told in forty minutes, which is likely if you are portraying someone about whom a lot is known, then ask yourself, "What makes a good story?" Here's a possible list: conflict, adventure, suspense, humor, romance, gore, and animals. These are components that a wide variety of audiences appreciate in stories told in a wide variety of media. Look back through your list of stories and decide which ones include several "good story" characteristics. Ann Birney's first story as Amelia Earhart is what she calls the "sled story." It competed with the "roller coaster story" when she was trying to decide which childhood story to tell. Both portray Earhart as creative and a risk-taker from an early age. Both had suspense, danger, and the suggestion of gore. Both involved her sister. In both cases, there was conflict with an authority figure. However, the sled story won out because it happened in a public space in Atchison, Kansas, where Amelia spent most of her childhood, and individuals familiar with the town can picture her hurtling down that very real, very steep street. Also, sledding is a near-universal childhood experience, so Amelia can bring the audience into the story by asking a rhetorical question: "It had snowed about this much the night before, and you know how it melts at midday and then freezes again overnight, so there's a crust of ice on top of the snow?" Another factor is that the roller coaster story, at least at that time, appeared in more children's biographies of Earhart, and she wanted to give her audiences something new. Oh, yes, and then there was the horse at the bottom of the hill. The roller coaster story had no animals.

People appreciate the conflicts in stories because we all have conflicts in our lives. We see and hear others making mistakes, while also making decisions that lead to survival. These stories provide hope and allow for the cross-time connections we all crave.

A story may be very good in its own right, but if it does not add to the discovery of the "real" human and the era, and especially if its contribution is redundant, for instance, both the roller coaster story and the sled story, then slip it into your story bag and use it later. (Ann tells me that often youngsters ask her as Amelia if she ever had a roller coaster, and she tells the story then.)

Sometimes stories are cut for time, but you put them into your hat, hoping you will have the opportunity to tell them later during discussion. For instance, as Calamity Jane I allude to Wild Bill Hickok, to having a daughter, to her horse, and "how [the army] found out that I was a girl." With any luck someone is going to ask me, "So how did they find out that you were a girl," or "I didn't know you had a daughter," or "Is it true that you were married to Wild Bill Hickok?"

## DETERMINE THE SETTING FOR YOUR PERFORMANCE

The concept of setting can be a little confusing at this point. You are looking at stories, each of which has its own place and time, but that is not what I am talking about. What I am talking about is the setting for the entire performance, for your script. We might call it a frame for the performance.

The setting of the script is important because you will be performing your first-person narrative as a direct address. Your audience will travel back in time with you. For audience members to be comfortable they must understand where they are, when it is, and who they are. If you have ever read a play you know that the setting is spelled out. No one in the play actually says what the setting is. Instead, the setting is given to the audience with the stage set, the costume, and words, just as it is gradually revealed in a book. That is one of the crucial jobs of your introduction—to give the setting. The worksheet on page 18 of the website asks for the date from which you will be speaking, the place, and the audience's role. Here is how I reveal the setting and my name in my Calamity Jane performance:

Calamity Jane comes swaggering into the room lugging a saddle and immediately engages the audience: "I just tied my horse up outside. A rider down the road told me there was good food here, but it seems I missed it. Some of you look like Easterners. But you've heard of ol' Calamity Jane, ain'tcha?" "Say now, are you a reporter?" [asked of preselected target]. "Thank goodness [or, "Well, doesn't that just figure?" depending on response] 'cause I ain't got no use for reporters." By this point we know it is inside and that the audience is not expected to know Jane, but is encouraged to interact

"I'll tell you why I ain't got no use for reporters. Here about two months back this reporter walked up to me and asked if I was Calamity Jane. I 'lowed I was, so he asked me for my story. I asked what he'd pay me for my story. He said 'Nothing,' so I said, 'Nothing's what you're gettin' out of me,' and I walked on down to the stable with my horse and settled her in. Then I stepped out onto the street and I was downwind of some mighty good-smellin' food. You know how it is when you're hungry and your belly just naturally starts to rumbling? I dug into my pocket and as is usually the case I didn't have any money. I watched as the reporter walked into the café and I got a bright idea. I followed him on in and I said, 'Tell you what, Reporter, you buy me a meal and I'll tell you a story. Of course, if you buy me a meal and a drink on a night like this I'll tell you a story, a tall tale, and a downright lie, and I'll let you have your pick.' You know how reporters are, he asked me to begin in the beginning. Now I'm an obliging woman, so . . . I was born May first 1852 and if this here year is 1900, that makes me . . . (excuse me for cipherin' on my fingers) . . . forty-eight. . . ." So now the audience knows the date of the setting and that their role is to listen and learn as if they were the reporter. The place could be any of those that Calamity Jane passed through or called home.

I chose this setting because most of what we know about Jane is from reporters. Based on the 1890 census the U.S. government declared the frontier settled. The Old West was no more. Before that time Eastern reporters could not get enough stories about the West for their Eastern audiences. They went West and interviewed colorful characters who later became our Western icons. Then between 1890 and 1900 interest in the West plummeted. By 1899 our nation's attention was fully focused on the new century, new technological frontiers. Jane, who had earned her living by telling her stories to visiting reporters and anyone else who would pay to listen, had no audience and therefore no regular source of income, leading to her illness and to her death in 1903. The year 1900 is, then, a transition year for Jane as well as for the nation. She is still telling stories, having memories of better times, but she has far fewer opportunities to earn money from those memories.

What should your setting be?

- After your historic figure has accomplished what he or she is most known for;
- When your historic figure is an age that you can physically represent; and
- At an event where they would be addressing a group of people (e.g., a press conference, a union meeting, a lecture, or an inspirational talk to the troops).

## HOW DO YOU CONVERT INFORMATION INTO STORIES?

As historical performers we always need to remember that we are limited in the length of our performance. Most venues will allow you an hour to an hour and a half, including your scripted text and the discussion. Your script might be a half hour, followed by about fifteen minutes each of you taking questions in character and fifteen of you taking questions as the scholar (more on how to do this in chapter 5). That first segment should be tightly scripted, like mine of Calamity Jane, giving audience members something they can readily grasp and follow as you move from story to story. The audience will want that too.

As you develop the stories you might realize you have a gap in your data. Revisit your research questions, as they often form a basic outline on which to begin the scriptwriting process. Think, write, restate, but always think of what the audience wants to know and what they might already know about your person or era. Link new information to their existing knowledge. Make sure you have included in your stories the richness of details that you originally craved when you began your research.

The act of scriptwriting for a historical performance should be perceived as not a onetime activity but rather an endless series of drafts until it finally feels just right. After your initial performance before friends you, of course, will tweak it, and you will repeat this after you have been out before your first real-life audience and subsequent groups of varying ages. Think of these as drafts or edits. Do consider revisions after additional performances based upon those audiences' responses and especially do so as you gain more confidence with your scripted lines. Never hesitate to rewrite parts of your script for greater clarity. Also plan to revise or remove whole parts of your script as your additional and ongoing research indicates that some of your earlier conclusions and hypotheses may not be as accurate as you initially thought. And, do these revisions especially when you find (and you will) additional data and new stories.

Think of scriptwriting as telling a series of stories. Your audience is used to following series of stories in novels, television shows, and movies. Stories, therefore, will be a part of the audiences' expectation when you come before them, so plan for that expectation and meet it.

Your whole script should comprise an introduction, a body of text, and a conclusion that allows you to smoothly transition into taking questions in character (or engaging the audience in a dialogue while remaining in character); then you need another transition into a discussion of the text with you in the role of researcher and scholar. At the very end, if the person who introduced you does not take over to dismiss the audience, be prepared, as the scholar, to say something along the lines of, "I have enjoyed my time with you; however, some of you might have someplace else you may need to be. If any of you want to continue our discussion, I will be here for a while. Thank you for inviting me. You have been a really good audience." This allows those in the audience who need to leave to do so graciously, while those who hesitated to ask questions in front of the group or want a more sustained dialogue may do so. Historical performers enjoy and are surprised by the extent to which some people crave interacting with them one on one.

Knowing that your script will have these components will aid you in the process of writing your script. Plan for three parts of your program with the first component being more tightly scripted and the other two relying upon your bag of stories and overall knowledge of the subject matter and era. By thinking of your script within these parameters you can convert your pile of research notes, folders, and books into a vital script with enticing stories. Always remember it is a process, a series of actions and changes that result in a really great performance and a really engaged audience.

Some of you will proceed from research to writing your script. The visual wordsmiths among you especially will eagerly proceed to the writing phase.

Some of you, however, would rather just talk the stories than be disciplined enough to sit down to write a carefully phrased script. If you choose to do *only* the talking, without the disciplined written phase of scriptwriting, you will deliver an inconsistent product from performance to performance. It does not mean that you must deliver the written script word for word, but it helps in refreshing your intention, those plans that you make when you create the best possible performance for your audience. If you *cannot* write but can read, use a voice-activated software program such as Drag and Speak that will record your verbal words for you. If you can neither write nor read, use auditory recording equipment and skip over the written text component (see trail story 4.1).

---

**A Trail Story**

### 4.1. CAN'T SEE IT? YOU SHOULD!

I have two historical performance friends who are legally blind. They use adaptive equipment for their computers. One has not only written her script for her own use but also published an award-winning book and a CD about her historic figure (who, by the way, was not blind).

---

If your learning style leans strongly in favor of the spoken word over the written word, then accommodate it. To be honest, I do this, too. I am a verbal processor. As I write my script I talk it into my computer. Sometimes verbal processors do not know what we want to say unless we hear ourselves say it. This means that we will do considerable talking into the air until we get our thoughts and words down. Feel free to prattle on, dialogue, and talk with your computer. One can always edit later. For some of us talking is crucial to the creation of a vibrant script. Talking, also, is the essence of how the audience will hear the final product, so eventually it needs to be produced in a way they will hear it anyway.

Revising your script is key to a quality product. Write it, print it, speak it out loud so you can hear the rhythm of the words; note changes, enter changes, print, and speak again. Repeat. By this repeated practicing with the written script, you can see and hear simultaneously where there might be a hole in the story line, illogical jumps in logic, and even research snafus. I have said it before and I'll say it again: scriptwriting is a process that requires many written revisions. Think of your script as a living, ever-changing, morphing organism that you will continue to change and revise as you practice it and use it. After you have spoken the script aloud, you know where it flows and where it needs to be edited. This is a very different process than writing a term or research paper with one or two drafts and then turning the paper in for a grade. Only you

A Trail Story

### 4.2. A CAUTIONARY TALE: DON'T BE A RAMBLER

A former reenactor who refuses to write down his script rambles and rambles and rambles. At one event he told about getting on his horse, going down the trail, and the Indians attacking him three times in the space of ten minutes. He knows his stuff and is enthusiastic, but he has not disciplined himself to order his knowledge. On at least one occasion he completely left out the subject he had been hired to cover. He is frustrated because he does not get as many bookings as he would like, but he is not delivering a consistently good product.

are grading your script, and you will do so as you practice it and as you observe what works and does not work for the audience. There is no final grade, only ongoing audience responses.

The written script is critical for recall of your story lines and themes. Also, because it may be weeks between performances or months before a seasonal series of performances, the written script is a lifesaver for preperformance review. Can you imagine having to create your performance from memory because you did not write down what you so carefully crafted nine months earlier? So, enter your script into a computer for ease of editing and keep saving and printing and saving and printing again (while computer crash stories can evoke sympathy, they are not the ones you want to tell). Print on the back of your first draft to save paper, but this is one time when not printing in order to save paper is deadly. I give you permission to "waste" paper. If you want to sit in your favorite spot and write on paper to sketch out your ideas, that's fine. I mean, that's what I do. Just get it into the computer or written in a more formal style before you begin performing for the public.

### SCRIPTWRITING HINTS

- Remember, "It's a process." Some of you will loop back and loop again through the steps below; others will check them off as you do them in a linear order. But let me reassure you, this is not a maze with blocked passages; it is just a path with a few twists and turns like any other complex task worth doing.
- Ask yourself repeatedly the following questions:

- What will most of the audience already know? List and use this very basic information to reinforce knowledge and the audiences' comfort zone as a base to build on, and then add new data.
- What do you want the audience to learn? What do you want the audience to know when they walk away?
- What are some of the really "cool facts" you learned in researching? Build in the "wow" factor.

- Build in the learning of data or information. The audience may or may not have the same common core knowledge base, so explain or tell or assist them in their recall of the details. One way to find out that core or base level of knowledge is to look closely at what is written in a high school and a college-level textbook. These will help you to not only cover that core but also give you ideas about the overall era's historical context that you may need to include in your script. Remember, just as you live in a world of people, economics, politics, and military concerns, so did "your" historic figure. Learn your character's historical context and include details in your script.

- Always footnote the stories as you write the script. These bread crumbs help you return to your information should you need to. And you probably will at some point in the future. Often this is long after you have thought you might need it—oh, you know, that file that is not marked or that book you had that you are just sure had a red cover but after hours of searching find it had a purplish cover. Or, the book you borrowed, or . . . ? Well, you get the idea.

- Define all terms and jargon within the scripted text by stating, "Let me explain . . ." or whatever language would be appropriate for the character and setting. This explanation provides the missing information within the context of the story and at the point-of-need learning. Never talk down to the audience; remember they are not stupid, nor is this the time for you to be the know-it-all smart aleck. If someone was reading your text they could pause and look up the new-to-them term in a dictionary. The audience is, however, hearing a stream of words and may not have time to ponder the meaning from the word's context before the story moves on. Two examples: One example is from my Calamity Jane script. I say, "The Captain called out, 'Cinch 'em down, boys! Columns of two, ho!' as we prepared to ride into the valley. I checked my cinch one more time." If the audience rides Western, this sentence works, but most audience members will not have a mental image of a cinch and its function, so I extend my hand downward, grab the cinch strap, look up, and say, staying in character, of course, "This strap is what holds the saddle onto the horse. It goes around the horse's belly just behind the front legs to keep the saddle on the horse. If it goes, you're rubbed out." A cinch is a Western riding term while Eastern riders use the term "girth." This takes far less time to say than it did to keyboard, but it greatly aids the audience and the story line.

Second example: Ann Birney subtly defines a technology that is key to one of her Amelia Earhart stories. "I checked my instruments one more time before flying into that cloud, and I saw that my altimeter had failed. Of course, on a sunny day it wouldn't make any difference. You could look down and see the ocean and know that you were above it. But I was going to be in the middle of a cloud, where all I could see was gray, just beads of moisture. And I might think I was flying like this [follows flat line with hand], when instead I might be flying like this [line slopes down], and if I hit the ocean, that would be it."

- Organize your stories as you begin scriptwriting. Bullets like those used here are very useful for organizing. Historical performers have commented on this technique as superior to the classic method of creating a standard or typical outline. Or write your story topics on index cards and arrange and rearrange them until they form a flow that works for you, be it chronological or topical. Think of this as plotting the story or as "story-boarding." Create a plan and then follow through until you find reason to change the sequence. Use index cards and a bulletin board, self-adhesive notes or tape and a wall, or organize on a computer. Fannie Flagg clipped notecards to a clothesline as she organized tiny chapters when writing *Fried Green Tomatoes at the Whistle Stop Café.*[3] Some of you will take a blank piece of paper and do a semantic web, or an octopus outline, or create some form of graphic organizer. The method of organizing is not the issue; it is, rather, that organizing occurs. As you organize you will start to see patterns emerge from the chaos of your research notes that will then lead to a mapped, scripted story flow.
- Put the stories in an order that will help the audience know your intent and focus. Cut and paste as necessary.
- Begin writing with one story, whether it is on computer or paper. I've said it before, but always take the time to write the stories down.
- If you are using paper and pencil, leave white space as you write to make it easy to add more data and details as the stories begin to flow in your mind.
- Write in active voice, never passive. Say, "My crew drove the cattle" not

"The cattle were driven." In the second example, there is no subject, no one doing the action.

- Remember you are not writing a typical history term paper or biography, so write in emotion as well as data and information. In "Cattle Tales," my composite drover/rancher shows her anger and frustration by throwing her leather chaps on the chair when she enters.
- Write in short paragraphs to move the story along.
- Write in sentences that will reflect the story line: several short sentences for rapid action, such as recounting a race or another very suspenseful event; languid sentences for fondly remembering a friend or a sunset, something of great beauty. Varying sentence lengths will keep the audience engaged. Slow down the pacing to emphasize a word or idea. This piece is from Ride into History's "Fighting beside My Brother" performance, but it also works here [pace is slow and easy]: "We have our orders to go from here, to there. I waited with the other men. We're waiting, just waiting. We smell the new grass, the sweaty horses. I hear a bird I recognize as a cardinal. [I take a deep breath, and then] Ka-boom! [pace changes to fast and choppy:] "I know I am supposed to look forward. That is our orders. But I look back, and I see a man without his head, still mounted on his horse, and blood everywhere. Then the bugle. That's our orders. We gallop into the field of battle."
- Watch your verb tense. Write in the present tense, remembering the past. This can be tricky as you must always remember when what is happening and to whom—and what you cannot know because it has not yet happened. (We ARE in 1870 [past], and I AM [present] telling you about what HAPPENED in 1858 [past]).
- Write in oral language patterns, dialect, jargon, or lingo as it reflects the era and adds flavor. Use some words that extend the vocabulary of the hearer of your script. Avoid words and phrases that are anachronistic. "Guys," for instance, is one that jolts me into the now when I hear it in a nineteenth-century setting.
- Give lots of details. Think about what you really like to read and how that author gives you what you want—then try doing it. And, of course, read some excellent writing. Note the differences between a newspaper journalist's quick wording style to the more, and much longer, detailed descriptions that are laced with layered contextual meanings.
- Think and write in word pictures—use details—what was the weather, how did you get there, who else was there. Even if you will not have time to write and tell every detail, picture it in your mind.

- Write sounds, such as the "Kaboom!" of the cannon mentioned above and the "Zing!" of Amelia's sled runners meeting the ice as she plummets downhill.
- Write smells, such as the cinnamon on the apple pie that Calamity Jane smells as she talks to the reporter.
- Help the audience hear, see, and smell your historic figure's context—in the next chapter we'll talk about how to use body language to show those sensory memories in addition to the words you use to describe them.
- Write all sensations, even the rush of air and hair standing on end as the cannonball whizzed past.
- In a historical performance the mouth and body of the performer carry the script and words to the ears, eyes, and body of the hearers, the audience—thus completing a communication loop. Information is transmitted, heard, stored, discussed, and recalled.
- Tell stories, letting one unfold into the next. Think of this phase as writing a plot line.
- Write transitions from one story to the next. Ann Birney ends the story in which Amelia Earhart describes her "first flight" as being on a sled by saying, "I like to say that was my first flight, but of course it had nothing to do with airplanes. I didn't get interested in flying until the war." Then she tells the story of listening to pilots during the war.
- Briefly and boldly sketch other characters as they relate to your plot line. Calamity Jane says, "Wild Bill Hickok was a fastidious man. He washed his hands for no reason other than to have clean hands."
- Make sure that everything you say (just as with anything you carry physically onto the stage) carries your narrative toward your goal; if it doesn't, then set it aside.

**WHY DO WE TELL HISTORY AS A SERIES OF STORIES?**

How recent audience members have responded to two of my narratives follows: "It went by so quickly I didn't fidget like I usually do. I got caught up in the story of trailing cows and the dust and their bawling and . . . well, wow!" said a young man with attention deficit disorder, after a one and a half hour performance of "Cattle Tales." "I saw your brother fall and his amputation! I forgot we were in the classroom!" said a student after an in-class presentation of "Fighting beside My Brother."

However, especially when we create a compelling narrative, it is our responsibility to tell the truth. If we need to interpret because one truth is not

---

**A Trail Story**

### 4.3. THE HORSE THAT WASN'T

A school principal heard from another principal about an all-school assembly at which I had performed. "I want to book the performance for our school. The one where you as Calamity Jane rode your white horse into the school gym and then shot a buffalo—right there on the gym floor. How did you get the buffalo in the gym?" The truth was my horse was not there; rather, there was just a white-painted saddle stand with the saddle on top. There was no horse, no buffalo, and no gun! Just stories, but obviously people "saw" because of the words.

---

agreed on, or there are gaps in the collective knowledge, then we have the responsibility to discuss that during the scholar's portion of our program.

- Stories embedded in scripts have a mystery, a power to reach into and touch the audience, each of us, to command emotion, to compel involvement in your character's life story.
- Stories transport us into a timeless suspension of "now-ness."
- Stories transport the audience from where they are sitting to "wherever" you as the historical performer can mentally carry them.
- Stories are a structural abstraction, the same as historical data, built into human memory, that structure our ways of thinking and our primary ways of organizing ideas, data, and information.
- Stories are centered around conflict because people identify with the problem solving that goes with conflicts. These stories provide hope because we see others making decisions that eventually lead to survival. We see and hear them making decisions and making mistakes, like all of us. This allows for the cross-time connections we all crave. We then see and hear them, like us, recover, go on, and survive.
- Be aware of specific magic or mythic ties to one's historic thread of human awareness of past events.
- A series of stories becomes, when told well, its own reality, a configuration in memory. This is what can and does occur. These stories become independent of the specific details of the given event. Historical performers thus carry the ethical need to tell the truth, as they discern it to be, and

do not add to the myths that already float around in the human mental ether of "textbook history" that one learns from elementary school. Sometimes the facts may be different than the "storied" ways of recall, which often take on archetypal dimensions when it comes to "mythic" events.[4]

- Historical performance is the action of telling stories, not reconfiguring real historical events into some kind of scrambled hodgepodge of illogical "weird" reality that someone tries to pawn off on the audience. Our audiences are by and large intelligent. As an audience member standing next to me said during a streetside performance (not Ann's of Amelia) during the 2007 Amelia Earhart Festival, "This is crap, not history!" While he did not state his observation eloquently, in my humble opinion he was right on target.
- Tell real stories and historical events. Never lie to the audience or fabricate events.
- Combine your stories into a series of stories that allow the audience to share the experience of transcending time and place.

Before you begin to write or create your script let me remind you that you have been reading historians' writings. These have a very different tone than that of a first-person narrative. If it is true, as we are often told, that our body is affected by what we put into it, then think about what you are putting into your mind and brain. If you are reading only scholarly historical analyses, you start to write (and sound!) that way. This is fine if you, like many historical performers, have a day job at an institute of higher learning or a historic site where this is how one is expected to speak, write, and present. While a formal academic style has its uses, and is appropriate for a conference or lecture, ask yourself if this style of writing and speaking will convey the intimacy and magic that you are seeking in your scripted historical performance. In other words, this is no place for the term *hegemonic*, except as the scholar and then only with extensive explanation, so why bother?

I suggest that you cross-train. Mix your reading diet. Read literature of your historic figure's era to get a flavor for the written language of the day. Add literature and historical novels to your reading mix . It is liberating to stretch and move now, isn't it? Think about how a good physical stretch feels when you've been curled over the computer for too long. So, breathe deep, stretch the body, reach for a piece of literature, and allow your mind to stretch, too. Note as you read how that author deals with details, language, and active voice.

If you are writing about the farming frontier, Great Plains, or immigrants' lives, read Willa Cather. She describes people, their values, and their living conditions as they tried to maintain homeland traditions, wherever home was for them, while carving out a new life, keeping what they defined as family, all with dignity as they dealt with realistic day-to-day problems. She was both a neighbor and a participant. Her power of observation during her childhood and adolescence in Nebraska at the end of the nineteenth century makes her work, although fiction, useful as a primary source. Read Cather to grasp how written language is even better read aloud—almost every page could be reader's theater. No wonder Hallmark produced *O Pioneers!* In a few bold strokes from her typewriter she carries us through time and place. We identify with "her" people. They are not one-dimensional characters on a book's page but rather people we know facing some of the same issues we face.[5]

After a decades-long diet of historical works and primary sources on the cattle frontier and the history of trailing cattle from Texas to Kansas, which I had inhaled with the goal of classroom and public lectures, I had to change that diet to create "Cattle Tales." I had enough factoids to choke the proverbial horse as I had been teaching versions of this topic every semester for over ten semesters, so I knew my data was excellent—but my lectures lacked the excitement associated with stories of trail driving. I was a long way from the old *Rawhide, Gunsmoke,* and *Bonanza* episodes that my test audiences seemed to expect. Trying to find the right tone I dipped into Zane Grey, Max Brand, and Louis L'Amour, staples of my youth, but they were not quite what I was seeking. I knew that Larry McMurtry's stories seem contrived to me, and, most egregiously, he ignores historical truth (I will spare you and not discuss here my thoughts about *Lonesome Dove* or *Buffalo Girls*). I headed to my local library, a place all researchers should routinely visit, if for no other reason than to see what everyone else is reading. There I found Ralph Compton's trail-driving series. Well written, and he had women on the trail. His novels helped me take information from such scholarly works as Joyce Gibson Roach's well-researched and well-written *Cowgirls* and craft a dramatic, emotionally moving historical performance. The factoids were still in my script, but my composite character of Georgiana Jackson did more, saw more, and experienced more, and thus was able to elicit audience empathy as she had conflicts with family, men, land, animals, weather, and above all, within herself, as a woman in a man's culture on the cattle frontier.[6]

As an academic, most of my reading is what my academic peers write, using their language patterns. This language is generally expected in my classroom lectures. After all, one of our goals is to sift out future professional historians. However, as I watch students' eyes roll up and their heads nod, or watch signs of panic that mark responses to my casual use of "hegemonic binary discourse," I am reminded that I have a responsibility to this audience, too. I have found

**A Trail Story**

### 44. CATTLE TALES

This example of script is from "Cattle Tales," my composite character Georgiana Jackson's story of how she came to create her own ranch in Kansas. She is remembering her emotions on coming home to Texas and a conflict with her parents' expectations. This aspect of this scripted story will demonstrate some of the items discussed above. Words in brackets indicate stage directions, while the quotes indicate spoken words.

[Move from the table to saddle on stand, putting hat onto head as I move, indicating by body or showing I am leaving the ranch house; let face show hurt and a huge sense of sadness.]

"I had just successfully herded a thousand head of steers all the way from our ranch in Texas up the long trail to Kansas, and sold them, too! I paid my men and myself, then put some into a bank; the rest of the money I put into a saddlebag to carry home. The first cash money our ranch had had since before the War of Northern Aggression, as we Texans call it. I purchased many desperately needed supplies for the ranch. I got every last man and horse back to Texas safe and sound. But what happened when I proudly handed Father a heavy saddlebag of money . . . . Father dropped the bag onto the porch floor . . . limping, thumping, leaning on his cane, he went back into the house. The saddlebag just lay there on the porch—If I had been born a boy . . . he would have had pride in me, but . . . well, appears nothing I can or ever will do."

[Sigh, almost a girl's sob, pick up reins of the bridle that is hanging on my saddle, and look to the porch.]

"I said to myself, "'Just nothing I can do that will solve the problem today—or tomorrow!!!! Well—the ranch will need to keep going. Horses need to be feed. Evening chores to do!'"

[Pause and look upward—sun's placement in the sky.]

"A few more hours of daylight! Guess I'll just ride out and start looking for cattle and planning. We'll have to trail another herd north and roundup will be soon. One can't cry over spilled milk, can one? Nothing to do but get back on my horse and go to work!"

that sometimes a story as explanation helps the audience of students understand what I wish them to know, and yes, data delivered that way is testable and meets assessment standards requirements, too. Sometimes professors need to remember to talk directly to the audience and think about using the above methods to go beyond the what and the how as they script their classroom lectures. Teaching is teaching, but the best way to reach any audience is by engaging their emotions with a story.

I not only want the audience to learn about my character's life, but also I always want the audience to learn historical details about a time, place, and era. Embedded details not only move the story along but instruct and delight

**NOTES**

1. Advertisement in *Architectural Digest* 66, no. 2 (February 2009): [29].

2. The fundamental difference between reenactors and historical performers is that the former get into costume, research, and perform informally for their own pleasure and that of a group of friends, while historical performers do so as individuals interacting primarily with strangers for the purpose of instruction and entertainment of the audience, using a crafted script. For more discussion on this differentiation, see chapter 1.

3. Don Swaim, interview with Fanny Flagg, CBS Radio Station, New York, October 6, 1987, at http://wiredforbooks.org/fannieflagg/index.htm (accessed February 9, 2009).

4. James W. Loewen, *Lies My Teacher Told Me: Everything Your American History Textbook Got Wrong* (New York: New Press, 1995).

5. Willa Cather wrote over fourteen books and numerous newspaper and magazine articles over her lifetime. Look, for instance, at *O Pioneers!* or *My Antonia.*

6. Ralph Compton's Western series books are still being published; Joyce Gibson Roach, *The Cowgirls* (Denton: University of North Texas Press, 1977).

# 5

# Telling History

IN the last chapter I told you how to create a script for your performance of a first-person historical narrative. Even before you as a historical performer first stand to practice your script, you have probably been saying the stories as you write them, trying out a phrase to see how it sounds, rejecting one word for another that sounds better. Maybe you have taken a break from writing stories to learn one really good story that you know you are going to use. The process, as I have said before, need not be linear, but all bases must be covered at some point of the process. Therefore, I offer here suggestions for learning the stories in your script, creating a convincing look (both clothing and body language), telling the stories, and taking questions both in character and as the scholar behind the historic figure.

Like many of you, I grew up in an oral culture, an extended family and neighborhood where stories were told as a matter of course. When information was exchanged it was most likely imbedded in an explanation that went far beyond "just the facts." I learned who I was by hearing stories about my family and about those who were "not us." I learned from listening to my elders how we fit into the larger picture of the township, county, region, and state. Those who grew up in a rich oral culture will easily make the leap into telling the stories, rather than the more stilted reciting of the script. Most historians tend to stand behind a podium and give protracted lectures (and I will admit that I have been guilty of this practice) because they have forgotten or never learned the tool of storytelling, a tool that will keep their students awake in a classroom. If you are a historian by training, learn this skill set and add it to the many tools you already use to reach the audience. Your job is to research the facts from primary and secondary sources, add your own informed interpretation, and repackage it all into an interesting narrative. After all, what is history if not stories, the stories of real people making real decisions?

## LEARNING YOUR SCRIPT

Let me remind you that a historical performance is not a play. Some of us want to memorize every word of every well-written phrase that we have crafted. The danger there is that if you forget one word it might stop your progress and you freeze on stage. What follows are some skills that will give you confidence, confidence that you have a well-created script that is worth telling.

Your preferred intelligences will affect which tools you will use most often to record your script to your memory and then recall. Your script is made up of an introduction, your stories, transitions between your stories, and your exit. You want to be able to remember the order of your stories as well as the content of each story and how to get from one to the other. Understanding which intelligences work best for you will make the process of learning interesting in and of itself. Scan table 5.1 and choose one or two intelligences that are most appealing, then experiment with them. If the first one you choose does not feel right, try another.

Research by Robert Krauss of Columbia University on how people use gestures when they talk suggests that using our hands helps us remember concrete words—or abstract concepts—that we conceptualize concretely.[1] For instance, if I was trying to remember the word "transition," I would gesture to the space between two of my fingers, probably sliding down the side of one finger and up the next, because that is where I "keep" the transitions between my stories. I remember each transition because I have put it in a particular place on my hand, but the concept of transition is also on my hands. Sharon Begley, *Newsweek*'s wondrous translator of scientific research, says that "if gesticulating is like wielding a key to the door of lexical memory, then someone who can't use his hands should have more trouble unlocking the door," and she says that studies have, indeed, shown this to be the case.[2] So when you are learning your script, especially if you are a kinesthetic learner, use gestures effusively, then edit them, keeping the more dramatically effective ones (more on that later). If you do not already have body learning in your toolkit, this is an opportunity for you to start using it—or use it more. After all, performance is about the whole body, and talking heads are so, so outré.

**Table 5.1. Learn Your Script Using Howard Gardner's Multiple Intelligences Theory**

| If One of Your Strongest Intelligences Is . . . | How You Might Use It to Learn Your Performance |
|---|---|
| Musical | Use rhythm to learn phrases and which words to emphasize—snap your fingers or mark a sentence with accents.<br>If appropriate for your historic figure, incorporate melodies in your performance—hum or sing a few bars of music if you know that your person was likely to do so. Play an instrument if your person did. Pick it up as a transition between stories.<br>If you learn best this way, but music is not central to your historic figure's life, use the music to learn, but drop it out as soon as you are able.<br>Use rhythm by walking while learning your stories. |
| Bodily-kinesthetic | Learn the processes, tasks, and skills that you are describing in your stories by actually doing them—actually fire a black powder rifle if you see that your historical person did so. Feel it, touch it, smell it, and taste it. Then you can describe it.<br>Write a few key words for each story on your thumb (introduction), pointer finger (first story), and so on. Touch each finger as you tell the story to aid your recall.<br>Signal each new story with a physical movement if appropriate to your character. A sports figure's first story might be about a failure he or she had, and an associated gesture might be looking down at the ground while rubbing a toe in the dirt; the next story might be about a victory, and the associated gesture is swinging the bat and sending the ball over the fence. |
| Spatial | You are good at sequence and have a mental map of your script. Draw the process, the stories as they flow from one to the other, as your figure moves from one setting to another in the stories. |
| Logical-mathematical | You don't need to hold the gun—look at its schematics to be able to describe how the gun works or how the airplane's engine failed. |
| Linguistic | Memorize the really fine phrases you wrote—repeat them over and over, trying for increasingly effective flow and rhythm of words. |
| Existential, philosophical | Give yourself time to articulate the reason you are giving your performance, and what you want the audience members to take with them. What is the purpose of each story? Why are you doing historical performance? Why is it important in the larger scheme of things? |
| Interpersonal | As your historic figure, picture the people you are describing and your interactions with them—their moods, temperaments, intentions, and motivations. Picture the audience as you practice, and how different audience members will take pleasure from parts of your stories. |
| Intrapersonal | Associate your own experiences and feelings with those of your historic figure and draw on those to express that figure's experience and feelings. It sometimes feels risky but can be very effective. |
| Naturalist | Associate a natural setting with each story—it might just be the physical setting of a building where a story takes place. Think about how the season and the weather might affect your person. See if you can tell the stories in a seasonal order (not necessarily a chronological order—it could be the winter of 1903, followed by a loop back to the spring of 1897, and followed by a jump back to the summer of 1910.) |

What do you think were your historic figure's strongest intelligences?

*Source:* Based on Howard Gardner's concept of intelligences in *Multiple Intelligences: New Horizons*, rev. ed. (New York: Basic Books, 2006).

**A Trail Story**

### 5.1. TWO LANGUAGES, TWO LEARNING STYLES

Ann says that she had an awful time learning Spanish prepositions. Finally, she translated them into a cigarette jingle from the 1960s: "Encima, debajo, alrededor y por" AND put that to hand gestures (over, under, around, and through) to learn some words that just were not working for her. It still takes both the music and the gestures (which she usually does in her head) for her to recall the words.

I put abbreviated stories on my fingers to remember the order of my script, but Ann Birney lists hers in a column on the far left side of a sheet of lined paper. She then folds the list under and tries to write the list from memory. She has used various mnemonics, such as the first letter of each key word, to get the order correctly. She keeps folding, listing, and checking until she gets the list right twice. Then she tackles each story, working from "head pictures" and memorizing her own phrases that she finds particularly pleasing, or quotes of her historic figure. For the latter, she once again uses the written word, with key word reminders, but combines it with walking along a country road with no traffic. Doug McGovern, a historical performer with an engineering background, uses index cards with key words like flash cards and studies them as though for a test. He also draws flow charts to map out and recall his script.

However you learn, you will need discipline. You have an obligation to your historic figure, your audience, and yourself to tell the story accurately.

## CREATING YOUR "LOOK"

Your look is important, not only to the audience, but also to us as creators. Donning an article of apparel helps me get into character as I work on my script and practice performing, and that has been the case with most of the people with whom I have worked. The sooner we have an article of clothing that we can put on while we work, the smoother the process.

Clothing and costume has been the center of debate within and between interpreters, reenactors, and historical performers. The items themselves and what they are called have been endlessly debated. One side says that if you have the walk and talk you don't need exactitude in the look. The other extreme says

**A Trail Story**

## 5.2. CREATING CALAMITY JANE'S LOOK

When I began to build my Calamity Jane look in 1990, I found a *True West* article asking whether the buckskin coat, pants, and beaded vest at what is now the Buffalo Bill Historical Center in Cody, Wyoming, were really Calamity Jane's. The author proved the authenticity of the outfit. I asked the curator to send me a copy of the museum's registration information with their notes as to material, measurements, and wear patterns. This was before we had the capability to send such things through e-mail, so I also paid extra for a large color photograph of the vest. My intent was to have a replica vest, complete with beadwork, made for me.

Clothing historian Kathy Brown measured me on Monday. On Tuesday I received the packet and found that my measurements matched Calamity Jane's exactly, even the way her jacket buttonholes had stretched when she had put on weight. I set aside my plans. The coincidence was too spooky. I just could not replicate her total look. So I went with the generic and accurate look of cotton pants, cotton shirt, and leather vest with metal buttons, all of which have passed muster with the thread Nazis and button turners, accurate-look fanatics who really like my boots, complete with mule ears, which were made for me from an 1895 Sears catalog drawing. In this garb I looked like her pictures.

that the look is most important, followed by the walk and the talk. Each knows its own intent and believes that this intent is self-evident.

Chautauquans would tell you that their audience is interested in ideas and overlooks or doesn't care about discrepancies in appearance. Of course, they might tell you, the 1800 person wears polyester because that's what is available inexpensively and everyone knows that humanities councils have very little money to spend on costumes. And it really is a costume, a representation of the appearance with little concern for accuracy.

Reenactors, on the other hand, are typically concerned with accuracy in their kit (military) or duds (Old West). They have coined terms like thread Nazi, button turner, and farb, which describe different players who police accuracy and those who are inaccurate.

Both Chautauquans and reenactors are facing an increasingly sophisticated audience, an audience that expects an experience as close to authenticity as can be achieved: accuracy in the look, appropriate performance, and an ability to share knowledge of the era.[3] The historical performer has the opportunity and challenge to provide the marriage of the two styles the audience craves. "The look" conveys the historical performer's accuracy of period clothing with their comfort in wearing and moving in it, as well as their knowledge of the context of how it would have been created. It also includes the material culture brought onstage, which we will address soon.

I have posed below questions that have been asked of me, with the answers that I have been offering. Scan until you find the questions that best describe your own circumstance at this time.

### What Did My Person Look Like?

Would that it was all as easy as "I see by your outfit that you are a cowboy." No, I don't really mean that—the world would be too boring. We like diversity in our clothing, but we also have icons to which we must give a nod.

You want to know what your person looked like so that you can approximate that person's look as closely as possible. If you found a photograph of your historic figure while doing your research, keep reading. If not, scan down to the section that applies to you. If the era you are researching is before the era of photography, scan even further.

Chances are you will have more than one image from which to choose. Things to consider when selecting your image follow:

- Occupation
- Social status
- Setting: time of year, geographic location, specific setting (inside, outside)
- What your audience expects the person to look like (the icon)
- What speaks to the era
- What looks reasonably good on you
- How much time and energy you want to spend on your look

Let's consider the above criteria for 1940s historic figures. If you are male you might be in the military and wearing a uniform. Homefront iconic looks are coveralls (mechanic, factory worker), overalls and cap (farmer), or a suit (businessman). If you are a woman in the military your uniform would be much the same as that of the men but with a skirt instead of slacks. Your factory and "farmerette" outfits would be similar except that slacks usually had buttons on the side, with prescription and actual practice varying as it has through time. You would have a scarf tying up your hair ala Rosie the Riveter. If you worked in an office you wore a skirt, blouse, jacket, and high heels. And, of course, you wore a hat to work but took it off once inside.

You want to use your look to convey your social status. In the early 1940s we are still in the throes of the Great Depression. Unless we are wealthy our clothing is probably showing wear. Women will not have nylons, especially during the war (they painted lines up the back of their legs to emulate the seams on hosiery).

Time of year: you cannot tell the audience that it is winter and not have a wrap or coat in evidence if you are coming in from outside. This is a strategy, though—if you have found the best look and it is a summer look, then if possible without changing the dramatic charge tell your story about winter from the good old summertime. If it is indoors and you are a male in the 1940s chances are you will have a hat, but it will not be on your head. If you are a woman of that time and you are hosting, your hat will not be evident, but if you are visiting it will be on your head.

Audience expectations: what do we think of when we form a mental image of Abraham Lincoln? Black suit, stovepipe hat, and beard. If we stray from those we need to tell the audience why, for instance, there is no beard—is it a young Lincoln, the railsplitter, before the war?

Know the look of the era: people think of the past as black and white because of the limits of pre-1940s photography. But clothing collections and drawings tell us otherwise: nineteenth-century women—and men—wore brightly colored, patterned dresses, vests, and jackets. The plaids! The buttons! The displays of wealth!

Just because you know that your historic figure preferred to wear green does not mean that you need to do so if you look atrocious in green. It is a minor point. You want the audience to enjoy your performance, not look away in pain. Wear yellow if it suits you better—and be ready to explain to the one person who cares why you are not wearing green.

The bottom line is either you will have to do the research to do the look or find someone to do it for you. If you enjoy the process you will want to wallow in the process of creating just the right look, including perhaps looks for each season. Some people even choose their character by the look that they like, including whether or not they have to alter their hairstyle. If you do not enjoy the material culture aspects of creating your look, you will keep the fuss to a minimum and use your script as necessary to explain what you are wearing. As long as you follow the criteria above and the look is accurate, how much time and money you spend will depend on you, keeping in mind that some investment on your part in both is crucial to the accuracy of your look.

You will probably start with an image of your person from which you will build your look. You probably have an image from your research, but what follows is more detail on finding historic images.

### Where Should I Begin to Look for Images?

Books are where most people find images as they are researching for data about the life and times of their subject. Check your research notes. What archives and research facilities have material on your era? Check their Internet site to see if they have listed their holdings online. Contact them and ask if they can send you a photograph, either through the postal service or e-mail. Every day there is more available online. You might be required—or be inspired—to send a small amount to help preserve that item for your future use and that of others.

### I Have a Photograph of "My Character"; What Do I Do with It?

Once you have one photograph, keep looking for others. Always document where you found your photograph and age of "your" person or the era in which it was taken. Every time you find a photograph of your person or of his or her family, carefully analyze it.

---

### A Trail Story

#### 5.3. AMELIA'S BIRTHDAY PHOTO

Two responses to a photograph of young Amelia Earhart's birthday party:

1. Isn't that nice? It's integrated. There's an African American boy in the picture.
2. That African American boy is standing and carrying a tray, while the other children are seated around a table. He is probably a servant. He is dressed differently than the other boys.

---

To analyze a photograph start with a careful look at the whole image. Move from the superficial to teasing out the details. Examine the whole photograph as a unit. What is the context of the image? Where was it taken? What were they doing? What were they wearing? Then focus on different parts of the image, methodically digging out all the clues you can see. Use a magnifying glass and different types of light while looking for minute details, specific data. Think how a crime detective would analyze the image for details that will include the clothing and material culture of the day or era, as well as suggestions about social relationships.

### I Do Not Have a Photograph of "My Character" Because None Was Taken or One No Longer Exists, at Least Not One that I Know of at This Time.

The best you can do for now is to look at other images and photographs of people of the same era, class, race, ethnicity, and status, doing the same types of activities in a similar geographic area. Extrapolate clues from the examples you are examining. And, of course, keep looking for that one picture you know is out there. On the other hand, if you don't know what they look like, no one else will either, so just get as close as you can. If you are going to be a blue-eyed Kanza, though, you need to be able to understand how genetics can make that happen and tell stories of tribal women marrying Anglo traders.

### I Am Working on an Era that Was before Photography Was Invented, and No Painted Portrait or Drawing Exists that I Know of at This Time.

This condition is both a blessing and a curse. It is a blessing because as long as it is based upon sound historical research your interpretation of what the person looked like is as good as that of the next person. If the historic figure has no iconographic image, then you look just like them! A particular buffalo hunter who was not painted and was perhaps photographed once in his life could look like anyone of his ethnicity. On the other hand, if you were to portray Buffalo Bill Cody, who made sure that his image was made widely available to the public, you need to create not just "the buffalo hunter" look but specifically Cody's look. Start with what is known (after all, there were written descriptions), and then keep educating yourself. Be willing to change and also educate others as you learn. Inform yourself through research. Be able to discuss with your audience how your research influenced your selection of clothing to reinforce your story line.

*I Am Working on an Era and Place Where There Were*
*No Visual Chroniclers—What Do I Do?*

Again, researching a tribal person or a "mountain man or woman" or any-one often labeled "The Frontier" is also going to mean digging for clues based on primary sources and items found in museum collections. Keep researching. You will find descriptions in letters and diaries, many of them in secondary sources.

*Where Do I Find Images of People in My Era and Place?*

Here are examples to get your juices flowing. Thanks to the Internet you can search just about any topic and find images *if* the images have been linked to key words.

- An excellent tool is Joan L. Severa's *Dressed for the Photographer: Ordinary Americans and Fashion, 1840–1900*.[4] Severa divides the photographs into decades. Each photograph is accompanied by detailed data about the image. Also very useful is her lengthy discussion of how women's, men's, and children's clothing was constructed and the nuances of the styles worn; her work is a useful tool for thinking about the social history of fashion. Severa discusses, too, how the knowledge of the newer styles was easy to come by, even by people out on the Plains. Newspapers and magazines showed what was being worn back East. Even if one did not have the circumstances to have "ready-mades" or acquire fabric and trim-mings, you might remake an existing dress and tat your own lace. On the other hand, remember that just because it is 1880 does not mean one is wearing 1880 fashion. I don't know about you, but I tend to wear cloth-ing I like no matter how old it is, and if I was in a financial crunch, as is the case with several of my characters, I would be especially likely to be "recycling" clothing.
- *Godey's Lady's Book* (for two years of the periodical go to http://www .iath.virginia.edu/utc/sentimnt/gallgodyf.html). This high-style mag-azine also includes menswear and is readily available in paper at li-braries and historical societies. Remember, however, that not all women could afford to be dressed at this level of style. Women were constrained, too, by their work. If they had to build a fire and cook over it, for instance, hoopskirts were out of the question. Think care-fully about your character's role in life. The same is true of men and boys.

- Newspapers from your era are available at libraries and historical societies and have illustrations and sometimes descriptions of attire. They also carry advertisements from local mercantiles listing "newly offered goods for sale."
- Catalogs such as those from Sears and Montgomery Ward were very common after the late 1880s as the merchandisers pushed to supply the Great Plains by railroads. Some have been reprinted for your ease of access, such as the 1908 Sears Roebuck Catalogue.[5] Just about every local historical society has a few catalog reprints, while some state historical societies or state libraries have whole runs. That way you can create a look authentic to the era and know what objects might have been in your person's home.
- Dover Publications offers compilations of catalogs in their series *Everyday Fashions of the* [Decade]: *As Pictured in Sears and Other Catalogs*, such as *Everyday Fashions of the Thirties: As Pictured in Sears and Other Catalogs* (New York: Dover Publications, 1986) by Stella Blum. All have useful selections of clothing, hat, and footwear images.
- For Great Plains life from 1880 to 1920, two collections from the Institute for Regional Studies at North Dakota State University contain nine hundred photographs of rural and small-town life at the turn of the century from the Fred Hultstrand and F. A. Pazandak Photograph collections (http://memory.loc.gov/ammem/award97/ndfahtml/ngphome.html).
- The Library of Congress collection of prints and photographs is at http://lcweb2.loc.gov/pp/pphome.html and includes Works Progress Administration photographs such as "Worker's wife washing clothes in front yard. South Charleston, West Virginia."
- Check online and onsite photograph collection of state historical societies.

### What Sources Are Available If My Era Does Not Have Photography?

Museum curators and registrars maintain very detailed records of items in their collections including prints and photographs. One very comprehensive source is the New York Public Library Digital Gallery (http://digitalgallery .nypl.org), which you can scan by individual collection or search by very general keywords. Middle Tennessee State University Library hosts a Web page: "American Women's History: A Research Guide, Clothing and Fashion" at http://frank .mtsu.edu/~kmiddlet/history/women/wh-clothing.html that includes lists of archives and collections.

**I Know How I Want to Look but Where Do I Go to Get the "Duds"?**

Count on spending money to get the most authentic look you can get. Remember, your audience craves accuracy. Most historical performers go to a supplier or sutler who specializes in clothing and accoutrement for their era. One caveat: just because someone is selling it does not mean it is accurate with the correct fabric, thread-count, or button style. Inaccurate garb is called "farbish" by reenactors. Always do your research before you buy as there are some interesting stories floating around among reenactors about their "not-so-correct" expensive purchases over the years. Based on your research, find vintage items or the most accurate reproductions you can afford, and plan on upgrading as you learn (and earn) more. If you cannot afford a custom-made pair of boots, get as close to the look as you can, know the difference between what you are wearing and what you should have, and make no apologies when you acknowledge the difference. Hold your head high as a knowledgeable person who is moving in the right direction. I know of no reenactor (and they are the ones who set the standard for accurate clothing) who did not begin with less-than-accurate garb.

Individuals who are knowledgeable about the era and the correct methods used during your era are out there. Part of the fun of researching is finding them and swapping information. "Hidden" museums include clothing collections at universities, such as the Kansas State University Historic Costume and Textile Museum (http://www.humec.k-state.edu/museum). Look for these in your geographic area—your state museum association should be able to help you. Fabric materials, treatments, and production methods vary over time but appear subtle to the untrained eye. Find those who know.

Here are three quick examples: leather, sewing, and metal. The difference between brain tanning and the chemical tanning process is readily apparent if you know what to look for. You can find someone to teach you. Likewise, if you have a leather garment, know that there is a huge difference between real animal sinew, artificial sinew, and thread. A 1770s look will use sinew, but if you are interpreting the 1970s, thread is appropriate for your leather moccasins. A quick word on buttons: no plastic, please, unless you are interpreting post–World War II. Metalwork should also be correct, so go find a knowledgeable blacksmith to hand forge your "mountain man" buckles. In other words, cloth, buttons, and buckles change over time.

This discussion could go on and on, and does around campfires and in the various reenactor listservs. The bottom line is that if you are doing a historical performance you need to think and be as careful about your "look" as you are about what you say. Professionally trained historians rant and rave about the accuracy of footnotes and information in the same way that reenactors rant and rave about the accuracy of "the stuff one wears and uses." While reenactors may josh about their "cool toys," they are every bit as serious about accuracy in their "stuff" as historians are about the accuracy of their words. So, yes, as a historical performer you are walking a knife's edge, but, hey, I know that with planning and preparation you can do it. One tool in planning is the chart in appendix C.

*Suppliers, Purveyors, and Sutlers*

Every war we have ever had has had its sutlers, its suppliers, which is why at reenactment events there is always a tent that is rather like a general mercantile. Sutlers are in a quasi-reenactment mode because their goal is to make a profit from the public as well as the reenactors. They are usually highly skilled artisans in addition to being entrepreneurs but often blend time zones by selling souvenirs as well as authentically made reproductions and books published across time. Blanket traders are for muzzleloaders and their public what sutlers are for war reenactors. Old West suppliers at events often sell out of tents labeled "Mercantile." All of these can be found at museum and historic site events.

The advantage of visiting a sutler or supplier is that you can see and handle the stuff, try on a hat, see how it looks, see how others respond to your new look. However, you do have to travel to the site. And generally you do not know who will be there and what they will have. Some suppliers have stores that you can visit. Maybe there are even some near you. You can also visit websites to familiarize yourself with what is available. There is a website for reenactors of any war, Revolutionary, French and Indian, Mexican, Spanish, World War I, and for virtually any historic group or era, such as Vikings, Renaissance, and Mongols. Start with the links on http://www.historyandreenacting.com/. If you will be portraying a Civil War figure, the directory to browse for your clothing is "Sutler's Web Pages" (http://www.angelfire.com/me/reenact/sutlers.html). If you will be a civilian of the last half of the nineteenth century, you might find the Victoriana website of use, at http://www.victoriana.com/, as well as that of Amazon Drygoods, at http://www.amazondrygoods.com/. Old West performers should look for Wah Maker and Scully clothing, which is carried by dealers who also sell hats, boots, and the rest of the look.

You might choose to make your clothing or have it made for you. Past Patterns (http://www.pastpatterns.com/) has been in business since 1979, creating patterns from an amazingly wide array of vintage clothing. Ride into History has had four of these made up. One caveat: when last we checked, you will have to do your own resizing, and a seamstress has told us that she found the lack of directions frustrating. Amazon Drygoods has the reputation of providing easier-to-follow, but still authentic, patterns from medieval times to 1950 but emphasizing the Victorian period. As of this time the catalog is not online, but it is relatively inexpensive and ordering information is online (http://www.amazon drygoods.com/).

Whether you call them "your duds," "your kit," or "your gear," remember, please—they are your clothing, NOT A COSTUME. Costumes are what actors can wear if they are on a stage thirty feet away from the first row of the audience.

### Other Considerations for Your Look

- Don't be a farb: check all of the details: your watch should be period correct, ditch the cell phone, and do not use anachronistic tobacco products in public.
- Eyewear: If you must wear glasses to see the audience, historically accurate frames are available through suppliers (above), and used frames can be found at antique stores. Opticians can put your prescription into those frames, although you might have to compromise trifocals. Or, better yet, wear contact lenses. Bifocal lens can be divided between the two eyes. Trifocals are a bit more difficult, but, again, compromises usually result in something pretty comfortable. Consider color, too, when you get contacts—if you are a brown-eyed person portraying a blue-eyed individual, here's an opportunity to get a little closer to "the look." Do not wear sunglasses or glasses that are not accurate for the period. The anachronism is disturbing to the audience.
- Makeup: Oof-da. This is one of the most difficult topics for many women. Makeup shows. It is not hidden. If women of your time and station did not wear it, don't you wear it. No eyeliner, no mascara, no lipstick, no foundation, and no blusher. If you are portraying a prostitute and the paint is era correct for a prostitute, fine (you have heard of "painted lady," right?). Paint often contained either arsenic or lead, though, and I won't fuss at you for not using those ingredients. On the other hand, just like people throughout time, you want to look the best you can with what is at hand and what is socially acceptable. You have to work with what is socially acceptable for your historic figure's era and what she would have had available. So use a little contemporary blusher

IF it looks like elderberry juice because many a woman has rosied her cheeks with berry juice—or, easier to achieve, pinching her cheeks. Tribal people ornamented their bodies with vermilion, ochre, and charcoal mixed with animal grease.

- Hair: Styles reflect the culture. But there are ways to get around it. When I told Ann that she had to grow out her hair if she was going to portray a nineteenth-century woman, she told me that her character, a composite, had had scarlettina recently and the doctor had ordered that her hair be cut off to bring down the fever. She wrote this into the script and it worked. For another nineteenth-century figure she stuffed a snood with hair, and under her wide-brimmed hat it looks quite realistic. Besides, Amelia Earhart, her signature character, had short hair, but Ann has to curl it . . . because Amelia did! Bear grease, buffalo grease—if you are portraying a tribal person or mountain man you need to have long hair, and it should be greased—or there should be an explanation about why it's not.

### A Trail Story

#### 5.4. AARGH!

At a festival muzzleloader reenactment, I saw a woman in a buckskin dress and moccasins, her hair very short and gelled into spikes, talking on a cell phone and smoking a filter cigarette. She checked the time on her wristwatch before closing her cell phone and tossing it into her tent. All of this was in plain sight of the audience. How is the public to know that very little about her was accurate for eighteenth-century fur traders?

- Double-check your look against the images you have found of your individual and others in their era. The audience trusts you to be accurate in your interpretation.

**Material Culture on Stage: How Much Is Too Much?**

If the audience is seated and your narrative is a half hour or so, the stuff should be part of the look and not distract from the text of the performance. *Anything on stage must be used to move the narrative forward.* Less is more for historical performance. Trust the words to tell the story. Amelia Earhart has a globe that she picks up occasionally from a very small table to demonstrate routes. Calamity Jane carries her saddle and bridle onto the stage where a wooden saddle stand, stool, and cup await. She interacts with all of these objects during her performance. Doug Watson as Will Rogers carries on only a rope, but it is almost part of his look rather than being a prop. The minimalist approach not only helps the audience focus on the performer and the words but is also a boon when the performer has several performances in a short time, say as many as four during a school day, and must set up and take down rapidly.

Material culture enthusiasts and reenactors tend to have wonderful stuff that they want to show off. It is more difficult to sustain a scripted story—and stay in character—with that much stuff on stage with you. The audience is wondering about the objects in front of them and not thinking about what you are saying. So unless you are really, really good you will lose audience interest when they do not have the opportunity to closely examine your stuff until you have completed your script. You have set up competing attention-getting devices. Use one or the other, not both. The best place to share historical knowledge through material culture is at a learning station, not with a staged production. That way you can have a sustained dialogue about the stuff and go into great detail with a very small group of people.

Ride into History has constructed a means of making artifacts and narratives work together, an artifact-based tour using first-person narratives, which we spell out in the final chapter. For a sustained narrative, however, we are sticking to the rule of either "much stuff" or "much narrative," not both at once. If you are telling history, use stuff strategically—to catch attention but not to hold it. You want your audience to focus on your words, not on your stuff.

## TELLING HISTORY IN CHARACTER

You have learned your script and created your look. Your look, however, is still developing because it is not just what you wear. Your look is also how you stand, how you move, how you use your body. This section will address those things, as well as how you speak to the audience and your interactions with them. You are ready to practice telling your stories, using your whole body. Then you will prepare to take questions, first as your historic figure, then as the scholar who is interpreting the historic figure.

As I said in describing the creation of the script, what you are performing is a first-person, direct-address narrative. Your performance actually has three parts: a monologue in which you are in character telling a planned sequence of stories, a discussion in which you are in character, and, finally, discussion as the scholar. You do it all while directly addressing the audience.

This is in contrast to the fourth wall that we usually experience in theater, including museum theater. The "fourth wall" is an imaginary structure that separates action on stage from the audience. In traditional theater, actors behave as though the audience is not there. As audience members we are unseen observers whose responses to their dilemmas are ignored. In contrast, our engagement as historical performers is intimate.

You have written the audience into the script. Planning ahead, you have written a script that tells the audience that they are friendly, and you, in turn, will bathe them in golden light. It is a mutual admiration society, so there is no fear on either side. The audience is comfortable if they understand their role, which is primarily to listen, but also to respond briefly to you just as they would to anyone speaking directly to them. They know they will have the opportunity to ask questions later. And you are comfortable because you know they do not care a fig about you. They are here to meet your historic figure. In other words, if I do my work right the audience does not see Joyce Thierer; they see Calamity Jane, or Grower, or Rosa Fix, or whoever I am that day. The greatest compliment I can receive is when people who know me well say they forgot they were watching me and were convinced it was my character in front of them.

**Performance Hints**
- Directly address the audience—the audience is always a part of the oral dynamic but especially so in a direct-address narrative.
- Use eye contact, or the appearance of eye contact. This is important as it pulls the listener into the story, and it also changes what might be perceived as an aloof performance into direct personal communication.
- Direct your total energy toward the audience; reach out to them with your voice, eyes, hands, and feet if necessary, body following mind. "Flirt" with the audience; projecting energy toward them makes them feel special.
- If you look confident, your audience will believe you are confident, and you will feel more self-assured.
- Reach the entire audience—look across, back, and forward.
- If you are nervous looking directly at specific individuals in the audience, pick focus points just beyond them, and the audience will feel you are looking at them. When Ann Birney and I conduct workshops we place sticky notes on the back wall, three notes placed widely apart, left, right, and center, and suggest that nervous performers look through the audience to those sticky notes.
- Audiences return the energy you give them—usually, most audiences (see trail story 5.5).

**A Trail Story**

### 5.5. GREAT PLAINS FARMERS

My background is rural. Part of my mission is getting quality historical performance to rural audiences. But for one of my first Calamity Jane performances, three hundred farmers sat with crossed arms, looking not quite at me, expressionless. I tried every trick in my saddlebag to get a reaction from them. Then I began to rush the script a bit so I could get outta there. Discussion consisted of a single question asked by the extension agent (an import from another county). I wanted to bolt; it was all so awkward, my having bombed with this audience. But I was expected to stay for coffee and cookies and discussion. Suddenly I was bombarded with individuals who looked me straight in the eye and said I had touched them emotionally, had made them laugh and cry. And they asked questions and offered observations. I was there for hours. A few followed me out to my truck, where they continued to talk, telling me their own stories.

Now that I think of it, in my experience high school students and German Lutheran farmers are a lot alike.

- Step toward the audience when sharing something more intimate and away for large movements.
- If your historic figure is known for a delivery style not appropriate for your audience, use that style to give a bit of the flavor, then move away from it. For example, instead of giving one of Abraham Lincoln's longer addresses, deliver the "Gettysburg Address" and move on to his other styles because he was also well known as a storyteller and raconteur. I coached a youngster who was creating Helen Keller. Keller's speech was difficult to understand because she learned to talk late in life and could not hear. We know that as we listen to an unfamiliar speech pattern it becomes easier to understand, so I used that—she told the audience in very stilted speech that in her experience they would come to understand her, and she rather quickly but gradually eased into what was for her a normal speaking pattern. By the way, that child will soon complete a master's degree in speech pathology!

- Varying your delivery in pace and volume spices up a story and conveys your moods as they change. "[proudly while gesturing toward my hat:] And it had a low crown and ribbony flowers. [looking down in embarrassment:] And a . . dead . bird . right . [hand to hat] *there*." Each dot represents a short pause.
- Use silence to bracket a word or phrase you want to emphasize—silence will get the audience's attention even better than a loud word will: "I saw that my . altimeter . had failed."
- Use silence to "remember"—look up and away as you say, "It was [look away, 'remembering'] . . . [nod to yourself] yes, [pace is slow] almost twenty years ago, [look back at audience] during the war. [pick up pace] I was in college near Philadelphia and"
- Use your voice and body to add the nuances of what "you" hear, see, smell, and experience. Nonverbal techniques such as posture, gesture, and facial expression add richness to your story. When Calamity Jane remembers smelling a fresh apple pie, my hand goes up my nose, and I grin with the memory of the cinnamon and sugar, all of the senses engaged. My grin also allows the audience to see Jane's inner trickster shine through as she plots how she is going to get a piece of that apple pie.
- Speak from the immediacy of your experiences. Be "there," whatever place or time you say "you" are in. Do not let your mind wander from your historic figure's setting. If at all possible, stay in character if there is a problem you need to solve (see trail story 5.6).

---

**A Trail Story**

### 5.6. STAYING IN CHARACTER

One of the more challenging problems Ann as Amelia Earhart faced was a child with projectile vomiting on the first row of bleachers in a grade school gymnasium. Luckily, she was just out of range and no other youngsters were involved, so she just helped clean it up and went on with her performance.

- If a historical anachronism occurs, such as a jet flying over, low, ignore it, or in the case of an intercom squawking out instructions in a classroom, stop your performance, then pick up where you left off or repeat a bit as you would if you were in any other discussion when that happened. Today's audiences are used to these disturbances. Do not call attention to them, but recall the audience to your story, and allow them to travel forward in your time line with you as if nothing had happened.
- Talk about your childhood, but do not regress into childhood. And above all, do not use chirpy baby/child talk. This is condescending; audience members become impatient and feel that you are talking down to them.
- If you feel you must use a dialect, do it well, get coaching, and consider the effect on the audience. A Confederate Civil War reenactor used a variety of racial slurs and stereotypes, mimicking black speech, while giving a canned talk to a small group comprising a black family, a self-proclaimed redneck, and myself. His goal was to be an offensive "bad boy." All but one of us walked off quickly rather than participate in a performance that should not have been.
- Consider the audience's expectations. When you walk or run onto the stage, greet them. This will tell them that you will be addressing them directly, that the fourth wall is not there, and that they have some role in what is to follow.
- One advantage of being a historical performer is that we have a vast array of tools at our disposal, including storytelling and theater. While storytellers do not directly address historical performance, their methodologies are useful in thinking about how to tell a story once you have written yours and in helping you think about the structuring of your story sequence and transitioning between stories. I very highly recommend Norma J. Livo and Sandra A. Rietz's *Storytelling: Process and Practice* (Littleton, Colo.: Libraries Unlimited, 1986). If it is not available locally, have your library borrow it through Interlibrary Loan. Or buy it for your professional bookshelf.
- Harriet Mason, author of *The Power of Storytelling*, suggests practicing with familiar stories to become comfortable with using more body language and voice emotion than is your custom. For example, read aloud and then practice telling the "Three Little Pigs." Note the story's ritual opening, rhythmic story line, sequence, pacing, anticipation of events, and conclusion.
- Mason says, however, that "if you like the story you are telling, and you want to tell it, you don't have to worry about techniques. Concentrate on the story instead of yourself, and your enjoyment will be contagious. Ges-

tures, facial expression, voice, and timing will take care of themselves and will be appropriate. I urge you to take the risk."[6] In other words, *enjoy the telling.*

- Observe storytellers and learn from them. Go to the café and listen to people as they tell a really interesting story for the umpteenth time. Professional storytellers perform at libraries and arts events. Attend one of the many storyteller events, festivals, and conferences. There are many opportunities. Check the Internet—one of our favorite storytellers, Priscilla Howe, has great storytelling hints on her site, http://www.priscilla howe.com/, and the National Storytelling Network's site (http://www .storynet.org/) will help you find events near you. Attend workshops and spruce up your skills. Storytelling, when done well, is truly performance art. Historical performers tell stories, so use those skills. As you listen and watch, analyze the structure of the story; the way they modulate their voice; their use of timing and pace, gesture and movement, and facial expression; and the way they project their energy toward and around the audience (see trail story 5.7).

## A Trail Story

### 5.7. AN INTIMATE MOMENT

I was performing my composite farm woman, Rosa Fix, outside the barn on the Morton County Museum grounds in Elkhart, Kansas. Unbeknownst to my audience, thunderheads were rapidly approaching from behind them. The wind was stirring up dust and sand. I stepped in toward the audience so they could hear me, and as I did so I felt myself starting to speed-talk. I knew I needed to wrap it up and move to safety, but they were a rapt audience. I was talking about the harshness of plains farm life, which most of them understood. Then, as I talked about how my German husband just did not understand what life out here meant for a woman, I talked about his angry words. I had my hands out in front in a defensive gesture, and then I curled up into myself as if I was protecting my pregnant belly. As I looked up, an elderly woman on the front row reached out to me, patting my hands. She looked directly into my eyes and said, "It will get better." We held hands and eyes for what seemed like a long time, and then the speaker blew over. I said, "Yes, it must," and we rushed for cover from the rain and sand.

- I NEVER practice my stories in front of a mirror—I find the "audience" distracting, but many people do so and find it very useful.
- Play in front of the mirror—assume poses, make funny faces—take risks; you really do want an expressive, mobile face when you are in front of an audience.
- Videotape practice performances and performances along the way—you will need them not only for self-critique but also for jurying onto arts rosters and, if it's a digital recording, for your website.
- I am feeling pretty confident (my dog, cat, horse likes it). I can walk or move and talk at the same time. Now what? Ehaaaa!!! It is time to invite in friends to celebrate with food and your first friendly dress performance. Let them meet your new identity.
- My best measure is by telling the stories to real people, people who will take notes and gently but firmly critique me. Everyone needs outside feedback, preferably from several people. Practicing by yourself and then on the animals is all very fine and good, but you will not catch some of the goofs, gaffs, miss-speaks, and illogical leaps that are very clear to you, who knows the stuff inside and out.
- I learned a lot from theater people, but I also rejected a few suggestions (no hands in pockets, never turn your back) because what we are doing is not traditional theater. I want to look as natural as possible for my setting and my character.
- Here's a good theater tip: when pointing use your whole hand or your first two fingers so that it can be seen from a distance and so that it cannot be misinterpreted as a middle finger gesture.
- What if you do forget something? That is when you ask yourself, "What would [insert your historic figure's name here] do?" Probably, they would do just as you would if you were being yourself in front of a group of people—you would take the story in a different direction, perhaps apologizing for forgetting what it was you were going to say. You would be secure and know that the audience has had it happen to them, and if they have totally suspended their disbelief they will think it is part of the script, cleverly written to make the historic figure more human. Unlike most actors, you have done your own research and written your own script, you have the picture in your mind as to what happened, and you can describe it without using the word you forgot (see trail story 5.8).
- Dare to tap into your own experiences, your affective memory, to evoke moods (a method identified in theater with Constantin Stanislavsky).

**A Trail Story**

### 5.8. WHERE IS "ALTIMETER" WHEN YOU NEED IT MOST?!

It has never happened to me, of course (cough), but Ann Birney says her worst case of forgetting a word was when she forgot "altimeter," mentioned earlier as crucial to the story of Amelia Earhart's solo transatlantic crossing. Can you imagine having to say "the instrument that tells how high you are above the ocean" every time you want to say "altimeter" (five times, I believe) in a very dramatic scene? And imagine, having to perform on the fly, so to speak, editing out as redundant the description of what an altimeter was. But she did it! The audience, of course, was none the wiser. And she was grateful that it happened only once in her fourteen years of being Amelia. She says that there have been other small "forgets" but none quite so challenging.

• When building emotion, enter the moment and actually forget the audience. See the event and speak it in the present. Here is one of my most emotional Calamity Jane scenes:

Their parlor was the size of four of our cabins out here in the West. [with awe:] The divan was as soft as a new colt's hair. The draperies . . . . I look up and see my Janie on that balcony. She has her daddy's hair. Oh, poor girl, she has my nose. Then Jim O'Neil calls up, "Jean Irene O'Neil, please come down to meet Calamity Jane, a friend of ours from out West." She comes down the stairs with her rustly crinolines. They've changed the name I gave her [first wave of sadness as I realize that this most intimate connection has been severed]. She tells me about her pony and I talk about my horses, and she looks up at me and says, "Oh, yes, my mother told me SO much about how you ride like the wind in the West," and then she starts to cry, telling me how her mother, Helen O'Neil, died a year ago. I reach out to her [doing so with arms] and hold her close [I allow my face to crumple as I think of how I, Joyce, once lost a child], thinking about how the last time I held her was out along the Yellowstone, facing life without her pa. . . . [I look up and outward, pushing the memory away, shake off the emotion, get my bandana from my saddlebag, and mutter:] I didn't plan on telling you that story. [more collected:] Most people don't want to know what it's really like to be a woman in the West. [transition to next story]

- If you step out of the now to really see and feel an emotional event, the audience will join you in your emotion, whether it is joy or pain. Confession: I even cried writing the above, and I have performed that story hundreds of times. I do not include it in every performance, but it often comes out in discussions after the monologue.

And speaking of discussions . . .

## DISCUSSION AND QUESTION-AND-ANSWER PERIOD

You need to draw your monologue to a close and make a transition to the discussion. Check what you wrote for your exit. How are you going to clue your audience that you are willing to take questions in character? The idea that you are going to take questions should have been planted in the audience's minds by the sponsor's introduction, and perhaps if the setting is that of a talk, you can say it as your historic figure during your introduction: "What I will do is tell you about ——, ——, and —— and then let you ask me any questions that you may have." Then, as you end your monologue you can be as blunt as saying, "Do you have any questions of me?" or "I promised to take your questions; does someone have a question or comment for me?"

The most difficult thing is to be patient, to wait until a question is asked. Count to ten on your fingers, staying open and accepting of your audience while running your gaze across the room, looking for people who want to ask but are hesitating and will do so if you meet their eyes and nod at them. If all else fails, tell them something that you expected them to ask about your character. During my Calamity Jane story about her time as a scout for the U.S. Army, I punt to what I call one of my "encore stories" by saying, "There's a story about how they found out I was a girl but that's not the one I'm telling you now." Then give them another opportunity to ask questions of your historic figure. If you still see no desire to ask questions (it happens rarely, but it does happen—think of my Great Plains farmers), then step out of character, preferably in part by taking off an article of clothing such as your hat or shawl, or putting on your glasses, and introduce yourself. The audience needs a visual cue at this point, and permission to ask *anything* of you.

Of course, I am not really Martha Jane Cannary. My real name is Joyce Thierer. I am a member of Ride into History, a historical performance touring troupe, and a professor at Emporia State University. I love to discuss why I do historical performance, women in the West, history, and just about anything to do with the West. Maybe you have a question that you did not feel comfortable asking Jane, or were not sure she could answer, and you would like to ask me.

If they still seem reticent, tell them something about her life after your setting, like the circumstances of her death. And that's the advantage of a historical performance—the audience gets "the rest of the story," a rich analysis and filling in of context. What was Calamity Jane's influence? Why do we hear so much about her but know so little?

Another advantage of historical performance is that you can move in and out of character during the question-and-answer session. For instance, the classic case is if you are taking questions as your historic figure and someone asks, "How did you die?" The response is, "Do I look like I'm dead?" Then smile quickly and warmly to diffuse embarrassment, step out of character, and explain how your person died, or why we don't know how the person died. Practice this because it will happen. In fact, sometimes when I make the transition to the scholar, I praise the audience because no one asked about "my" death.

Sometimes, on the other hand, it is easier to answer a question in character even though you are now the scholar. In that case, move back into your character's look by putting on your hat and assuming your in-character stance. Then use your character's voice to answer the question. The audience will love it. It's a neat parlor trick, and they will delight in your ability to move back and forth at will, as will you. At that moment you think, "All that research, all that practice, and it all came together perfectly at this moment, one fine successful performance." But maybe you don't trust self-evaluation, so you are going to ask someone else, maybe the person you brought along to set up your sound equipment, or give you your cue, or just drive you home while you are flying with your post-performance high: "How did I do?" and they will be glowing with you—but maybe share a few suggestions on the way home.

To prepare for taking questions, have someone interview you in the role of a reporter to find out what you know and what you do not know. This is a good thing to tape, or you could take notes: what questions were you not able to answer. NEVER fudge an answer, UNLESS you are doing so in character with your best finessing (that is, doing as the politicians do: answer instead the question you wish they had asked) and are willing to then step out of character and explain as the scholar why you equivocate.

Did you hear me hedge on that last question? I let Amelia answer the question I wished you had asked instead of the one you asked. Let me explain why. Of course, Amelia Earhart would have known the answer to that. She had a highly technical mind and knew her airplanes inside and out. I, on the other hand, am a humanities scholar, not technologically talented, and am still learning about aviation. Does anyone else here know the answer? I would be glad to look for the answer and contact you.

Or you could simply say, "That's a very interesting question, but I do not know the answer. I am still researching." We cannot know it all and would not be accurate if we said we did. We wear the mantle of authority, but we do not hesitate to show its lining of humility.

Once you have put it all together: the script, the look, the walk, the talk, and especially the knowledge, you try it in front of a few audiences. And if you find that you really are enjoying this sharing of history's stories, maybe you want to build what you are doing into a business—you want to earn some money so you can afford to take it on the road, upgrade your look, and buy more books. The next chapter addresses the "how to" of creating a historical performance business.

## NOTES

1. Ezequiel Morsella and Robert M. Krauss, "The Role of Gestures in Spatial Working Memory and Speech," *American Journal of Psychology* 117 (2004): 411–24; Frances H. Rauscher, Robert M. Krauss, and Yihsiu Chen, "Gesture, Speech, and Lexical Access: The Role of Lexical Movements in Speech Production," *Psychological Science* 7 (1996): 226–31.

2. Sharon Begley, "Living Hand to Mouth," *Newsweek*, November 2, 1998, 89.

3. Susie Wilkening and Erica Donnis, "Authenticity? It Means Everything," *History News* 63, no. 4 (Autumn 2008): 18–23.

4. Joan L. Severa, *Dressed for the Photographer: Ordinary Americans and Fashion, 1840–1900* (Kent, Ohio: Kent State University Press, 1997).

5. Search for "Sears catalog Schroeder" because Joseph Schroeder edited many of these reprint compilations.

6. Harriet Mason, *The Power of Storytelling: A Step-by-Step Guide to Dramatic Learning in K–12* (Thousand Oaks, Calif.: Corwin Press, 1996), 12.

# 6

# The Business of Doing Freelance Historical Performance

WHY would you want to start a historical performance business? We asked this of ourselves and others. Here's what we came up with:

- "To get the stories to the people who need them." But we can do that without charging money.
- "To preserve the stories for the future." "To correct faulty knowledge." Again, possible without having a business.
- "For the fun of it." True, it's great to work at something you enjoy.
- "To be able to deduct the cost of this book when calculating your income tax." Not bad.
- "To earn respect for knowledge." Right; generally our society uses money to place value on services and goods (and we are not only a "good" but also a service), so if we want to be valued . . .[1]
- "To earn enough money to have the time to get the stories to the people." Ahh, there it is: because it's our passion, and life is good when we can support ourselves with our passion.

As we have discussed elsewhere in this book, sharing stories with those who need and want them while preserving the stories for the future motivates most historical performers, along with the great adrenaline rush of being onstage before a receptive and responsive audience. This chapter is about the business of doing historical performance—how to make sure you have the resources and the venues to accomplish your mission. It takes money to fund your time and your research expenses, and it takes marketing to find the organizations that will provide you with an audience and fund your endeavors—and, of course, put food on the table.

Historical performance—researching a person and her or his historical context, crafting stories that are both insightful and entertaining, practicing telling the stories for greatest impact, and building a costume—is all a lot of work and can be costly. And then the idea of also creating a business entity within which to operate . . . well, it may be daunting. It also, however, provides endless opportunities for you to tap into the creativity that led you this far.

Here is my suggestion: start small but with grand plans. Open as many doors as possible but only as many as you can shut again as your time and your changing interests and the interests of your market suggest. Take it one step at a time, but keep your eye on several staircases and be ready to make relevant leaps.

Only you can define success, but one definition is that you identify the resources that enable you to reach as many people as you want to reach with your performances—and maybe also be able to afford insurance, self-employment tax, and, dare we hope, a little put away toward retirement. To do that you need to create systems that will help you market your great product, keep track of upcoming performances, and keep track of income and expenses. You will need to figure out what works for you, but we're willing to share what we use, most of it having been in place since the mid- to late 1990s. Ann Birney admits that while she never thought she would have a career that directly involved selling herself, she has found a great deal of creative expression in making Ride into History work for us and for our presenters. Here are the basic activities that we have identified:

1. Create a business identity that is recognizable to clientele ("branding").
2. Create an office space.
3. Determine your business structure and make it official.
4. Create a system to book performances.
5. Determine fees and costs.
6. Create a system to keep track of and report income and expenses.
7. Market your identity.
8. Create relationships.
9. Keep your vision in front of you—where are you going, why, and how will you get there?

You may notice the word "create" used several times. The process of establishing a business, especially a very small one that involves arts and education, is of necessity a creative process. Entrepreneurship should be creative—and fun.

## STEP ONE: AN IDENTITY

Start by creating an identity, one that will make you look and sound like a business, a really interesting business. You are creative or you would not be entertaining the possibility of making a living by educating in an engaging manner. Spend a good deal of your creative energy on finding a name and a logo that allows you some flexibility but brands you as unique. Brainstorm with friends and family. Try your ideas out on other people—historical performers, presenters, and especially those who haven't the foggiest about what it is that you will be doing. If they get it, you got it! Think about the long run—you do not want to work to establish your brand only to find that it does not fit after a few years and you have to introduce it all over again.

Think also how the name will sound. You (and everyone else who answers the "business" telephone) will answer with the name of the company. Is the name one that can be said easily by whoever answers the phone in your home or office? I was not sure that I would like answering my home phone "Ride into History; this is Joyce," but the worst that has ever happened is that a long-lost acquaintance queried me about what on the earth is Ride into History. After I filled him in, I mailed him a postcard; maybe I'll get a booking from him someday. We do get people who hear our name as "Write into History," and we get people who think we give trail rides. But it's a talking point and an opportunity to explain who we are and hand out our marketing materials.

In Ride into History's first years all of our performances were done on horseback. We were doing nineteenth-century figures, mostly in Kansas, and performances were done with vintage saddles on the backs of old-style (high-withered) horses. When in our second year a cattle-hauling trade organization booked us for their annual meeting at the Dallas-Fort Worth Airport Marriot, horses were out of the question, but we carried our saddles and referred to horses that were not far away. Today, we do few performances with horses, but we have decided that's okay because the horses are still symbols of how our historic figures moved through space and how our audiences move through time so that historic figure and audience meet in some limbic, mythic place and moment of "could have been." So the name still works, even for

Amelia Earhart and Rachel Carson. It means, though, that we must continually resist being pigeon-holed into the Western theme suggested by our logo and explain that we are not the Wild Women of the Frontier, a fun group always on horseback with lots of pageantry but slight on history (see trail story 6.1).

---

**A Trail Story**

### 6.1. THE TRUTH

How Ride into History got its name was actually a little more complex. Somewhere around the spring of 1988 the history honorary at Kansas State University, where I was working on my doctorate, was charged with creating a student recruitment fair booth that might entice incoming freshmen to consider a major in history. I decided that the "sexiest" resource we had was my collection of vintage Western and military saddles, so we displayed them invitingly under an old red barn board with the words "Ride into History" painted in white. The sign gathered dust for several years but came to mind when we were looking for a name for our troupe. It now, several times repainted, graces the drive of the Ride into History ranch.

---

Nolan Sump of Sod-Bustin' Kansas History, on the other hand, has a name that tells it all—at least for now. His focus is on Kansas settlement, especially agriculture. His teaching job limits his availability, so it is appropriate that his name reflects where he is likely to seek—and find—work. If, however, he decides he wants to travel further afield, he will probably want to drop the "Kansas" in his name—after all, his dust bowl farmer of the 1930s also tells the experience of farming in Nebraska and South Dakota.

When it came time to create the artwork for our logo, we took our concept and my knowledge of the specifics of how a cowgirl and horse should look to an artist friend. I helped her shape the horse and lasso, and our friend made it look good. And of course we paid her for her work because we are a business and we do respect artists as entrepreneurs of their own work.

We have our logo on the shirts that we wear to and from our venues, and on vests and winter jackets. The weather is always right for the Ride into History logo. The logo is also on license plates that my brother had made for me, as well as, of course, on our cards, flyers, workshop materials, and letterhead. Talk with your lawyer or check online about protecting your logo from use by others—we went the route of a service mark instead of a trademark. Of course, you will likely want to copyright material you write so that, if you find that your script, for instance, is being used by another performer, you have legal, and not just moral, recourse to tell them to cease and desist.

Who are you and what do you do? Every business must be able to state its mission quickly and succinctly. We have struggled with this many times. Our first marketing was at the Kansas Sampler Festival, with thousands of prospective presenters walking past our booth. We were in costume with our horse-and-roping-rider logo nearby. We found ourselves saying what we weren't more than we said what we were: "No, we don't give trail rides." Ann came up with, "We're a historical performance touring troupe," and if people hesitated because they were not sure what we just said, we gave them a brochure while we explained they did not have to come where we are but that we would come to them. And if they hesitated longer, we went into character to show them a first-person narrative.

Several years later when we applied for the Kansas Arts Commission's roster, on the other hand, we had to decide into which of their preexisting categories we fit. Having come to performance through scholarship, we already felt uppity calling ourselves "art." And now we had to decide if we were "storytellers" or "theater" or "performance art." We approached it from a business point of view. We wanted as wide an audience as possible. "Storytelling," especially twenty years ago, had the stigma of being for children, that is, childish. Theater, on the other hand, was about drama, which was serious stuff. And as scholars we wanted to be taken seriously; so even though our theater did not involve complex sets or memorized lines written by bona fide playwrights, we categorized ourselves as theater, and to our knowledge no one challenged it.

You will also want really good photographs of yourself in costume, preferably ones in which you are performing in front of diverse rapt audiences. Having said that, we use posed photographs to represent our "group" because unless we are conducting a workshop we are not onstage together, and the opportunity to have Amelia Earhart, Calamity Jane, a horse, and an airplane in one publicity shot was too good to miss. Therefore, we have the "Ride into History" photograph that is on our postcard (a detail is on the cover of this book and a variation is in figure 6.1), single posed shots, and a few candids with audience members. While we have good performance photos, none match up to the posed ones. My favorite publicity photos are those of storyteller Priscilla Howe at http://www.priscillahowe.com/. They really give a sense of her energy.

Figure 6.1.  Horses and Airplanes: It just doesn't get any better!

Create letterhead. You don't need to have it printed, but do have the footer ready to use on your word processing package. Likewise, make sure that every e-mail you send out has your contact information. We also put a note about public appearances. A hint: the signature inputter is hard to find in our version of Microsoft Outlook. Maybe this will help you find yours: Tools: Options: Mail Format: Signatures, write in lower box, and be sure to click Okay on both screens on your way out!

## STEP TWO: AN OFFICE

Ride into History has worked out of many spaces, most of them in our farmhouse, at one time having components of the office spread between a corner of the living room, one full bedroom, and half of another bedroom, with books throughout. And most of the planning took place on the kitchen table. Recently, we built on an addition for a 28' by 18' office. The office was designed to fulfill specific business functions. It even has a smallish sofa and chairs (actually outdoor furniture) for reading and consulting, and has been used for planning as we wean ourselves away from the kitchen table. A twenty-foot-long countertop for sorting, writing, and calculating travel expenses is lit by eye-level horizontal windows that are perfect for watching the sun set. Above and below the windows are bookshelves for research materials—books, journals, and maps. There are lower shelves with plastic boxes for temporary projects such as this book (a box for each chapter, some items in folders and others loose); for ongoing projects such as the 2008–2010 Kansas-Nebraska Chautauquas; for Ride archives (which need to be transferred to archival quality boxes); and for piles of papers that need to be sorted.

---

**A Trail Story**

### 6.2. THE BUSINESS GETS THE BEST

My friend Kay married into a Mercedes dealership family. Kay soon learned that her husband's income was less than her own as a medical technician. He had a small salary, and when he needed something more he would approach his father who would give him the money if he thought the cause was justified. Profits went into the business first, not into the pockets of the owners. While she did not get her husband to negotiate a higher salary, Kay did manage to negotiate a new Mercedes sports car for her daily drive to work.

Another friend was appalled at how Kay's husband's family treated him, but that was exactly how I was raised on the farm—the family business had to come first. One of our efforts at farm diversification was a museum with lovely antiques. We, on the other hand, lived with minimal furniture. And we never did have running water in the house, only in the barn because it was rented out for dances. When I went away to college my parents and brother moved into the barn. Before a dance they knocked down their beds and carried them to an outbuilding. And during the dances our living room furniture lined the walls to be sat on by fraternity members (and absorb their spilled drinks). Unlike many parents in the late 1960s, however, my parents gave me an elderly car so I could get home to help on weekends, and in between in a pinch.

A portion of the countertop is the correspondence, booking, and marketing area, surrounded as it is by shelves with a Fellowes pigeon-hole box for flyers and booking sheets, a box with the booking folders filed chronologically, an atlas and phone directories, and financial records in notebooks and accordion files. There is a "mail room" that is another short countertop with a basket for bills above and tubs for recycling and a shredder below.

The desk is a computer table with, supposedly, current projects (dare we at least say that the piles are chronological?) at hand. Snuggled up to the computer are two printers: one a fast, dependable Brother laser printer that is fine for our black-and-white documents, the other a small color Canon printer that we take with us when we do workshops, primarily to print programs with a color picture of the performers. The office also has a built-in space for a small, ancient, leased (cleaning/repair/toner contract) photocopier. Oh, yes—and a closet for our costumes and Amelia Earhart's props. My props are too large for the closet, so they are in an outbuilding that is sparsely climate controlled—something to consider when you are planning both space needs and "stuff" desires! Will you consider your antique props "consumables" that you can let people handle and not worry about when humidity threatens, or will you plan to provide protection from all elements as you travel?

Our big new office is, admittedly, a luxury. When our contractor started putting in electrical outlets, he said he had never even seen a place with so many outlets. There are twenty-two double outlets, and that is just about right. Of course, the rest of the old farmhouse gets by largely with extension cords. The bottom line in creating your business is that you have easily accessible space for the following:

- A computer to produce your materials and for e-mail
- A telephone (preferably one with speaker-phone capability) and answering service
- Marketing materials
- Financial records (expenses and income)
- Calendar and maps
- A file for prospective bookings/contacts
- Research materials, including a copy of Nolo Press's *Legal Guide for Starting and Running a Small Business* by Fred S. Steingold and information from your state's Small Business Administration

We use our mobile phones for most outgoing calls but list the office number (which is also our home number) with answering machine for incoming calls.

---

## THE "NOW GET TO WORK!"
## RETREAT AND STUDIO

In addition to our office at the ranch, we have a fifty-by-thirty-foot studio in Admire, a town so small that there are no paved streets (and no distractions). Rent and utilities average $250/month. We conduct several workshops a year there, occasionally rent it out as a scholar's retreat, and store exhibit materials and costumes that we loan to workshop attendees. The costumes travel to "away" workshops in our portable "green room," a (cleaned-up) twenty-four-foot horse trailer with dressing room.

---

Using the cell phones for outgoing calls saves on long-distance bills. Using the office number for incoming calls ensures the caller will get a high-quality reception. There is nothing more frustrating than trying to communicate with a stranger who wants to book us when reception is poor, as often happens when we are on the road. On the other hand, if we check messages on the landline and then return the call when we are in an area with a strong signal, the outcomes are much better—we appear competent, and they can hear our outline of terms and that we are, indeed, available on their date. The goal is to present a businesslike presence at all times. You might be in your jammies drinking coffee, but that is not how you want potential presenters to picture you. Your answering machine message should be professional and include your business name. Never have a generic message greet prospective customers. How do they even know if they got the right number? They just might go down their list to the next performer.

Our telephone answering machine has a cordless extension. We put the main station where we can see the flashing light when we come into the house and the extension in the office itself. Our message says, "Hello! If you are calling for Ann, Joyce, or Ride into History, leave a message and we'll get back with you as soon as we can." Often we'll get a message, "Actually I'm calling for all three. Are you available to . . . ?"

### STEP 3: DETERMINE YOUR BUSINESS
### STRUCTURE AND MAKE IT OFFICIAL

When you get to the point where you are making more than an honorarium to cover your travel expenses, you are ready to formalize your business, and to do that you must determine what structure you will use: a pass-through sole pro-prietorship or partnership (the easiest to set up and maintain); a corporation (protects your personal assets if your business is sued); or a not-for-profit cor-poration (requires a great deal of work to establish but lets people get a tax de-duction if they donate to your endeavor). You will also need to check with your county and state about registration requirements. And you will need to con-sult with THOSE WHO KNOW about these things and are licensed to share what they know.

Have I said it already? I am neither an attorney nor an accountant. I advise you to spend time and possibly a little more money than you might have with both. I also advise you not to spend money on the business until you know you will be earning money. When you have your first few hundred to invest, put it into costumes and props. It is still a hobby. In the meantime, consult with a free service like the Small Business Administration. They might be focused on get-ting you into the position where you can qualify for a business loan. Avoid this. Avoid overhead. Be humble. Work with what you can afford and gradually im-prove that. When you sign a contract for $500, then you can go to a printer and contract for postcards to advertise and bring in the next ten contracts. Rent a minivan for the few days in a year you need one, and for the less cumbersome gigs use your ancient fuel-efficient Metro Geo. Of course, if you have sizeable savings or receive an inheritance or a $600 gift from the government and you have had your eyes and teeth checked lately, indulge. But otherwise, if your business is not going to bring in an income, do it as a hobby and do not create a business. Having said that, there are risks involved even with hobbies, and es-tablishing yourself as a business structure can help you minimize risk, includ-ing the risk of getting it wrong with the federal government.

What if, for instance, you have the opportunity to get a pretty good paycheck for a performance, or you do several paid performances in a year for one presenter—say, a museum. The presenter files a 1099 MISC with the IRS, indi-cating that they paid you and did not withhold income tax. You file your 1040 EZ, forgetting about the "extra" $1,000 you earned that year, and then receive a "whoops" letter from the IRS (never panic; always communicate early and of-ten). If you think of yourself as a business, as, say, a sole proprietor, you will keep records of your income in part because you also want to report and deduct your expenses, and you cannot claim to be a business unless you are sincerely trying to make money. You will fill out a Schedule C (Profit or Loss from a Busi-ness) in addition to indicating on your Form 1040 what your income was other than for wages. You will also calculate Self-Employment tax, which takes care of your Social Security and Medicare contributions, and hopefully you will make enough to pay estimated taxes quarterly throughout the year. Another artist told us to plan to send 30 percent of our self-employment income (less expenses) to the government, and that has kept us from underestimating what we owe. In my other life as a university professor, half of that 30 percent is paid by my employer, the state of Kansas, as part of my benefits. I am only responsible for about 15 percent. In my life as a partner in Ride into History, however, I need to take care of the entire 30 percent of my share of the partnership income myself.[2] Please do NOT call me with tax questions. You are, however, welcome to come to look through our books. Just know that because we have not been audited I cannot recommend anything specific to you (see trail story 6.3).

### A Trail Story

#### 6.3. PRACTICING BUSINESS PRACTICES

When we were starting our business we discovered role models in unusual places. Some of you may know our friend Jane. Jane had at that time not only her ranch but also a retreat where women could drive a tractor, ride a horse, or just sit in a hot tub and look at the stars. The IRS was skeptical. They sent an agent to check out the operation. All of the expense receipts were in a shoebox, chronologically. It wasn't fancy, but it was adequate and satisfied the demands of the audit. It made me feel much better about our annual chronological notebooks with travel expenses stapled to booking forms. Somewhere in there, too, we found we had friends who were years behind in their taxes. We found out that the government does not care if you file if they owe you instead of the other way around. AND we found out you can file for an extension—again, it helps if you don't owe but are owed. But don't take tax advice from us, of course! We have made a few bumbles, but humility and the IRS help number (oh, yes, and several public libraries with their notebooks of forms and their photocopiers) have saved the day—and our hides.

A very different sort of risk: a couple who portrayed Annie Oakley and her husband harmed an audience member during their act while shooting blanks from a gun. Suddenly, a wholesome activity turned into something dangerous not only to the audience but also to the financial future of the performers. (We strongly recommend, by the way, not using firearms or other weapons—or animals—except with great forethought and very controlled audiences.) Had they been taken to court and an award made against them, they might have lost personal assets, even their home. On the other hand, if they had created a separate legal entity, a corporation, the suit could only have involved the assets of the corporation. Being a separate corporation would also protect individual assets from bankruptcy if the corporation defaulted on a debt. Of course, I do not know this for sure because I am neither an accountant nor a lawyer.

Because Ann Birney and I were starting the business together, we opted to form a partnership as our legal entity. We have always divided any income fifty-fifty, but that is certainly not the case for all partnerships. The most important thing is to get as much advice as you can, then sit down and talk openly and honestly with anyone who will be taking this financial adventure with you. Remember, no matter how sincere your mission, it is important you have an income that will let you honor your commitments, including that commitment to book a flight and motel so you can be at the Smithsonian in the fall.

### STEP FOUR: CREATE A SYSTEM TO BOOK PERFORMANCES

While we have been tempted to adopt a computer software system for booking and tracking performances, Ann, who doubles as our office manager, likes her paper calendar, booking form, and checkbook. She says she likes multiple tangible and very visible reminders of an upcoming gig. Personally, I think it's just so she can carry them from room to room with her, which would be fine, so long as she doesn't spill major coffee on anything. Besides, there is hope for our entry into electronic record-keeping: last year she hired someone to create a spreadsheet and periodically enter bookings so that we have mailing lists and can create reports while she herself does not have to type into those little boxes. I joke here, but of course, the message is that business practices need to fit those who will be implementing them, so make yours fit you.

Here is our system for booking performances:

1. Someone e-mails or calls with a request. If they leave a message, you need to get back with them as soon as possible, of course—or have someone else do so, or you might lose the job (after all, their board meeting might be this evening and they need to report on the program for the annual meeting, which is next month).
2. Check the calendar. If the date is available, pencil in the sponsor and time. Penciling is especially important if they cannot commit at that moment. Ethics then says that, if someone else wants that date, you contact the first presenter and give them a few days to commit before giving the date to

the second presenter. If you are not available on their date, suggest an-other date when you are. If their date is fixed, recommend a colleague who will in turn recommend you when they are not available.

3. If you are available, call or e-mail immediately—they might be working down a roster and will book the first person who can give an immediate and definite "yes." E-mailing is fine to begin with, but you will want to talk at some point so you can better understand how you can serve them

---

### BOOKING SHEET CONTENT

Program
Day, date, time
Presenting organization
Event
Contact person and person on site
Mailing address
Office, home/cell telephone
E-mail address
Fee
Our sound system?
Location/directions/lodging
Audience information
Invoice #
Contract and invoice sent [date]
Contact date and means
Funding agency(ies)
Schedule beginning with departure
How did they hear about us?
Number of people reached

[Circle if needed; mark date when sent:]
News release
Photos
Introduction
Curriculum packet
Playbill
Bibliography

(maybe it has never occurred to them to also book you into the school while you are doing their evening program, or maybe their idea of a sound amplification system and yours do not coincide). As you talk to them, record on the booking sheet information about the event and contact information, especially how to get in touch with them if someone else should want that date and you have not received a signed contract from them. Our booking sheet is at http://www.historicperformance .com/.

4. Tell them what your fee is and that travel is in addition, and ask if it is in their ballpark. If not, then neither of you need to waste time discussing program specifics. Also, tell them if you have specific technical needs such as a wireless lapel microphone, lighting, or a riser if they anticipate more than sixty in the audience. Determine who will provide lodging, and if they will, indicate such needs as that it be smoke free or have a pool or exercise room. This is the time to work out all of the specifics as it will prevent problems down the trail for you, keeping in mind, though, that you will want to remind them of these things again a few weeks before your engagement. Tell them you will get right back to them with the total fee, including a contract and invoice (unless they have to first check with a committee, as is often the case, in which case just call or e-mail with the *total* fee—do not break it out into parts).

5. Map out travel plans, figuring out your means of transportation: what time you will need to leave to make sure you arrive at least an hour and a half ahead, depending on the venue and how much setup you will have to do; where you will stay; and how many meals you will eat on the road— put these costs into your total fee, remembering also to include mileage to the airport, parking fees, car rentals, and tips. We also charge $25 per travel hour, as most of that time it is difficult to work, or truly relax.

6. If you are communicating by e-mail, reply, and make a copy of your reply as well as their message.

7. Clip together documentation and place in a pending file (ours is actually a binder labeled "Scheduling" that has pocket pages). Record-keeping is tedious, but, well, the devil is in the details (however that applies here!).

8. When you receive confirmation that the presenter is ready for a contract, write and print the contract and invoice (see discussion below and appendixes D and E), sign the contract, and send them to the presenter with your card or brochure (stick a card or brochure in with every post so if people lose the first one they can find you again, or pass it along to someone else).

9. E-mail (or send by surface mail) a photograph (it is fine to put on the back of it that they should return it to you, with your address, but don't depend on them to do so), a news release (see marketing), and a short (one-page) biography. I highly recommend sending e-mail attachments instead of paper copy. It makes it very easy for people who are creating newsletters and sending copy to newspapers. Small newspapers in particular often have room to print everything you send them, and if you make it easy for them, it is even more likely they will publish it all. So go ahead and attach photos to your e-mail message: one of you in costume and one of you as the scholar. Been there, done that: if the photograph's properties indicate that it occupies megabytes instead of kilobytes, you will want to copy it and save as a jpg file so it will not clog up your e-mail box or theirs.

10. Create a file folder with location, program, and date on tab (e.g., Jamestown, ND, "Calamity Jane," 10/5/09).

11. Place the booking sheet, a copy of the contract and invoice, and any notes or prints of e-mail messages in the file folder.

12. File the folders by date in a location that you see often (we used to have nightmares about missing a performance, and it did happen once, but I won't go into that—needless to say we learned from the experience); we use a cardboard Fellowes visible folder file box, but evidently they are no longer available. A plastic or metal step file placed on a desk or shelf would also work.

13. Record the event in chronological order on the Income Sheet. Ours is a single-month record, a computer-created table (Ann uses Word for this, but I am sure others would prefer Excel or another spreadsheet) with numbers one through thirty-one in the left column. Across the top are the headings Date, Sponsor/Place, Character, Invoice #, Child, Adult, Amount, and Mileage. We also have specialized columns that indicate whether, if it is a festival, horses were used.

14. The Income Sheet has three primary purposes: it allows us to monitor and anticipate Ride into History's (and hence also our personal) income; it journals income for IRS tax reports; and it gives us a backup to the calendar and file. The Income Sheets live in the front of the binder into which we put the booking sheet and other documents after the performance. (As indicated earlier, we contract with someone who takes information from the Income Sheets to maintain a spreadsheet for us so we can create reports, such as how many people I have reached as Calamity Jane in the last year—my university likes to know that sort of thing. And, of course, I like to know how my business is doing.)

A system is doubly important if you share space and a telephone with someone else (offspring?). They will need to know how to answer your telephone and where to leave a message, maybe even where your booking files are in case a presenter calls about a major change and you want to be able to resolve it while you are out of the office.

### STEP FIVE: DETERMINE YOUR FEES (AND COSTS!)

What should you charge? From the beginning our performance fee was closely tied to marketing. We wanted to spread the word that we were a great value but not that we were "cheap." Your first few performances will probably be free and in a workshop environment. Your next audience might pay an "honorarium" to cover travel expenses or to acknowledge the time you have spent on their behalf. Ask members of these audiences to give you feedback immediately, even taking notes while you perform. It is part of your training and part of what they can give you that is more valuable at this stage than money. If they like what they see, ask them to write a short testimonial that you can use in your publicity.

Some people suggest that the first "away from home" performance should be free, but I firmly believe that, by the time you take it on the road, even if it is only at your public library a few blocks away, you are providing something of value and, therefore, you should receive payment for same. If you want to donate that $50 honorarium back to the library, that is your decision, but you do not want the word to get around that you do freebies. In fact, when you write the contract for your first few performances and any others where you charge less than the going rate, you should include a clause that says your terms are "exclusive and confidential" (more on contracts later). Let your sponsor ("presenter" in the parlance of the arts, as in "ABC Arts presents Joyce Thierer as Calamity Jane") know that you are giving them a super deal.

Having said that, the year that we averaged two performances each a week we began allowing ourselves two freebies each per year. Those who receive our largesse (often Ann's mother's causes: the Marion Clinic where she volunteers or her Philanthropic Educational Organization [PEO] chapter) understand what a great deal they are getting and why they are receiving the donation. When we first began doing this we wrote a contract for the full amount, took their check, and then donated that amount back to the organization because we wanted them to fully comprehend the gift they were receiving. But then we realized that since we were paying income tax on their check we were actually losing money, and we really do not enjoy unnecessary paperwork, so we stopped doing that.

But what about after the very beginning? The answer is to charge according to what the market will bear and that means doing some research. We looked at our state arts commission's touring roster to determine what storytellers and small theater troupes were charging. We also talked to performers and presenters. I think our fee back in 1994 was $250 plus travel. We do not charge that much more now: $500 for a single performance of one character; $750 for a day in the schools or a workshop day; decreased rates for additional performances of the same character; and $900 for a piece like "Amelia Earhart and Calamity Jane: One Frontier Differently" that requires both of us. We also charge $25 per hour travel time per person when we are performing outside Kansas (our gift to our home state—we can be on the road for seven hours and still be in Kansas).

About that travel time added onto the fee: Travel costs and fees can be emotionally tricky to calculate. For instance, what if you really, really want to perform at this prestigious site, but when you calculate the cost, the travel is more than the performance fee. You panic and think, "They'll never go for this. I'd better eat some of this cost to get it down below the performance fee." Nonsense. If your presenter does not know that travel costs, you can educate them, or let them go because they will not be able to adequately host you. On the other hand, do travel. Not only can it be fun, but also it can increase your credibility. You have no doubt heard the axiom that an expert is someone who is at least sixty miles from home. I have never heard anyone say, "Really?! You've performed for Admire Middle School?!" But the fact that I have performed for the Smithsonian—or even for schools in other states—has enhanced my cache considerably. Historical performer Anna Smith (aka Revolutionary War soldier Deborah Samson) notes that respect is her primary motivator for charging for performances.[3] In our society we tend to value that which has a dollar amount attached to it. If she charges nothing for a performance it will be "that nice little skit that you do." About fifteen years ago Donald Dunhaupt, then owner of a furniture repair and refinishing shop in Lawrence, Kansas, was trying to decrease the volume of his business so he could sell it and retire. During a family gathering he observed that, when he increased the price of his service to discourage business, business only increased. His Uncle Ron, owner of an interior design firm, chided him, asking if he did not realize that the higher his fee the more valuable, and hence the more desirable, people thought his work.

It was not so long ago that you heard of a speaker who charged what seemed like an exorbitant amount for "a single hour" of work. Now, however, you realize that presenters are paying for hours upon hours of research, writing, and rehearsal, not to mention creating costumes, arranging bookings, and marketing.

Yes, presenters have to help foot the bill for what it cost you to get their attention, just as each time we buy any product we help pay for convincing us to buy that product. Oh, yes, each performance you give must also help you pay your insurance, your social security, and your income taxes. So, please—charge enough so you can do all of that, eventually.

It is hard for me to imagine doing historical performance without traveling. Travel, does, however, involve an opportunity cost. Ann says that she retained little from the Econ. course she took decades ago, but an invaluable nugget that lingered is the concept of (trumpet fanfare) !!OPPORTUNITY COST!! I am emphasizing this phrase because it is really important to you as a self-employed entrepreneur. When you agree to do a performance on a given date, you are agreeing NOT to perform for someone else on that date. If I drive to North Dakota to perform, it is going to take at least most of one day up and another back (almost that much if I drive to the airport and fly up), and I will probably not be able to perform during those two days—it takes time to set up, take down, and get settled in, so I will likely be staying two nights. Anyway, that ties up three days for what might be just one performance. If, on the other hand, I take a booking within four hours of home, I can get in other performances before and after. I can play three, four, or even five venues in three days instead of the one or two. Will that out-of-state performance for $500 still look great if an organization nearby wants to book you for a three-day workshop that would pay $2,250? You might come to resent the first booking—unless you charge them what it is worth to you to go to their location for that single performance. I believe it was a member of the rock band Kansas who said something along the lines of, "I don't get paid to make music—it's traveling and being away from my family I get paid for." On the other hand, if someone calls just a few months out, you can be reasonably sure you will not have any other calls this late, so if your calendar is free (no promises to dear ones on it) you can negotiate if they are in a financial bind, knowing that whatever they pay will be money that you would not have had otherwise.

If you are building your list of venues for marketing purposes, and you really want a particular opportunity, ask for thirty minutes to calculate travel, then call the potential presenter, give her the figure, and ask if it is within their ballpark. If she hesitates, let her know you might be able to "work a deal" if you can do other venues in the area while you are there, and ask her to make some contacts for you or give you a list of not only places but also people to talk with.

Ironically, large cities often pay less than smaller ones because they have ready access to more programs and so do not have to pay for travel. So do not think that you need to give a discount to the rural school district in order to present for their youngsters—they are accustomed to the tyranny of distance and may be willing to go to a foundation or their well-organized support organization. If the larger venues turn you down—eventually they will be willing to pay your fee just because your fame has spread and they really, really want what you have.

In addition to the performance fee, you will need to calculate travel costs and fees for any add-ons. To calculate how much we will be paid for mileage we use the number of miles one way times two multiplied by the current federal mileage rate. We find the number of miles on the map or using http://www.mapquest.com/directions. To find what the U.S. government has calculated as a fair rate for mileage, go to http://www.irs.gov/ and enter "mileage

## A Trail Story

### 6.4. AIRLINE HORROR STORIES

Always schedule flights preparing for the worst. A friend treated herself with a flight from Kansas City to Minneapolis instead of driving the eight hours. She arrived at the airport an hour ahead of time, but a problem with the plane (the coffeemaker?!) had her sitting in the airport for six hours before they got her on another plane. And then there was the time that Ann had to spend the night in Milwaukee due to drastic overbooking—they gave her a motel room, but she was on her way home so she had checked all of her luggage, so no toothbrush or other basic niceties. (Moral: always carry your small bag with underwear, toothbrush, and medication.) Let's see . . . and when booking connecting flights, make sure to allow time to get between terminals if the first leg of your flight is late. In spite of the advantages of the aerobic workout, it is better you should cool your hooves in Detroit for an hour and a half than run madly through buildings, lugging the carry-on bag with your costume (NEVER CHECK YOUR COSTUME when you have more than one leg on your flight) and dodging slow-moving traffic, only to find that, although the plane has not left, they have finished boarding and you will have to hope there is room on the next flight. The bottom line to all this is, IF YOU ARE FLYING, DO NOT SCHEDULE TO ARRIVE THE SAME DAY AS YOUR PERFORMANCE, even if you do not have high blood pressure or fear ulcers. Driving, yes. Flying, no.

rate" in the search box. In the first half of 2008 it was $.505 (fifty and one half cents)/mile; from July 1 through December 31 it was $.585/mile. Of course, you can charge ten cents a mile if you want, or a dollar a mile if the market will bear it. Checking with the IRS suggests we are being fair to ourselves as well as our presenters. The Kansas Humanities Council's (KHC) reimbursement rate in 2008 was $.36/mile. (Their budget was, of course, set long before the $.505 was determined, and they probably figured that the scholars, believing in their mission, would not protest and, besides, were probably driving fuel-efficient vehicles.) When we figured mileage for our income tax report we kept track of KHC mileage and figured it separately at the difference between the reimbursed rate and the allowable rate (that difference was $.145 and $.225/mile for the first and second halves of 2008—it all adds up). I'm figuring that most of you are glazing over at this point, but hopefully we have done a good job with the index and you'll be able to find this advice when and if you actually need it.

We have a set dollar amount for meals. The number of breakfasts is multiplied by $6, lunches by $7, and suppers by $12. The meal allotment is skimpy for anything but smaller communities by the time we add taxes and gratuity (it is based on the Kansas Humanities Council's reimbursements, and if you are really organized you are going to keep your list of tips separate because, generally speaking—again, I AM NOT a tax attorney or CPA—you can deduct 100 percent of tips on a business trip). Remember, though, that this becomes part of the single fee. Therefore, if you choose to lunch on a peanut butter sandwich and soy milk you packed at home instead of buying lunch on the road (we often take our own cereal, fruit, and veggies because they are difficult to find in restaurants), you get to keep the $7 (once you receive the check from the presenter), but you do not get the business expense tax deduction (50 percent as of this writing) that you would if you had a restaurant receipt. And before you complain about only getting to deduct 50 percent, remember, it would have cost you something to eat at home, too. Federal allowable per diem rates for major cities in the United States are at http://www.irs.gov/pub/irs-pdf/p1542.pdf (which is often updated and only available online). This will give you an idea of both motel and meal costs.

City and state convention and visitor bureaus or travel and tourism divisions are potential online sources for lists of motels if you do not have a preferred chain. If you are really going on a shoestring, or into a tiny community, low-cost motels (we're talking in the $35 range) might not have an online presence or even be on a Chamber of Commerce list. So call the library and ask. Typically, local people do not know what motels rooms are like because they do not stay in them. Out of community pride they would rather send you up-

---

**A Trail Story**

### 6.5. B&B OR MOTEL?

In the early days we tried to support local bed and breakfast establishments and small motels. We still give them serious consideration, having a few favorites sprinkled throughout the country. Unfortunately, though, we tend to avoid those we don't know and go with known chains because too often they just do not fit with our needs. Bad: rooms so cluttered with collections (dolls everywhere!) that there is no place to put our things; breakfast at the host's preferred time, not mine (not often, but what if I want to just sleep in? or wake up early?); no coffee and a book before breakfast; having to dress for breakfast; hearing the neighbor pee and flush in the wee hours; worrying about coming in late at night; no desk or table in the room; and an extrovert host who wants to trade stories. Sometimes the last point is good. If I have some extra time and am not worried about being too exhausted to give a good performance, it is fun to swap stories. But, please, no talking politics or (shudder!) religion. Or the economy and how on the earth am I making a living doing what I'm doing. Good: a residential area in which to take a walk; hosts that map out the boundaries and tell you, "Yer on yer own; help yourself"; experiencing interesting building recycling projects, such as sleeping in a barn; and meeting local people, although usually they are too busy hosting to come to your performance, which is a downer, so you end up giving them a mini-performance, and maybe some of the other guests decide to come to the performance as a result and that's great!

---

scale than down, so you might have to insist that the sleazy-appearing strip (single-floor) motel where the construction crews stay will be fine. "Just give me the phone number, please." But be ready for the sound of diesel trucks warming up just outside your room.

If we are not going into a larger city, we build into our fee $70 for a single room. Then if we decide to treat ourselves to a business suite for $25 a night more, it is on us, not on our probably not-for-profit client. On the other hand, if a venue offers to provide a room, and it is in a city, we jump on it because chances are it has a relationship (perhaps through a board member) with a nicer motel than we usually stay in. You will be in a $150 room, which is pleasant

A Trail Story

### 6.6. ALWAYS MAKE A RESERVATION
### AHEAD OF TIME—AND GUARANTEE IT

Ann tells me that she and a friend drove from Manhattan, Kansas, to Houston, Texas, to attend the political event of the midseventies: the International Women's Year conference. Wanting to be on hand to support friends who were delegates, they nonetheless got a late start. After getting off work they had to take the friend's dog to the kennel and run several other such errands. They drove most of the night but finally reached the conference hotel, where they had a reservation. But no room. Ann did not know that the only way to have a room still available at four in the morning was to guarantee it with a credit card. They set camping gear (for the Padre Island excursion to follow) under the car, hoping it would not be stolen, and slept in the back of Ann's AMC Hornet hatchback in the parking lot of the posh hotel. These days if a desk clerk does not ask for a credit card, she insists on giving one and getting a confirmation number—or, in the case of very small motels, the name of the person to whom she is speaking!

occasionally, and is a bargain even if you tip the valet who parks your car. If we are quoting a fee for a venue in a large city, we check motel prices online, often using AAA, before quoting a fee, and then we reserve our room (see trail story 6.6).

And, speaking of AAA—road insurance is a must. It is well worth the fee to be able to call a toll-free number at 2:00 a.m. and be told that a tow truck is on the way. We get the super-duper package because we are often more than the standard miles away from a city with a service station, much less our own mechanic, and so we can have the truck and trailer towed if necessary. It has more than paid for itself. But then, for several years we put about fifteen thousand miles a year on our vehicles.

The travel costs, as I have said, sometimes add up to more than the performance fee. For this reason, when I am going a distance and am time-and-day flexible, I encourage the presenter to line up other venues for me (and I do what I can to make that happen, too) so the cost of travel can be shared. Usually, though, a venue has adequate financial resources and would rather spend money on me than time putting together a tour.

Oh, yes—while I might talk generally to the presenter about the cost of travel during negotiations, when I e-mail the final figure and put it in the contract, it will be only one number: the one that will be on the check. This is from experience: once upon a time, wa-a-ay back when we used to include in the contract an itemization of what went into the fee, I had successfully negotiated with a presenter's representative, only to have another member of the group, seeing how I reached my bottom line, second guess it and say that motels in their area were less than what I had budgeted and that they would provide me a plate at the banquet where I would be performing, so please adjust my figure accordingly and rewrite the contract. Not only did I have to take the time to research motel prices in their town, but I also had to have the motel figure local taxes (and if you have been staying with friends when on vacation, know that communities are charging a lodging or entertainment tax on top of the sales tax, so don't max out your credit card—you will need some wiggle room). And this was before the Internet was quite so accommodating. As for the banquet, I do not eat right before I go on stage, and often the promised plate is gone or forgotten by the time I finish visiting with audience members (and it is surprising how many communities have no restaurants open after 9 or 10 p.m.— always pack your peanut butter). So now to avoid hard feelings on anyone's side, we lump it all into "fee."

And, by the way, until I have a signed contract I do not book the flight and rarely the motel—although even in smaller communities earlier is better in case there is a high school sports tournament or college homecoming that eats up all of the rooms.

### A Trail Story

### 6.7. YES, A CONTRACT, BUT . . .

Even *with* a contract there is no guarantee. The U.S. government still owes us $320 for a flight never made to perform at a conference (which was supposed to encourage small business development!) for which costs were severely cut only a few weeks before! Fortunately, the airline was generous so it was not a total loss. Now we let the governmental agency buy the flights, as some of them prefer anyway.

*Extras, add-ons, additional.* These may be materials—perhaps you charge $10 per teacher for that classy teachers guide you mail out in advance to every teacher whose classroom you will be visiting (we e-mail our guides and hope they are printed and distributed, but mailing hard copy sounds like a good idea). Or maybe you have giveaways for the youngsters. Or you charge extra for discussions with the audience after the performance. Horses are one of our optional add-ons. Almost all of our performances can be done either from horseback (Amelia Earhart was an excellent equestrian) or with a horse modeling vintage tack. If we are taking a horse, we will probably need to take a wrangler who will need to be paid, and we will need to take care of their lodging and food. We will also need to charge a higher mileage rate for the truck and trailer.

The add-on that we provide most often is sound equipment. We are somewhat unusual in that we provide our own sound equipment unless we can be guaranteed a system with a comparable wireless lapel microphone or excellent acoustics. We don't charge for that because we don't want it to be optional. There is nothing worse than an amplification catastrophe (see trail story 6.8).

---

**A Trail Story**

### 6.8. SOUND ADVENTURES

You haven't lived until you have been performing on horseback as Calamity Jane at a small-town festival and heard coming through your speakers the sound of hog judging two blocks away, the words you are speaking into your concealed wireless microphone being vetoed by the airwaves. The moral of this story: invest in a really good wireless that will search for a clear channel instead of leaving you to duke it out for the airwaves with the county extension agent, the city police, airport authorities, or even someone talking to her son on a cell phone (we were there when it happened to actor and Kansas native Ed Asner as he was accepting the Kansas Arts Commission's Governor's Award).

---

### STEP SIX: CREATE A SYSTEM TO KEEP TRACK OF INCOME AND EXPENSES

Of course, none of us REALLY minds paying taxes. We want Social Security and Medicare there for us and ours. And we want the government to do those things that we are too busy to worry about or lack the skills to evaluate, such as educating our young of all ages (in Kansas, auditing state university classes is free for those over sixty-five) and building roads. On the other hand, we want the system to be as fair to small businesses as it is to large corporations and so, like them, we need to keep records that reveal how very much we are putting into our business. Mistakes can mean we have nothing left to show for our hard work after we pay taxes. There are many guides for identifying expenses that small businesses can deduct when calculating taxes. Attorney Stephen Fishman lists fourteen types of expenses at one such guide on http://www.nolo.com/. But we can't deduct those expenses if we do not have the records. Okay, we could deduct them, but at what risk? Do you want to explain undocumented expenses to an IRS auditor? I didn't think so!

I am going to recommend an IRS publication to you, but I will caution that it, like most other small business services, ironically (after all, they are providing a service) presumes that you are selling goods not selling a service. So they are going to be referring to keeping track of the sales of thousands of widgets, not (hopefully) a few hundred performances, a year. That said, IRS Publication 583 Starting a Business and Keeping Income Tax Records will be useful to you, and, of course, it is available online: http://www.irs.gov/pub/irs-pdf/p583.pdf.

I highly recommend you open a separate bank account for your business. The checkbook will be your basic record of expenses and income. Receipts (to prove to the IRS that you really did have expenses) can be tossed into an envelope at first. Look into deductions involving space in your home as an office. That is explored in part in Publication 583 (above). Allowability for this has shifted a great deal over the years. Even though we are theoretically paid for the performance we do away from home, none of it would be possible if not for the far more time we spend in the office.

Having said that there is a need for good records, except for a brief flirtation with QuickBooks software we have never used the two-column system of bookkeeping. Our first records were the booking sheet with check stub and/or receipts taped to it—income and expenses. We were so in fear of an audit that we photocopied EVERYTHING and sent it with our partnership paperwork (this was no doubt why the IRS repeatedly states what NOT to send with your report). Ann managed this for a few years before she realized that, when it came time to do taxes, she had to do a lot of page flipping to find all of the travel, meals, office expenses, and so forth, so she could add them up in the categories the IRS wanted. And one of the things we found by talking to an accountant and a couple of tax preparers early on (we confess that we do our own now that the system is in place—that way we know exactly where we stand) was that as long as we were organized and transparent—in other words, as long as it was evident we were not trying to hide any income or manufacture any nonexistent expenses, the IRS, should they ever audit us, will not really care about our format—we do not have to master methods taught in accounting classes, which is a good thing.

So now Ride into History has an accordion file labeled with expense categories that work for us in terms of volume of receipts and how we do our reporting. These include:

- Contract labor (computer work, horse wrangling, workshop intern, etc.)
- Dues
- Horse expense
- House expense
- Office expense (rent and utilities of our Admire studio; photocopier rental; etc.)
- Supplies (things that get used up)
- Travel

Please do not ask us for details—we are not accountants and would hate to get you into trouble. Set up what you think will work for you and then bite the bullet and consult a tax preparer or accountant, preferably one you know who both understands what it is that you "do" and is creative enough to make their models apply to your unconventional endeavor.

Instead of the journal we use an Income Sheet to track income. The income sheet is monthly, with a line for every day. After all income for a month is in (our state humanities council pays mid-month for the month before, so we are usually a little behind), we total the month and add it to the last month's, which makes us a little more prepared when tax time rolls around.

So if you want to get serious about this business, take a break from reading and go dig through the recycling bin to find your receipt for the purchase of this book. But what you really want the IRS to know is that you are a business, not a hobby, which means you expect to earn an income. So keep track of all of your business-related expenses, but also record everything you earn and proudly state those earnings when you do your taxes, even if for the first couple of years you spend more than you earn—the IRS seems to expect that of a new business. Keep overhead low, provide a quality product, and you will soon be in the black.

**STEP SEVEN: MARKETING**

I never thought I would be involved in marketing myself, and yet to some extent most of us are involved in just that. For example, twice a year I file reports with the university that not only list my accomplishments but also tell in narrative form why I should be retained, promoted, or given merit pay. I cannot, however, imagine any of my colleagues describing what they do as "marketing"—even when applying for a position at another academic institution.

If you think you cannot market because you are somewhat shy, not to worry—that is not a bad thing because it might give you an air of humility, which is useful when you knock the socks off people with that really, really great product that is your historical performance. On the other hand, if you do not toot your own horn no one else will because no one else knows your work as well as you do, or probably has the time to dedicate to telling the world about what you do, or wants to be that close to your spit (continuing the horn metaphor). You must be convinced that what you do (not who you are but what you do) you do well, and that it is an important product that has the potential to change lives for the better, so prospective presenters will want to know about it. Arrogant fools will not read this book, so we do not have to warn them to tone it down. I am more worried about those of you who will be hiding your light under the basket.

### A Trail Story

#### 6.9. ARTISTIC SNOBBERY

Early in Ann's historical performance career, she presented a ten-minute showcase during a statewide theater conference. It was her first showcase, but she felt good about it—she did Amelia Earhart's sled story, which felt risky to her because she was Amelia imitating her disapproving grandmother, and she said "zing" very loudly as she described "flying" down a very steep hill on a sled. Afterward, a colleague who does a more formal stage presentation of Amelia very generously told her that a famed director who had been brought in to do a workshop had muttered, "Oh, no, not another monologist," and then, "She's actually very good." Ann was glad he had been processing out loud—and that her colleague shared the experience with her. For one thing, it told us where we fit in, in theater terms, and it warned us of a bias against the form. And, of course, it gave her the positive feedback that keeps us all going!

Aside from any predisposition toward not putting themselves in any lime-light that is not on a formal stage, why is it that the work of some really, really good artists does not receive much attention? The explanation might be the difference between playability and marketability, as described by *Los Angeles Times* film critic Kenneth Turan in an NPR review of the French thriller *Tell No One*. The book, according to Turan, was written by a best-selling American author, and the film had great success in France, but it hit a wall in the United States. After two years, though, a small American distributor picked it up, and even though there was virtually no paid advertising, word of mouth made it successful.

> *Tell No One* had playability—people who came to see it, loved it, but without marketability, like big stars or a fancy director that could lure people into the the-ater in the first place, no distributor wanted to take it. But *Tell No One* is catnip for audiences who love smart thrillers the way they used to make them. People who see it and love it tell their friends and that word of mouth is making *Tell No One* into a success.[4]

We must consider not only marketability but also playability and how it can work for us.

Historical performance, with the exception of Hal Holbrook (Mark Twain), "lacks big stars or a fancy director that could lure people into the theater." Knowing this, we focus not on marketability but rather on playability. And very targeted marketing. Marketing is simply letting people know that your prod-uct (in this case, your performances) exists. There are two forms of marketing: telling people about a product they already know they need and convincing people they need a product with which they are completely unfamiliar. We are often in the position of having to do both. People are likely to know they need a program—they have an event, a venue, and an audience for which they need entertainment, or a school group that needs educating. What they don't know is how we can solve their problems and meet their needs—because they are not familiar with our genre, our format, and our art. In fact, they do not know we exist. So the first step in marketing, unless we have the opportunity to SHOW them what we do, is to find language that will tell them, and get that language and photographs that will back up our language to the people who will want to book us once they know how great we are.

Showing what we do is called "showcasing" and usually involves a brief (five- to fifteen-minute) sample performance. Showcases are often sponsored by groups representing organizations that hire performers. Regional arts organizations like Arts Midwest (http://www.artsmidwest.org/) have annual conferences with competitive showcases and opportunities for more informal showcasing. Library districts or systems, school districts, storytelling organizations, and other entities might also sponsor showcases. People who come to these events are looking for "acts" to book. Chances are they will want to talk to you. You will register ahead for a slot, go onstage in costume with minimal props, give your performance within the time limit, and then step out of character to talk briefly about how you will go anywhere anytime and play for any audience—or whatever your parameters are. Then you will try to get your literature into the hands of anyone who looks the least bit interested.

## A Trail Story

### 6.10. "NO-SHOW" SHOWCASE

Twice that I can think of we have driven over two hours to get to a showcase where there were far more performers than potential presenters. Two positive things: we got to know other performers, and it is always good to know and be known among one's peers; secondly, they had extras of the dandy catalog/roster of those who appeared, and we handed them out for several years. My own philosophy of such events is that if I get one new idea or meet an interesting person then the trip was worthwhile (good food helps, too).

Every year the Kansas Alliance of Professional Historical Performers meets at the Kansas Sampler Festival. The annual festival, which moves to a different community every two years, is designed to show Kansans what there is to see and do in Kansas, especially in smaller communities. Ostensibly, we are there to entertain, but our real mission is to showcase—to convince people to bring us to their community. We are given our own stage and a tent (one of about thirty large tents in the park) in which each member has a display. We talk with parents of school children, teachers, and other community members attracted to our tent and stage, but the challenge is that the people we need most to reach are stuck in tents of their own, representing their community's venues, not walking around to see what we have to offer. Therefore, in between our two fifteen-minute stage performances a day, we each walk around to the tents and

hand our materials to chamber of commerce staff members, museum personnel members, and whomever else we can find. And if they are REALLY interested in us, we can tell them what time we will next be onstage so they can find
someone to watch their table and sneak away to see us.

In addition to formal showcasing, it is important to be able to demonstrate
your talent in person and spontaneously. Before we knew the term "showcase,"
we learned to play "tape recorder" (see trail story 6.11). Conversation with a
prospective presenter turns to this really cool thing that my colleague does, portraying Amelia Earhart. I say, "Would you like to see?" Of course, the "prospect"
asserts the affirmative, and I push the imaginary play button on Ann's shoulder.
Ann ascertains that this is, indeed, something that interests our acquaintance,
and if so, goes into character and tells a story. The nice thing about the exercise
is that it allows the performer to be both humble and brag. It is also very
portable. Warning, though: it only works if you do, indeed, change body posture and voice when you go into character because you do not have the visual
costume clues to help your audience quickly suspend disbelief. You should be
able to do a showcase piece in virtually any setting with no preparation, no costume, and no props. It should show off what you do best, and especially demonstrate how quickly you create rapport with the audience. It should be no more

---

**A Trail Story**

### 6.11. THE "PLAY" BUTTON

The first time I remember doing the "tape recorder" routine was at the
National Cowgirl Hall of Fame when it was in Hereford, Texas. Ann and
I were researching rodeo women for upcoming lectures and got to talking with the director. We told her that I performed as Calamity Jane. She
was not familiar with the Chautauqua-style first-person narrative genre,
so Ann told her I would go into character and show her, and she tapped
my shoulder saying, "play," as one would push the button on a tape player.
I will admit that my first reaction was anger that she had put me in a situation where I might not be successful, but we got the gig—I became
Jane, told a story, and won over the director. Each member of our troupe
of three (this was before Ann was on board officially) entertained during
that year's induction weekend.

than five minutes long. The five minutes will feel far too short to you, but if you are demonstrating your skills to only one individual who is not accustomed to being the sole focus of attention for as much energy as you might have, then that five minutes is plenty long—leave her or him wanting more, not overwhelmed. And by all means give them the opportunity to summon others to listen, too, and maybe ten minutes will feel very comfortable to you all.

If you have several characters you portray, you should be able to move in and out of them quickly so you can demonstrate your versatility. One of the things I like to do in a workshop is show how I establish the setting when I greet audiences in character. So I give the opening lines of boisterous Calamity Jane, followed by gentle, beaten-down Mary Fix, followed by proud Grower.

Beyond occasional showcasing, and often arising out of showcasing, word-of-mouth advertising is our number one marketing tool (see trail story 6.12). It tends to be passionate, and it is free. In our early days when we had no money for advertising other than photocopied handouts, we set a goal of two bookings from each performance, and we quickly achieved that. Word of mouth does require a little work because, generally, members of our audiences do not think of themselves as presenters, or as influencing presenters. However, those audience members have many, many contacts and organizations that would want to bring us in if only they knew about us. We need to spark their imaginations while we have their attention. During the discussion following the

---

**A Trail Story**

### 6.12. WORD OF MOUTH AND A SNOWBALLING PERFORMANCE

Thanks to the urging of Kansan-moved-to-Wyoming clothing historian Kathy Brown, Museum of the Mountain Man in Pinedale brought me in to do Calamity Jane one summer. I did not think it was one of my better performances, but National Geographic staff members took it back to Smithsonian colleagues, who invited us to the National Postal Museum several years later, which led to a National Air and Space Museum gig shortly thereafter. And, because of an impromptu workshop Pinedale had us do for science camp middle schoolers, science teacher Elaine Ullery wrote a grant and brought us in for a weeklong school workshop the next year.

performance, both during the staged Q & A and during the one on one following, we can mention the range of audiences for whom we have performed, and the range of historic figures and workshops we do. I love it when someone at an annual soil conservation meeting asks, "Would you work with my class of learning disabled kids?"

We also distribute our postcards. If the venue and sponsor are appropriate, there might be a playbill with contact information at the door or a postcard at each place at the table. And I always have a few on my costume or tucked away in my props. After all, I may be a performer, but I am also an entrepreneur, and if I don't promote our group, then the good work that we do will not continue. So say it to yourself again: what I do is important, and I need to let people know about it.

To be able to market yourself you have to be able to put into words what makes you the best thing out there. You need to establish your credentials, both in your content area and as a performer. Write a few lines that describe what it is that you do, what makes you especially qualified to portray the person/people you portray, to work with the audiences you hope to reach. If you want to perform for young people, are you a teacher, or a youth group leader? Are you an expert because you grew up in the area you are going to be talking about, or have you written a book about your topic? Have others said you are an expert? Will they let you quote them?

Janet Burnett Huchingson's entry on http://www.historicperformance.com/ first describes her character: "In October of 1704 Sarah Kemble Knight began a four-month business trip by herself on horseback from Boston to New York and back, the first recorded female business trip in the American colonies." After a few more sentences, Huchingson describes herself as the author of *With No Little Regrett,* a 1995 novel based on Knight's journal. She then lays out her academic and education credentials: "Huchingson received a B.S. in Education from the University of Kansas and Doctor of Arts degree from State University of New York at Albany. Her special interest is how history can be learned through literature. In thirty years as an educator, she has taught kindergarteners through adults, in the U.S. and abroad."

Actor/director Graham Thatcher works with attorney and spouse Anna Marie Thatcher to produce, primarily, one-person shows for lawyers. They have Clarence Darrow, Thurgood Marshall, Sir Thomas More, and Justice William O. Douglas. Their credentials are an impeccable match for their audience. As a result, bar associations have validated the couple's Periaktos programs for attorney continuing education credit.

Consider the niche you want to fill, the market or audiences you want to reach, and get the credentials that will give you credibility in that market, or look at the credentials, the experience and education, that you already have, and think about audiences and organizations that would respect your credentials. The Thatchers caution, "You don't have something for everyone!"[5] Of course, when Ride into History began we so wanted to get our stories out there, and earn the experience and money to be able to continue, that we tried to convince everyone we could provide them with something. Since then we have pulled back somewhat: we do best with audiences third grade and older, and no (well, almost no) arena performances with the horses.

Part of describing what it is you do is using the wonderful things that other people have said about you. When someone says, "This is the best time I've had in a long time," ask if you may quote them. Write down exactly what they said (or have them do it for you), and write the date they said it, their name, and a little about who they are. For instance, when a fourth-grade teacher says she never had her youngsters sit so still for so long, or ask so many questions, you need to get that in writing. And get those responses from the many types of audience members you hope to attract.

An Internet presence, or more than one, is crucial. People want you to send them your classy promotional material, but until they have it in hand, and before the program committee meeting, they can look you up and send the website's address to other members of the program committee. We are told that now we should have a Facebook page, and that is no doubt right. What we really need is someone who truly enjoys daily updating . . . maybe a blog?

When we do a mass mailing we send a black-and-white flyer customized for the audience. We also send at least one copy of our color postcard. More than once someone has told us that it is the color postcard showing Ann and me as Amelia and Calamity Jane—her crouching on the wing of an airplane, and me with my buckskin mare, both of us looking at a globe—that is what made them really look, that our mailing would have gone in the wastebasket but for that postcard.

Before you conduct a mass mailing, get the rules from the post office, or hire someone who knows the ropes to do it for you. The U.S. Postal Service is constantly updating the rules on such things as which address in which format, to the point where I worry about its continuation, with "service" being so deemphasized. If we mail to three hundred schools, we might get five responses, and that is plenty to pay for the mailing. We recently sent flyers and postcards to about thirty aviation museums, and Ann has since performed at three. We'll send another round out, in case people were intrigued by the first and the flyer is buried on the education curator's desk.

Speaking of education curator, it is important to send material to the right title. People come and go in institutions, but titles not so much, and they are sufficiently generic that if, for instance, a museum does not have an education curator, they do have someone who does programming, and your envelope will be tossed in that person's in-box. In schools, we have found that, while principals hold the checkbook, they generally leave it up to their faculty to plan Kansas Day activities and assemblies. We find that if we send two envelopes with the same material to each middle school, with one addressed to "librarian" and one to "social studies teacher" we are more likely to get a hit. Librarians are great. They specialize in passing along information to those who should have it. An envelope addressed to the school MIGHT get opened by a secretary who might keep the cool postcard and toss the rest (purely speculation, not a scientific study).

"Marketing" reminds us that we are entrepreneurs. We have a product that we are passionate about, so of course, we want everyone to know about that product. Unfortunately, we are often too shy to adequately represent ourselves. Most of us have at one time hoped that someone else would do the hard work of shouting our praise from the rooftops. Unfortunately, though, that "someone" seldom materializes—or at least does not have enough time to get the job done. When we were first applying for the Kansas Arts Commission's (KAC) touring roster in the mid-1990s, we knew if we reached this zenith we had it made. I mean, this was a list of the crème de la crème of Kansas performers. We would be besieged with calls and never have to do another mailing. The KAC staff was very careful, however, to emphasize that their list was the beginning, not the end. At that time they required that all applicants not only prove with a list of presenters that we already had a track record but also, by submitting our marketing pieces, prove we were able to get the attention of presenters without being solely dependent on KAC's subtle advertising. After we were on the list, we realized its greatest benefit was that of their endorsement, a super supplement to our marketing. And, of course, it also helped that we could promise presenters that KAC would pick up 40 percent of the tab, if they submitted the grant in a timely manner, so of course, we learned how to write the grants for our presenters. But we still had to make those calls and mail those materials.

We have had a couple of brushes with agents. One school lyceum owner was ready to sign us on and promised lots of work, but when I did the math I could not figure out how anyone who was not collecting a pension and social security and did not already own their own recreational vehicle (and this was before gas got *really* expensive) could possibly afford to travel for them. In addition, because the first goal was to make money for the agent, they scheduled people very closely, so we would be limited to a forty-five-minute assembly at each school with no time for additional interaction. Their catalog verified my math—people were older, and their "acts" were just that, entertainment with a moral message tacked on.

A comic group insisted that we contact their agent, but we soon realized that that agent, and another we met at an arts conference, would not be able to represent us because it would take too long for them to tell their venues just what it was that we do. "Trust me, you'll love them" might or might not work, and there were other, easier acts to place. So we just decided that since we were having pretty decent luck making our own luck we would continue doing so.

Titles are important (see trail story 6.13). Mary Wade has recently created a compelling portrayal of Sister Xavier Ross, Mother Superior of the Sisters of Charity of Leavenworth, Kansas, and founder of a large number of Catholic institutions west of the Mississippi. She addresses audience members as novitiates, new nuns. The theme that goes through her portrayal is "What Can a Woman Do?" and, indeed, the Sisters themselves have written a play with that title. Such a title would play well with women's groups and, perhaps, with pious mixed-gender Catholic audiences. If, however, she wants to attract a broader range of audiences, she might select a title that refers to the Wild West or settlement. Maybe her framework will be that she is going to tell the audience how to raise money for churches and hospitals from a lawless public, as she and her Sisters did repeatedly in Leavenworth and also in Laramie and Denver. Being subtle, leaving spaces in which audience members can imagine themselves, lets them reach the conclusion that Mary hopes they will reach. The

---

**A Trail Story**

### 6.13. "AMELIA EARHART, LIVE!"

This was the title on the downtown theater marquee when Ann appeared there one weekday. A woman drove by, did a double take, got her daughter out of school, and brought her to see her daughter's hero, who had, she was convinced, been found. Unfortunately, when she found out that it was not the real Amelia Earhart, she took her daughter back to school, much to Ann's regret.

question "What Can a Woman Do?" as a title implies that the speaker will tell them the answer and lets the audience sit back and receive it. Including the question as part of the text, however, lets the men ask themselves, "What should I be encouraging the women in my life to do?" "Are there Sister Xaviers in my life that I am impeding?" "Am I being like Sister Xavier's father and not understanding my daughter?"

Make a list of types of prospective venues. This might include the following:

- Libraries
- Regional library consortia
- Statewide library organizations
- Museums
- Specific types of museums such as aviation museums, science museums, or transportation museums
- Statewide and regional museum organizations
- Schools
- Home-school organizations
- Organizations that might relate to your character

Then go online and get addresses.

Also, find out about nearby conferences. Choose your two top markets, perhaps schools and museums, and find out about their annual conferences. If you cannot afford to have a booth, maybe you can nip into the motel or convention center and put your cards out on a table. Or send your cards with a friend who is going (that librarian you gave a special deal?). Try to get a gig performing at the conference banquet but only if your text is one that people will enjoy as well as learn from. My Calamity Jane, for instance, is a great banquet performance. "Fighting beside My Brother," however, with Bleeding Kansas and Civil War stories, is not—it is too serious. On the other hand, "Fighting beside My Brother" is a great mid-afternoon program for a Civil War Roundtable or even (they still do this, trust me) a conference program for spouses of an organization that is mostly one sex or the other, so, for instance, while the guys are learning about surfacing roads their wives need to be entertained. Convention and visitor bureaus (CVB) often advise visitors on this sort of entertainment, so get yourself known by area CVB staff members and your materials into their hands. You might not want the really big shows, but Amelia Earhart had a great time with such diverse groups as county clerks, National Space Grant Consortium Directors, and Kansas Red Hat Ladies.

Some organizations, especially women's clubs, provide great audiences, but they have a tradition of free programs, buying the speaker's lunch, or paying a very small honorarium. Do not, however, write them off altogether. Find out if there is a statewide, regional, or national organization and suggest that the local group (for which you did a freebie that was very well received) recommend you for its conference.

**STEP EIGHT: CREATE RELATIONSHIPS**

I have already advised you that one way to market is to go where there are groups of people who might want to hire you, such as museum personnel (see trail story 6.14). Part of that process is gaining credibility with them. Usually, it is not expensive to join a state museum or library association. Go to their annual conferences. Be where a whole lot of the people you want to meet are congregated. Offer to share your expertise (not necessarily a performance but perhaps an educational session—we have done well-received sessions on gender and museums, for instance) in a way that costs the group nothing but helps them get to know you as a scholar and someone who understands their setting.

---

### A Trail Story

#### 6.14. HANDS-ON MARKETING

Shoulder rubs at the end of a long, hard festival day. Now that's creating a hands-on relationship. The Kansas Alliance of Professional Historical Performers wanted to create an impression on exhibitors at the Kansas Sampler Festival (mostly the chamber of commerce, convention and visitor bureau, museum, historic site, and small-business staff). We decided that a country club reception with one free drink (obtained with a coupon from our exhibit area) and heavy hors d'oeuvres would make them grateful, and we would be there in costume to reinforce our marketing. Then we added the shoulder massages by historical figures. Almost all of the exhibitors showed. Lines were long but convivial; the chef had to get out more food as people got in line for seconds; and the bill ended up being huge, but it was a delightfully memorable event (*and* paid for by a grant). Did it result in more bookings? We cannot document it, but it definitely increased the personal relationships that led to a willingness to talk about booking us!

It is important that presenters experience your goodwill with them all along the way. Contracts, invoices, and other communication and records are a part of that, as is your flexibility during the process, as long as it does not threaten the quality of the performance you will provide the audience. Everyone wants to hire someone who shows their competence through their confidence. No matter what is thrown at them they can handle it. No whining, only negotiating. Seldom "No" but, more likely, "Here's what we need to receive from you to feel good about that change and do our very best for your audience."

The most important thing you can do for presenters is to get to know them and their needs. Even before you have a contract, you want the presenters to like you well enough, to trust you enough as a professional that they will go out on a limb to bring you in. You want them to think of you not only as a performer but also as a partner, as a colleague, and as a friend. But, of course, the most important thing is that they think of you often and well. Therefore, listen to what is on their mind, what is their challenge, today, and if you can help out by offering contacts from your network, or your knowledge of your field. You might not get that booking with this call, but you just might hear from them— or someone to whom they recommended you, later. For instance, we often get calls from presenters who have a particular need. Once, they really wanted a male performer. Well, we are women and find plenty of opportunity and inspiration as women "doing" women. We could, however, refer them to male colleagues whom we know well enough that we know they will do a great job and reflect well on us.

The contract is crucial in making sure that all responsible parties are on the same page because a representative of both entities signs it, and both have a copy. Contracts should have the following components:

- Names of the legal entities (what organization will be the source of the check that you receive?)
- Title of the performance
- Description of add-ons, like "followed by discussion with audience"
- Dates of the performance
- Location of the performance
- Time of the performance
- Time of the sound check or stage setup
- Who will provide
  - Sound
  - Lighting

- - Transportation
  - Lodging
  - Meals
  - Props
- Amount of the fee
- When the fee is due (usually at the end of the performance, but some want an advance)
- What happens if one party or the other has to cancel or chooses to cancel?
- Will photographs and other recording be allowed?
- Signatures of both parties
- Request to make a copy and return original to you

It is also important because many, if not most, of your venues have never drafted a contract for a performer. It also gives you a more detailed document to accompany your invoice. Occasionally, we work for larger organizations that prefer to use their own contract. While that is fine, we do not hesitate to have them add such things as our recording clause (or when fee is due!) if those are not already included. Most contracts from such organizations as library systems are to decrease their liability should you do something illegal or immoral. I have actually signed a contract from a public institution that stipulated that my clothing cover certain portions of my anatomy and that I will not use obscene language. There's a story there, no doubt!

And, by the way, always carry a copy of both contract and invoice with you—we take the booking file with us to make sure that we have directions, times, motel information, and such data. A few times in schools we have had a secretary who was willing to write our check but needed an invoice, which we were very glad to provide (again).

Some things are tempting to put in a contract, but we do not want to scare our presenters. One presenter warned us she would not bring us in if she had to hire a lawyer to read our contract. Some things we intentionally leave out of contracts for just that reason—we do not want the contract overinterpreted and thus putting people off. The provision of a dressing room, for instance, is amazingly complex when one performs in a wide range of settings. I will need a place to change. That place does not need to be a dressing room. Dressing rooms are luxuries, and seldom do our venues have real dressing rooms with a place to hang clothes, chairs, a mirror, lighting, and, dare we even hope, a bathroom of our own. Instead, we will be offered a bathroom that our audience will also be using, and we will turn it down because we do not want our audience to either see us first with our suspenders down or, if it's a one-holer, have to wait for us to dress before they can take care of their very urgent needs, hence forming an unfavorable impression right off the bat. Therefore, I mention on the phone that I will need a place to change costumes and that I will check out the possibilities when I arrive. What I occasionally encounter and personally need to avoid is a location with a superabundance of dust or cleaning chemicals. Those block my breathing apparatus and make it difficult for me to project my voice (see trail story 6.15). Other than that, I have changed and loitered in a good many commercial kitchen hallways, closets, stairways, offices, rooms-next-door, spaces behind stage curtains, and horse trailers. One time, I even changed shirts outdoors, next to the horse trailer: I have lost my extreme physical modesty because it just is not practical.

*Access issues.* You might be taking the lead and you might be following. Either way, be aware, and be willing. For instance, you have taken great care with your costume, to make it era authentic. You have your own wireless lapel microphone, which you have carefully hidden in your costume, and you are just

### A Trail Story

#### 6.15. A LOSS OF VOICE

Probably the only thing worse than losing amplification is losing your voice, and often the one leads to the other. Ann (as Amelia Earhart) and I (as Calamity Jane) were to do two libraries and a school in a day and a half in a neighboring state. Not a strenuous schedule except that Ann was battling a cold. And the electricity went out in the school, so she had to perform in a large carpet-and-book-filled space without amplification . . . twice. That evening, at the second public library, we did not tell the librarian that Ann literally had no voice. We kept hoping it would return. I ran interference, talking with the librarian while Ann "got into character." We could not experiment with the sound because the performance was to be in the reading room of the old Carnegie building, and people were reading there until evening. And sure enough., when Ann went on I cranked the sound up as high as I could, but the audience could not hear her amplified whisper. So "Amelia" made her apologies in character and Calamity made an early entrance. I don't know *what* would have happened had I not been there to take up the slack.

ready to go onstage when someone rushes up, says, "I hope you don't mind," puts another microphone around your neck, and looks for a place to put the transmitter, another box the size of your carefully hidden transmitter. What do you do? Hide the second transmitter and microphone as best you can and as time allots (is the MC even now giving you your cue to go on?), while making sure that the microphone is in a place where the hearing-impaired listener will

---

**A Trail Story**

### 6.16. THE SHOW MUST GO ON

Ann remembers one time that she could hardly talk for all the phlegm running down her sinuses into her throat. You've probably been there—when you think you're going to drown in the stuff? Luckily, it happened in a nursing home and the audience was very forgiving as she kept turning her back to blow into increasingly gross handkerchiefs.

And then there was the spring of 2003, when Ann, who is allergic to red cedar, tended brush pile fires that had her breathing red cedar smoke for five hours. A few days later she flew to Saipan, where the Northern Mariana Islands Humanities Council had invited her to do eleven performances in seven days on three islands not awfully far from where Amelia Earhart had disappeared. This was during the severe acute respiratory syndrome (SARS) pandemic, and other airplane passengers gave her dirty looks and leaned away as she chewed gum and swilled Dayquil in vain attempts to avoid coughing.

On the islands, she started coughing about three-quarters of the way through each of the performances, but it was not a big deal because each audience was different and each time she managed to stay in character, control it, and continue. A few days later, we went to Deadwood, South Dakota, where we gave a workshop to middle school youngsters in Calamity Jane's old stomping grounds of Deadwood, in and around a blizzard and while staying in a smoke-filled casino, and Ann (I'm sure she wouldn't mind me telling you this) kept disappearing from the classroom because her coughing wracked her so badly that she was in danger of peeing in her pants. After going to the Pacific, she went to Ireland, and the coughing quit during her second week there. "I just took it one day at a time," she says.

be able to benefit from the FM transmissions of your great performance. In my experience, this is most likely to happen in schools. I have also had American Sign Language (ASL) interpreters onstage with me, but only once have I had a request to have a copy of my script ahead of time in case there was language with which they might not be familiar. I usually make some small reference to the interpreter in character and then generally ignore their presence. Personally, I enjoy watching ASL interpreters when I am in the audience, so I might have a twinge of jealousy at sharing the stage or fear they will not "get" what I am saying, but I remind myself that my mission is to take the stories to ALL the people and get on with it.

I have add-ons that I love to do if the schedule allows it. I may offer to go to a nursing home to do a performance for individuals who are unable to travel to the regular venue. (On the other hand, an assisted-living center is usually able to arrange transportation, and I will expect to be paid if they want me to go to their site.) Or I might take my saddle in to the preschool classroom since they did not get to attend the assembly.

Think twice before turning down an engagement. When we need money or exposure for our new endeavor, we are tempted to take anything that comes our way. When we are not dependant financially, or not desperate for new friends, we might be tempted to turn down something that is outside our comfort zone, but if it is a serious request from a presenter that just might want you to do what you feel is in your strength, and is willing to pay what you need in order to be comfortable, see if you can accommodate.

Very early on, we were asked to open a new strip mall that had a frontier theme. What they really wanted was atmospherics—people strolling around in period costume engaging prospective customers. We, however, were not able to think outside our box. First, we priced ourselves so they might turn us down, but they did not blink. Then we said that we would do short scheduled performances on the sidewalk. This was a mistake—we did not get audiences. We should have just done the strolling thing and gotten over our concern that someone might see us! Since then we have occasionally, maybe once a year, been paid to appear in costume at an event such as a museum exhibit opening, a themed festival, or a conference reception. We use our performance setting (1900 frontier for me as Calamity Jane, 1937 for Ann as Amelia Earhart) and visit casually with the public, being willing to step out of character whenever appropriate. If attendees are at loose ends, for instance, children at a largely adult gathering, we tell them a story. If someone wants to know where we got the "cool duds," we step out of character and tell them. It's casual, and the goal is for everyone to have a good time—education is way down the priority line,

A Trail Story

### 6.17. SPEAKING OF NURSING HOMES

Ann tells me that everyone should at least once do one of the grueling eleven-performances-in-four-days residencies in which we get paid as much as we would for two performances in one day. I don't know if it will make you a better person, and I have not yet done this, only because of my teaching schedule, you understand, but Ann assures me one time is worth what you learn about yourself and the "war stories" gained. These underpaid tours are arranged by agents. Ann's as Amelia Earhart was an intriguing cooperation between a two-year college that needed student credit hours to justify state dollars and seniors services that needed programming for their accreditations. All of the residents of the local assisted-living centers and nursing homes were enrolled in a community college humanities class. Several artists came to the community at different times during the semester and gave a performance at the college (for the community and for the few traditional students enrolled in the "class"), followed by ones at nursing homes (Ann found the Alzheimer unit folks the most engaged), assisted-living centers, and area high schools. The community is small, and several hours from an urban area, so artists had to arrange for all of their living. Ann stayed with a friend, but there was also a woman who rented a room to the artists. Having, however, been warned that she liked to "share," and after long days of schlepping sound equipment from place to place and talking over clanging pots from nearby kitchens, Ann decided that she needed the quiet of her friend's space. Now, however, she "kind of regrets" that she missed out on part of the authentic experience. "But that's okay."

but that's okay because maybe we will be brought in by someone we met there (always secrete a few cards in your costume) and be able to meet some of those same folks under circumstances that better fit our mission.

One of the more gratifying aspects of this kind of work is that often we can recommend other performers, thus benefitting the performers financially, the presenter, and us, providing the opportunity to visit a bit before or after. Most recently, Ann "mingled" as Amelia for the opening of the Ulrich Art Museum exhibit of Jeffrey Milstein's photographs of jet airplanes. The Ulrich is in

Wichita, Air Capital of the World, so she suggested they also hire Teresa Bachman, who portrays a World War II Boeing worker ala Rosie the Riveter, and
Gary Krehbiel, who interprets airplane builder Clyde Cessna. The artists got
paid, the presenter was pleased, and the corporate sponsors were pleased to
have "their" history represented.

Historical performance can be lonely. Unlike reenacting, historical performers are usually on the road, and on the stage, by themselves. This works
fine if you are an introvert, someone who recharges by getting away by yourself, but not if you recharge by plugging into other people.[6] It also helps to have
someone to keep you motivated in such tasks as marketing. Ann Birney is my
partner. She works full time and exclusively for Ride into History and has done
so since 1993. Admittedly, for the first four years there was mostly expense and
very little remuneration, but she says that the lifestyle was good. And in turn, I
have finally convinced her that my professorial work is not a "day job" but,
rather, another venue—an ongoing contract with a single presenter, if you will.

Prisca Krehbiel is Gary's representative, booking agent, and significant other.
When they are not doing historical performance, they farm, and Prisca is a social worker. Like many of us, on stage Gary is more comfortable in character
than out, but Prisca has a true talent for marketing Gary while Gary as Clyde
Cessna is marketing airplanes to us.

You might, however, find a great and irreconcilable divide between a wage-
paying job and your historical performance work. Historical performers have
as a group tended to be "older" because many individuals are growing a weekend project into a retirement job, especially those who can retire early and want
to escape "the desk."

It could be that you will want to join a storytelling organization and find al-
lies there. After all, what we do is to string stories together to create a portrayal.
In fact, Ride into History was the "keynote" for the National Storytellers Association conference when it was held in Kansas City. The move was somewhat
controversial among the board, we were warned: it was their practice, if not
policy, that they did not pay storytellers, and the opening slot had always been
in lecture format, not storytelling. But we have had no finer audience for
"Amelia Earhart and Calamity Jane: One Frontier, Differently." Storytellers are
wonderful people.

## STEP NINE: KEEPING YOUR VISION IN FRONT OF YOU

Where are you going, why, and how will you get there? Starting a business is
the kind of process that has to be a labor of love, an immense process. Why go
to all that trouble? When asked why they do historical performance, several

members of the Kansas Alliance of Professional Historic Performers replied that it was because the stories should be told. Anna Smith, an army veteran who portrays American Revolutionary War veteran Deborah Samson, reminds us that "forgotten history dies." Gary Krehbiel, aka airplane builder Clyde Cessna, says, "The story needs to be told." Yvonne Larson, who travels with a vintage wagon and accoutrements that would have been used by settlers on routes such as the Oregon Trail, takes a stand for accuracy, saying that she wants to "correct some faulty ideas" about trail travel.[7]

It is important to keep in front of you the "why" of your performances and also that you create opportunities to measure your success. Anna Smith might want to ask her audience members a month later what they remember from her performance, as might Gary Krehbiel and Yvonne Larson. In fact, Yvonne might want to give teachers a simple pre-test for their students to find out what "faulty ideas" they have about trail travel, and then give another simple test after Yvonne has been to the school. Granting agencies often request evaluations from presenters, and this information would be helpful to you, not only in changing anything that should be changed, but also in providing testimonials to use in marketing.

Share your goals and celebrate your successes with others. Even self-actualized introverts can appreciate the motivation of having someone ask, "So, how is that script coming along? Would you like me to listen to you?" And when Ann (2008) and I (2007) were recognized by the Kansas Arts Commission with mid-career fellowships, you'd better believe we celebrated with family, friends, and colleagues.

Identify opportunities that will make you a better performer, and figure out how to make those happen. It might involve research, like getting a grant to travel to a research institution such as an archive or library. While some such grants are limited to faculty members, contact the organization and see if it has funds to help you defray costs—or lodging for visiting scholars.

One year we received an arts commission grant to develop math curriculum material to accompany Ann's Amelia Earhart performances in schools. Our arts commission has provided excellent workshops for artists. One or both of us attend as often as we can. Usually, they are free and held in several places across the state, although never in our village of Admire, so we always have to drive! When the University of Kansas' Lied Center brought in John F. Kennedy Center for the Performing Arts teaching artists for a free six-day "Artists as Educators" seminar (cosponsored by the Kansas Arts Commission), Ann was there, and as a part of that workshop created a curriculum that integrated Kansas Department of Education standards and benchmarks for social sciences, language arts, and theater—a package we can market to schools. She also renewed friendships with other performing artists and met new colleagues.

We read arts commission and humanities council newsletters and attend grant-writing workshops so that we can spot opportunities for programs, but also so that we can advise prospective presenters on possibilities for funding and can help them write their grants. And because (I know I have said this before) it is important to be where the presenters are.

Of course, part of the development of our own business is developing not only ourselves but also our infrastructure, which means that we talk to our legislators about why it is important to continue to support arts and humanities programs for the public and in schools. As historical performers we can be very convincing advocates because not only do we witness the effect that our work has on our diverse audiences but also, with a little planning, as performers we are the ones best able to tell that very compelling story to those who most need to hear it. If we are not excited about what we do, why should other people be? Project that excitement not only while you are in character but also every time you talk about what you do . . . and why you do it!

## NOTES

1. E-mail poll of Kansas Alliance of Professional Historic Performers, July 2008.

2. I did this for years before figuring out that I always got a refund because I was having the university overwithhold. And Ann, whose only income is Ride into History, did not earn enough after expenses that she would have to pay a penalty. So while it is an interesting exercise, make sure it's an exercise that you need.

3. Anna Smith, e-mail to author, June 20, 2008.

4. Kenneth Turan, "French Thriller *Tell No One* Gains Momentum in U.S.," *Morning Edition* [audio], August 12, 2008, at http://www.npr.org/templates/story/story.php?storyId=93522536.

5. We met Anna Marie and Graham Thatcher of Periaktos Productions LLC (http://www.periaktos.com/) in 1998 at the regional Art beyond Boundaries conference in Chadron, Nebraska. They presented a workshop on Self Employment Issues for Artists, emphasizing the need for artists to wear many more hats than just that of creator.

6. The Myers-Briggs Type Indicator personality assessment instrument is useful in understanding others and self and so is often used by work groups—officially it can only be administered by a certified counselor.

7. E-mail poll of Kansas Alliance of Professional Historic Performers, July 2008. More on the Alliance later and at http://www.historicperformance.com/.

# Enhancing Museums and Historic Sites with Historical Performance

Historical performers have two responsibilities:

- to be accurate—true to the time period being portrayed
- to be entertaining—to hold the attention of their audience

—*Ride into History*

BY now, reader, you are either ready to try doing historical performance yourself or you are contemplating, as a program planner or a presenting organization (henceforth "presenter," meaning the organization that brings in the performer), using it to entice people to your site, thus enhancing the audience's enjoyment of your museum. Let me pose a series of questions and then offer responses as a means of elaborating. First, I will address the programmer's museum and historic sites needs. If, however, you are a historical performer or transitioning into historical performance, please read on to see what the presenters are seeking so you will know if, and when, they can use your product. Second, in this chapter I will address issues about working with freelance performers and why, or when, you may wish to considering growing your own troupe. Therefore, this chapter is both descriptive and prescriptive about the roles of historical performers.

## WHY USE HISTORICAL PERFORMANCE?

You are going to want to incorporate historical performance into your long-range program planning because it will enhance the overall experiences of visitors to your site or museum. It will increase first-time, nontraditional visitors, who will, in turn, talk about it in their communities with excitement and then return with their friends. Word of mouth is the most effective (and cheapest) publicity. Historical performance has the ability to reach new audiences because it appeals to diverse learning styles and tells compelling stories.

What are the advantages of historical performance for museums and historic sites?

- They use narratives to involve people emotionally.
- These narratives in turn enhance experiences for visitors in either single-age cohorts or intergenerational groups.
- This style increases both individual and group learning by using multi-sensory techniques. Any time multiple learning styles are met, one reaches a wider percentage of the audience's learning wishes, and thus their satisfaction increases.
- This style provides human connections to bridge the "past era of a performance" to the "now times of the audience." It evokes thinking through the emotional connections of the human story line; also, on the part of the "hearer" (that is, the audience members), it leads to a deeper level of post-performance questions of "the character" and "the scholar." These deeper questions lead to a real dialogue that readily and easily crosses time. Really, more thoughtful why and how questions are asked by the audience than the type that can be answered with a quick yes or a no.
- Historical performers can offer alternative stories and perspectives—think about gender, mixed heritages, as well as different age takes on an event. Programmers routinely take into consideration the diversity of audiences when they plan events.

These stated advantages of using historical performers apply primarily to museums and historic sites and their audiences. But, if you are an individual thinking about doing historical performance, look carefully at these advantages and think how you can use them too. For an example, imagine individuals who are considering a change, from, say, a third-person lecture on nineteenth-century mourning clothing and customs to a first-person performance on the same topic.

## WHEN SHOULD ONE CONSIDER USING HISTORICAL PERFORMANCE?

At the point of dreaming, of course! At the point of planning programming and at the time of writing grants for funding those dreams. Now we have a plan, but even if it is "pie in the sky" wild dreaming and brainstorming, it does make visible the components of the larger plan. And components can be found, a part here and a part there; perhaps this year do this part. Plan to make it happen, and focus on the parts you want to see happen. Do not let the big picture scare you; rather, look for the small parts and work from there.

And, of course, planning is everything. If you don't plan you will have to settle for what you can get, so planning is crucial. What will be your overall tentative time line and the tentative date of the event? Will you be writing a grant? How many programs are you offering, and how many historical performers are your wishing to have? Do you wish to bring in one or two freelance performers? Do you wish to bring in a troupe? Do you want to plan a Chautauqua event for your site? Do you wish to grow your own troupe? Do you want to include youth in your programming or presentations? Breathe! Dreams are big, as they should be, so let us look at the smaller components.

Count on booking some performers at least a year ahead, which means you need to plan. Generally, if it is a major event, you are already planning a year and a half ahead as you finish out one project and are midway though several others. Using historical performance is just incorporating another element into your already established planning process. Before you can plan a "tight locked-in-stone" type of program, you need to analyze your needs and your site's goals. But you also need to dream! This helps you offer new, fresh programming ideas.

## HOW ARE WE GOING TO FUND THIS EVENT?

This question always sneaks into the conversation. There are partners out there—corporate sponsorships for all or part of the overall event—and there are granting agencies. Another thing presenters will need to consider when they apply for grant moneys—are they going to be working with arts or humanities grants? And is historical performance art, humanities programming, or both in your state? If you are already familiar with your state granting institutions' definitions and styles, you can just begin the process. If this is your first time at writing a historical performer grant, consider this an opportunity to learn. Each state has slightly different nuances, so do look at your state's grant guidelines. Remember, too, these agencies are used to getting calls about how events fit their options.

## HOW DO WE FIND REALLY GOOD HISTORICAL PERFORMERS?

Ask colleagues and humanities council staff members, "Whom do you know who performs in character with an accurate script and accurate look, has enough knowledge to be able to take questions about historical context, AND can hold an audience?" Make sure that your colleagues know that you want all of those things. If the scholar-performer has the knowledge base to be an authority and can tell a compelling story in character, don't worry about the clothing "look" as this is the easiest part to improve. Talk to the performer and see if they are willing to make the acquisition of appropriate period clothing (not "costume") as a condition of the contract. In fact, find a clothing historian for the performer as it may require consultation, if not constant monitoring, since you expect authenticity of both words in the script as well as the "look." The total package is what is important to your site's needs because the audience, your visitors, expect authenticity. To settle for less is settling for second rate, and this is never best practice in applied public history theory.

There are many performers with websites and many open rosters. In your selection process, note, too, that not all websites are deeply or evenly juried, meaning anyone can be on the site for a fee. Or, one can create one's own Web presence. Some websites are better designed than others. Some have a better marketing plan and are thus downright seductive in what they say the performer can do. (Standards for a deep roster, including the jurying process, are listed in the last chapter.) Look for disclaimers, as in this one example: the National Women's History Project (NWHP) warns that it "publishes these listings from information provided by the performers and is not responsible in any way for the performers, a performer's negotiations with clients, or the performances."[1]

One of the mistakes that presenters can make is to decide whom they want to have portrayed before they see who is actually available to do the portrayal. The Kansas Humanities Council (KHC), known for their Chautauquas, celebrated the sesquicentennial of the Kansas-Nebraska Act[2] in 2004 with a Chautauqua. A committee determined who should be portrayed: Abraham Lincoln, Stephen Douglas, Frederick Douglass, John Brown, Clarina Nichols,[3] and David Rice Atchison. Nichols is little known outside Kansas, but Atchison was the real problem. Not only is he a minor figure, even though he was technically president of the United States for one day, but he is also known as a villain to Kansans because Rice advocated for slavery and was a leader of the Missouri border ruffians. The list was set in stone, but finding a scholar to portray Atchison turned out to be impossible, so an actor was hired. He had a tough row to hoe with little scholarship available to him to research, and he also had little overall knowledge of the historical context from which to draw a deeper take on Rice's life. He memorized his script. Did he research and write it? I do not know as he kept to himself, not talking to the other scholars of the troupe or participating in the numerous informal discussions about our collective people—so he portrayed Atchison stereotypically as a villain, rather than attempting to interpolate Atchison's motivations from knowledge of others of his political stripe and persuade the audience that his motives might have been sincere. His discussions were disappointingly short because he lacked information, whereas others in the troupe could hardly be contained because they knew so much depth of knowledge and were so eager to share it with their audiences. Had KHC widened its call initially to include more possibilities for historic figures, perhaps it would have had a scholar-based performance. David Matheny, on the other hand, who played John Brown, was a retired theater professor, not a history scholar, but he had been researching and portraying Brown for decades and was trained by historian Loren Pennington, founder of the Kansas Chautauqua of the 1980s.

Once presenters have the dream or a plan, they then begin asking among their larger network of colleagues if anyone knows of quality historical performers on the topic they are thinking about for their event. They also tend to publish a call for historical performers, listing the criteria: for example, knowledge of the era (the thirties, Great Depression) or on a broad theme (history of sports) in which you are interested; have experience in creating and performing a historic figure; and available during the dates of the event.

Some presenters require auditions or visuals in a media format so they can preview the quality and suitability of the scholarly work and accuracy of the look. These are also watched for style. Are they watching a scholarly historical performance that is true to the person or just, well, watching a theatrical over-the-top actor in representational clothes and makeup. Just scan some of the sites on the Internet under keyword terms such as History Alive! or Chautauqua, and you will readily observe the differences. Some of the images are not up to the best practices standards you want for your site. They, well, how do I say this tactfully, are not accurate in their look or style. Note makeup as one quick marker. Note, too, the style the performer uses. Playing a person or setting for laughs may bring snickers from the crowd, but is that really the thoughtful scholarly take on that person your site wishes to promote? There is a huge difference in providing an accurate, serious characterization and a caricature, comic, or grotesque take on that same person's life story. In the spirit of Everett Albers, the father of the modern Chautauqua, when it is good it is good but when it is bad it is horrible.[4]

How do you know they are good? How do you know they are the ones you want? Here is a checklist (more is written on standards in the last chapter):

### Checklist to Help You Plan Your Selection

- Check rosters. Are they on juried rosters? Who does the jurying process? What are their standards? Do the rosters comment or take into consideration what you are specifically looking for as you plan your event? Do they comment on accurate look or representational look? Is the look even a consideration for that roster? For many of the Chautauqua sites this is a nonissue. Do the rosters comment on the quality of the scholarly work behind the script? Does the roster classify them as scholars or actors? This often is a flag for public history venues.
- Can the historical performer provide references? Do compare as there may be several to choose from, and they will have varying abilities and credentials.
- Interview informally those who look interesting.
- Things to look for in a historical performance:
  - Are they using the accurate wording for the era?
  - Can they send you photos or images in another media format?
  - Do they have the accurate look and props (properties)?
  - Are they offering a good or historian's scholarly take on their persons and those persons' lives and times?

One can attend one of their presentations, rely upon word of mouth of a colleague, use some media format to see their presentation, or use a standard telephone discussion to determine their ability to answer questions about their characters and historical context. Visit with them over the phone, much as you would for an early-stage job interview, to get a sense of how they will answer questions.

Ask them a series of open-ended questions:

- How would they describe their program/performance?
- What do they consider their best audience demographics?
- Can they send you publicity images? What types? Can they be reproduced?
- Can they provide a contract if you decide to hire them?

If they are not able to tell you concisely and precisely what they do, then maybe they are not the best for you. If they do not have enough experience at marketing to have thought through theses basics—at least why they are doing what they do—then will they be able to answer questions adequately from your audience?

Also, pose a few questions as if you were in the audience at your site.

- Ask what primary (of the time) and secondary (written later) resources they found most useful, and what they would recommend for a first-time reader.
- Ask which archives, special collections, and museums they visited to do their research. Professional historical performers are lifetime learners who enjoy sharing their resources with others. Ask what they have read recently or what they have most recently added to their script.
- Audience's interaction with the historical performer needs to be considered. Do they answer questions from the audience? Do they show respect? Arrogance has no place on your site.
- Are they known as team players? Or, at least, do they have a willingness to be members of your team while they are with you? There is no room for prima donnas.
- Are they operating alone or as part of a troupe?
- Are they operating as a business? Can they offer you a contract? Your organization will need one, so if they do not know how to provide a contract, they may not be the professionals you are looking for, or are you willing to write one for them?
- Do they have a tech sheet? How much space do they need? What do they really need?
  - Riser/stage
  - Electricity
  - Sound—do they have their own or will you have to provide? (Remember trail story 6.8 about sound problems.)
  - Space restrictions

If they can't answer these questions adequately and succinctly then maybe they are actually an impersonator or perhaps they do a dramatic monologue or fit into some other portion of the taxonomy discussed in chapter 1 (review figure 1.1 and table 1.1).

I pose the above points as these are the standard type of questions Ride into History receives from museums, historic sites, festivals, and libraries. Perhaps not all of these points or questions are covered at each initial contact point, especially if they have seen our presentations, but more often than not one or more of the points is posed to us, and if we take out a new character we will get these asked. If you are a working historical performer you need to be prepared to answer these. Conversely, the public history site planner needs be prepared to ask these questions. Planning a quality event is based on open and repeated communication.

The presenting organizations (meaning the organization that brings in the performer) and the performers start to discuss things such as the dates of the event. The historical performers will need to be able to say if they are available on your dates; if not you can seek elsewhere and not lose staff time. The programming plan will determine tentative dates as the possible performers are identified. These dates become firmer with funding. Once you as the presenter have identified your possible performers, do have the performers you want pencil in your dates. The protocol for penciling in dates is that the performer will call you if someone else wants that date and they do not have a contract. This gives you the opportunity to firm up the date or let them go.

The next step is to apply for funding and seek funding partners for your event. A few of you may have an adequate budget, but . . . well, money is always tight. As I commented on earlier in another portion of the presenters planning time line, now is again the time to contemplate the use of one, two, or more freelance historical performers, or bringing in a troupe, or "growing your own." Do you as a program planner wish to have youth involved? Each of these will be discussed in more detail below.

### What Is Good? And How Do You Find Out If They Are?

In my early years of performing I, like many, went to others' performances with great hopes of sitting at the feet of someone who was better than I was. Over and over again I was disappointed. Most were concerned with authenticity in their clothes or their words, not both as I was. Too many did not stay in character or in the correct time zone during their monologue, switching from first person to third and from present tense to past. More than one carried a plastic water bottle into the eighteenth or nineteenth century. If they did not care enough to find a representationally reasonable drinking vessel, could I trust them to give me accurate information verbally? If they took questions they were likely to be vague. It was obvious they did not know the answer but would not humble themselves to say so. I was embarrassed for them. Audiences deserve better. Your organization and your audiences deserve the very best.

Initially, I thought it was because I was in Kansas, and no Oz jokes please. I thought perhaps my observation was just too limited. Ride into History had a gig near Richmond, Virginia, in the early 1990s. We decided to extend our stay and do research on costumed interpretation styles by visiting Jamestown, Colonial Williamsburg, and Carter's Grove. I had made research appointments, talked to a number of interpreters informally, and did quite a bit of observing, but the only interpreter I actually talked with formally was Rex Ellis, one of the head interpreters and creator of the other-half tour. His comments were similar to his comments made in the video *Digging for Slavery*, so I recommend you view it to gain insights into Colonial Williamsburg styles.[5] Virginia or Kansas, both had similar issues, a wide range of styles and quality of historical performances.

I am a stickler for quality. For example, when an individual wants to bill herself as a historical performer who sings and her character is a singer, great. But, when she sings and it is intrusive or ahistorical, I cringe. Then it is not correct. Heaven forbid that Calamity Jane should sing. The Deadwood, South Dakota, newspaper described her singing as being akin to a mule's braying.[6] So much for Doris Day's portrayal (which, by the way, I did enjoy because it was pure unadulterated fiction, much like Larry McMurtry's novel and movie).[7]

### What Should You as a Presenter Expect of Historical Performers?

The best freelance historical performers comport themselves as professionals, act as a part of your team on the day of the event, and come prepared to and expecting to deliver to your audience a quality program on the day they said they would. That is why you hired them.

Always get a contract? Let me say it again, in working with freelance performers—contacts and contracts. Without one, they may not show up any more than the one lone reenactor story in chapter 1 in this book. Write into your contract if you want accuracy, then if they do not give you this, put it into the evaluation or reference responses and send it down the net so that others will know.

The contract and letter of agreement is where the specifics are stated. Both presenter and performer need to know the following:

- Who is doing the program and what is it about?
- Where?
- When (date and time of program)?
- When is the estimated time of arrival?
- Where will we meet?

- Where will we load and then park?
- Staging considerations:
  - If outside, weather considerations: discuss, in advance, options for rain, wind, wind direction, seating, sunlight, sunset time, lighting, and so on.
  - Logistics in general: ambient noise and wind direction (tent sides can be adjusted).
- What time is sound check?
- Whose sound system?
- Personal needs issues: place to change clothes, restroom, water, and food issues.

One more concern is the issues of sound systems and authenticity. Today's world is ever noisier than the past; just listen—the hum of air conditioners, furnaces, cars, and so forth. If the audience members cannot hear they will leave not only dissatisfied but also cranky over the money they spent. Our audience members' ears are also getting older. They will forgive much if they can sit and hear. Audiences don't expect to see speakers in anything but a staged setting, so place the presenters in a prominent location. Provide chairs out of the sun, and they will come. Earlier, I had a trail story called "Sound Adventures" (see trail story 6.8) that I would like to call your attention to again. Let me also note that whether you are the presenter or performer you both need to think about this aspect of logistics. If the performer will not be close to the audience, if there is wind, or if there is one of the many little things that go on at events (kids yelling, people talking loudly about something, cell phone conversations, the train, the plane, and the list goes on), you will want a microphone. If the performer uses a handheld microphone, think about the anachronistic look, let alone the problem of talking naturally with one's hands. You also do not want them to have a headset singer's microphone unless they are singing (think: Garth Brooks). I was once told not to bring my sound system as they had a good and big one coming. I should have packed mine. My contract stated a lapel clip-on microphone with a battery pack. The DJ of the day stated when I arrived for a sound check that they were too expensive for him; then he muttered about how difficult they were to fine tune because he did not know how, so—the singer's headset mic look was my only option that day. What if my flesh had not been his color? And talk about the visibility of that mic under my hat. Best practices is a clip-on/lapel microphone; if the presenter provides sound, they also need a knowledgeable technician, brand new batteries, and a microphone/transmitter that has been tested in time to be replaced if it crackles. Do not let your technician say "good enough" (trail stories are rampant among presenters and performers alike; beware of DJs who work with bands).

Once all the particulars are worked out between both parties and expectations are stated, the contract is written, two copies. Both copies are signed, and one is mailed to the other party. Now both parties have one on file in their event folders. Sure, this sounds terribly legal and much more time consuming when a handshake might do, but again I refer to the story of the lone reenactor in chapter 1. You as a presenter are counting on there being historical performance. The audience is counting on it—so if it is not there, it is your and your site's reputation that suffers. And in turn so does the historical performer's reputation.

Presenting organizations need to continue to contact the performer after the contract has been signed by both groups. Consider this as the tickler file concept. Reminders are good on both parts in case changes occur on either end. What I have found as a historical performer to work best for me, and is the same as what works well with presenters, is a contact one month in advance of the event—e-mail or call. Do not leave a message along the lines of "Call if something has changed." Perhaps telephone tag occurs at times, but do ask them to return calls or e-mails. Many grants, as part of their best practices, require this as a part of their time line for planning events.

Some museums and sites require insurance. A few years back this was an issue at the Kansas Sample Festival (KSF). Aaargh! Insurance! KSF began to require certificates of individual insurance, and thus, as the event date got closer, there were no vendors or performers. Therefore, they returned to having the city park's insurance cover the festival. However, some groups do carry their own insurance, so it never hurts to ask them.

### Horse Hugs Are Free

"Survey after survey has shown that museum visitors want to see and interact with animals," according to Chuck LeCount, president of the Association for Living History, Farm and Agricultural Museums. He also notes, however, that animal programs are expensive.[8] There is no doubt that keeping livestock is expensive. Unless animals play a central role in programming and are, in fact, at the center of your revenue-generating programs, you probably do not have them routinely on site. Yet, it is hard to imagine a setting before 1950 without animals. Until you can provide funding for an animal program, freelance performers and living history interpreters can sometimes fill the bill by bringing in livestock that are accustomed to being around people.

Ideally, you as a presenter can work with the performer to provide a controlled situation in which animals and public can interact. It can also add to the authenticity of an event. (I am thinking here of the times I have ridden my horse into a remote site or though the city park, arriving in time to present on horseback, as opposed to the times I have been delivered on a golf cart! Ah, yes, authenticity.)

Horses and guns and reenactors can at times make for an interesting mix. Do you want guns at your event? If yes, make sure someone does a complete ammunition safety check to the same level as if your site was doing a reenactor event, and have someone knowledgeable from your staff with them when it is done. If "no guns" is the decision, make sure they can talk about the gun without bringing it onto the grounds. Sometimes this requires extensive conversations with your local security and police. If they do have guns, find out whose insurance will cover it. If half of the horror stories I hear floating around my reenactor friends are true, then think about your audience and safety.

Horses—Kansas has a domestic animal law; does your state? I know I comply, and yet I am overly careful as I take one of my horses out and about into the crowds. Yep! You can give my horse a hug, but stop a minute and look at my horse first, see the size, and then listen as I launch into my horse and safety lecture and confirm an adult is with you—then the hug.

As veterinary pathologist and freelance interpreter Barbara Corson says, "Even one disaster is one too many. . . . 'An ounce of prevention is worth a pound of cure.'"[9] "Know your audience and know your animals."[10]

The bottom line is, do your overall planning of the event around your theme and then try to find historical performers who match your concept. The biggest disadvantage to having this type of historical performance is the cost: cost of time of volunteers, cost of your own staff time, and money. But do look at all the advantages you reap with the single planting of the idea—"Let's do . . . !" This is why most presenters use freelance historical performers to fit the concept or theme of the event or fit the mission of the site.

Another option is for presenters to use a mixture of outside freelance historical performers and members from their own troupe. This is pleasing to the audience to see new programming as well as their friends and family members. Presenters can also opt to try the next model.

## CREATING YOUR OWN TROUPES FOR SPECIFIC SITES AND EVENTS
Usually, presenters think of this role because of the types of events listed below. These events lend themselves to the type of local enthusiasm necessary to create a troupe and because they are adaptable to creating an onsite group:

- Anniversaries
- Centennials
- Festivals
- Your dream event

These special events have the primary advantage of specifically fitting the theme and mission of your site because the historical performers have only this one venue. The other advantage or disadvantage, depending upon how you look upon training and maintaining a quality troupe, is that they are local and have emotional ties to your site that encourage them to want to help out and thus be willing to make the effort to enter training to become a historical performer. But training is a must, and someone will have to do this and monitor the quality. One caveat here: it can be really hard to tell a volunteer that their centennial dress is old but that it is not the right look. Some museums and historic sites hire outsiders, under contract, as trainers. These trainers not only train but also nag them into the correct way, and the museum does not have this stress. Ride into History has been hired numerous times to do the training and to be the enforcers of standards. We provided the training as well as the encouragement, always a key with volunteers and beginning troupes. This leads to confidence in their ability to do historical performance. That is one of the reasons behind the writing of this book. Staff repeatedly said they wanted a manual to train their staff, so have fun using chapters 1 through 5 to train your troupe or individuals.

The Lecompton Players is an example of a troupe created to support one specific museum. They were created to be geo-area and topic specific. They work primarily in the area around Lecompton's Constitutional Hall and focus upon the anti-slavery and pro-slavery issues of the Kansas-Nebraska Act. When they present a program, their troupe comprises as many members as could be there that day, at the time and place of the program. They agree to divide the time allotted between the number of their troupe there to present. One of the members, a proud reenactor, wrote the scripts that the various members deliver. Their looks range from accurate to ever so representational. They are sought to perform as they were the first to become players, the advantage to being the first to try in the area. They are reasonably cheap to bring in if you are close to Lecompton, Kansas, and they love to perform and are flexible in the numbers of people and thus the roles or views to be given at an event. The disadvantage is that, say Osawatomie is planning their annual Freedom's Festival on the same topic. The Lecompton Players are invited but will not sign a contract, and only two present one year and five the next. This can be frustrating to the planners, presenters, and audience.

This situation led Grady Atwater, director of the John Brown Cabin and Os-awatomie Museums, Kansas, to plan how he would create his own local troupe. Atwater contacted Ride into History to see if they could help him with his frustration over finding or training quality historical performers. He knew what he wanted because earlier he had attended one of our Preserving the Past through Performance workshops. He knew the skill concepts but did not have the time to train and do everything else the typical busy museum director has to do and plan the event, too. Also, he wanted an outsider to come in to train some of his potential reluctant reenactors to either stay in first or third person. He also had attended the Kansas Museum Association Conference where we had presented on a youth historical performance and artifact-based program. Atwater wondered if we would consider doing an intergenerational training workshop so he would have a local troupe to call upon. Atwater used grant money to have us come in and train. One caveat: none of the reenactors signed up for the training even though he called them all to see if they wanted to participate in this free workshop. Grady himself had paid for his earlier training. We had five afternoon sessions to train. This group, three high schoolers and six adults, their ages ranging from thirteen to eighty years old, came and left more than when we have captive youth. But the groups were so enthusiastic about what they were doing that they met us for lunch and at times for supper, too. Media coverage was good. The tours were solidly booked, one Friday evening, one Saturday afternoon, and one Saturday evening. Grady and another docent led the tours through two museums. Mannequins at first glance to the touring people turned into real people with a story to tell about artifacts. Doors opened and in walked someone to claim an item and tell the story of it and his family in the community. One man stepped out of the tour group to tell about his World War II uniform. The train whistled as a woman rushed in to tell us about a train wreck that had just happened. And that was just at the vintage-style Os-awatomie City Museum. At the physically small John Brown Cabin, really owned by his relatives the Adairs, the Reverend Samuel Adair met the group at the door. As the tour moved from room to room, they learned from the costumed historical performers much of the story of early Osawatomie and its roles in the Bleeding Kansas era. I say costumed because we supplied the clothing out of our horse trailer green room/costume shop. Part of the grant Grady wrote was that we would supply the representational look for this event, like we do for the Youth Chautauquas. For this group we were also to help them know what they should really have. One of the women was hand stitching before we left. Grady evaluated it as a success in that he got bodies in the door and garnered much media attention. And to Grady's joy the tour members stayed to talk and do evaluations and talk some more to the troupe, asking excellent questions and sharing. And, Grady noted later, "Osawatomie's Very Excellent Time Machine" has presented for several senior events, bus tours, and Osawatomie's Freedom Festival, 2008. This was all in three months after the August training, and they are still going strong.

Granted this is a long story about only one museum, but it is actually representational of the power of local troupes. Museums and historic sites have to make decisions. Perhaps one of the biggest as it affects the theme of the project and who might sign up for training is, do you want to pay a historical performer to develop a local historic figure, or identify a local person to do so? Logistics also need to be planned. This is part of the why behind the last story.

A slightly different variation is in Dexter, Kansas, a rural community; some might call it a ghost town except for the locals. Dexter dared to dream "big" with historical performers. Their committee decided they wanted to keep the local history story alive with all local people researching and performing the past's local people. They too contacted Ride into History about helping them. No one in the community had ever written a grant, but with our help and suggestions, they were successful. Since that initial grant Dexter Community Foundation was begun; several grants later, their dream continues. We conducted a long and intensive weekend workshop. Then later we went back to Dexter for a dress rehearsal about a month before their planned event, all agreeing that would give them time to make changes. What a joy to see their enthusiasm and depth of knowledge of the local area, but the gaps in other areas were tackled and they too were up and functioning as a local troupe. They have now for five years been performing at the annual festival in their city park on the date of Dexter's annual reunion day. The town is full of people hearing the stories, learning about the community's rather colorful characters as well as rather ordinary people who made decisions that changed their town's history. The report is that it is the best thing this little town tried as the stories are being kept alive. Now does it get any better than that?

Other examples could be given, but I want you as reader to know that there are options in using local historical performance troupes to your advantages regardless of the size of your site. You are limited only by your imagination in where one uses quality historical performance.

For one last example, consider a variation on this same theme before we talk about the more formal Chautauqua style of troupes. Leavenworth, Kansas, representatives met Ride into History at a statewide tourism event. We were part of a panel talking about Kansas tourism and the role of historical performance potentials. Their county commissioners had just informed them that they wanted some type of Christmas event in the courthouse, other than just Santa Claus for the kids. After the panel, they had what they thought was a wild idea—telling Leavenworth's stories via historical performance. Intriguing, we had not thought about a courthouse Christmas party as a venue before. They wrote a Kansas Humanities Council grant, and the Leavenworth county commissioners made the monetary match. We trained these adults, one sixteen-year-old, two ninety-year-old women who were delightful, and the whole age range in between. One of the ninety-year-old women declared that learning and performing this way was the best mental activity she had had in years and maybe we ought to take our methods to senior centers (so I hope someone takes up that challenge). The event was scheduled for December 7. These women pointed out that would be the anniversary of Pearl Harbor day and launched into stories of themselves and their families. After about an hour we came up for a plan for those two and their stories. They, with two younger women, would sit around a quilting frame, discussing this theme as a current event. They represented one of the local ladies clubs; thus five local stories grew out of this one station. The other two floors of the courthouse had performers in chronological sequence telling the story of the county. The audience loved it. And, more to the point, the county commissioners loved it. One said it was great publicity for the courthouse and the county. Part of the group wanted to try this format again but only on one floor this time. Three stages simultaneously, even if in one building, were a bit much; even if the group did several sequels that day, it was hard on the troupe. They regrouped for the second year, lost members, and gained members. This is typical. More training was sought. Another grant obtained. This time the makeup of the group was very different with different challenges. And this too is typical. Troupes evolve, morph, and change.

I truly understand because Ride into History once had two other women in the troupe. Their interests took them elsewhere. Then Ann Birney joined the troupe, and we pushed even harder on the professional status of the troupe's standards to the point that now both of us are recognized as award-winning professionals.

I hate to even bring up this next topic, but I would be remiss if I did not.

### Disadvantages

- Whether your performers are in-house or you hire them as contractors, the **performances must be done right** or visitors will leave with erroneous information and your reputation will suffer.
- Even the shortest historic performance, such as the young docent performance discussed later, is more **complex** and requires more preparation than a third-person description of an artifact.

- Performers must be knowledgeable about their subject area even if they are storytellers and actors.
- The performance is limited to the perspective of the character presenting the information—although this should be overcome by stepping out of character following the monologue and answering questions from the audience.

Other presenters, reading these disadvantages and thinking about training, opt to contract with their state humanities council for a Chautauqua. This is like partnering for a performance package. The theme is selected. The scholars are selected to meet the theme. The presenter follows the humanities council outline of what to do, and they offer some assistance and funding. This is a very different type of programming. There are advantages and disadvantages to this. Specifically, Chautauquas are for the community, thus they tend to be held in a big tent in a city park with the museum or historic site in the role of providing satellite or shoulder events. These circuit Chautauquas are on tour in the summer, so the funding agent, the humanities council, sets the date they will be in your community. A few communities run their own, so they control for the date and place factors.

For Chautauquas, scholarship is their key concern. Under the tent you will hear wonderfully researched and nuanced presentations. But if you are a stickler for the look, well, do not look at their clothes, only listen. They have the words but not the duds. Worst practices: they have gone to a theater costume shop to get a costume that vaguely represents an era and somewhat fits. For the Chautauqua performer it is a costume. It does not look natural, or believable, from even twenty feet away. Since the revitalized modern Chautauqua in 1980 was reborn, the focus has been on scholar performers who typically went to their university theater costume shops and got a costume that would be suitable to a stage. It therefore only needed to be representational and one that the scholar could wear every week and wear out in the traveling the scholar would undergo. One needs to remember, too, that in the early 1980s some of the reenactors were not as careful in their look as they are in 2009. A disclosure here, please. I have been a participatory observer over the years. I have noticed some changes. The scholar and performance style has improved a bit, the clothes for a few have consciously changed and been upgraded, but for some it is still a costume. For them it is all about the words. A few have moved beyond the classroom-engaging story line, while a few have eased into a full historical performance.

Let me elaborate with a brief history of the Chautauqua Movement.

## HISTORY OF CHAUTAUQUA MOVEMENT

"Chautauqua is the most American thing in America," noted President Theodore Roosevelt.[11]

The term originates from the educational seminars first held in 1874 at a site near Chautauqua Lake in southwestern New York State. From there the concept radiated outward and especially westward. According to Loren Pennington, "Father of the Kansas Chautauqua," "Attempts were made by different Chautauqua groups across wider regions to coordinate their organization, fund-raising, and scheduling of program content. . . . Private companies that offered packaged programs appeared after 1900. These companies coordinated the performers and the themes and then booked their Chautauquans in strings of communities."[12] These circuit Chautauquas filled a niche.

Ticket sales and attendance stated declining on the Great Plains during the 1920s. I assume it was also in part due to the Agricultural Depression as this event greatly affected not only rural dwellers and their towns. Also in the 1920s this population as well as urbanities started to have more leisure options. Automobiles, radios, and motion pictures provided competition for the entertainment needs that the circuit Chautauqua met usually once a year for a week.

The Great Depression basically terminated the circuit Chautauqua's movement. The radio met the people's need for information and entertainment and was cheaper to produce in the economic situation of the era.

Former Dickinson [ND] State University humanities professor Everett Albers sparked the revival of the touring-tent Chautauqua soon after 1973, when he became the first executive director of what is now the North Dakota Humanities Council. Clay Jenkinson, now best known for his Thomas Jefferson portrayals, describes on his website the programming model established then, and still followed today:

> The Chautauqua Method divides the performance into three phases. First, the historical interpreter will appear before the group in costume in the persona of the character. He [or she] will begin by speaking for 5–25 minutes (depending on the group) on a specific topic or in general about the character. . . . Following this portion, [the interpreter] opens the floor to any questions the audience may wish to ask. . . . [T]he final portion of the Chautauqua begins, with the performer breaking character and answering questions as a scholar himself.[13]

North Dakota scholars such as philosophy and religion professor George Frein of the University of North Dakota became part of a successful troupe. By

1980 Albers had also inspired and involved Oklahoma, Kansas, Nebraska, and South Dakota humanities councils into the cooperative Great Plains Chautauqua Society. A century after the original circuit began, Chautauqua scholars were once again touring, this time presenting characters from the past organized around a central theme. Oklahoman Doug Watson, an early and long-time member of the Great Plains Chautauqua, said that Albers was passionate about making the best of the humanities available to the public.[14] Every June through 2007 the troupe of scholars began in Oklahoma, setting up a tent and establishing a weeklong residency in first one community and then a second, moving north at the rate of one state every two weeks.

The Great Plains Chautauqua Society produced a written informational souvenir program or reader containing primary sources written by the various individuals being portrayed under the tent and including biographical information on these historic figures as well as about the scholars behind the Chautauqua style performances. Major support was from the National Endowment for the Humanities with significant local match and no fees charged to individuals. The scholars and support staff were paid.

Several Great Plains states, and some communities, in turn, developed their own Chautauquas. Some followed the model of the Great Plains Chautauqua and created annual series (Tulsa Chautauqua), while others have been episodic (2004 Bleeding Kansas Sesquicentennial Chautauqua). The basic pattern developed in North Dakota, however, is the same followed nationwide and emulated with varying degrees of success.

### THE PATTERN OF THE MODERN MODEL OF CHAUTAUQUA

- A theme ties the four to five scholars together in an approach that allows for attendees to hear different sides of the same issue. It encourages the audience to read primary and secondary source material and discuss the material with scholars while they are in residency.
- Funding is through grants and local money as well as in-kind match of time or goods.
- The theme affects the makeup of the troupe.

Remember not all Chautauquans have been trained as historical performers. Many answer a request or a call in the same way as an actor for a part does, and not all actors in the role are of the same ability. Please think again about the standards you want.

Regardless of the state there is a pattern.

- Chautauqua evening programs have four set parts.
  1. Local musical entertainment, to build the local crowd, entertain the early arrivals, and encourage others to be there on time for the primary event. Their performance is followed by a short break to remove their things and to set the stage for the moderator to begin.
  2. The moderator and the evening's Chautauqua program. A local master of ceremonies introduces the event, thanks the sponsors, and then introduces the moderator. Many of the states have the moderator in costume as a historical figure, really another Chautauquan role. The moderator's role is to set the stage for the centerpiece of the evening, the featured Chautauquan who presents a text for about forty minutes.
  3. The audience begins discussion with the characters. The audience is encouraged to ask anything of the "characters," with the moderator repeating and rephrasing as necessary for about fifteen to twenty minutes, or as long as the audience is in engaged in the discussion.
  4. The audience then meets the scholars behind the characters as they step out of their roles to answer additional questions.
- The scholars are in residency in a community because they also offer daily programming.
- All Chautauqua programs, like all humanities programs, are evaluated.
- No admission is charged.
- Venues range from under the tent in the city park with a rain-site backup to an air-conditioned auditorium with theater setting.
- Communities get the word out through various advertising efforts.

George Frein, in addition to being in the first wave of this revitalized Chautauqua, starting in 1986, continued to be a part of the current Chautauqua in North Dakota. When he retired to South Carolina, he helped establish the Greenville Chautauqua, and the Asheville, North Carolina, Chautauqua.[16]

Frein also wrote "Historical Characterization: Some Ideas for Scholars," which was part of "Reflections on Doing Chautauqua." Frein outlines how to research and prepare your script, but he advocated that "the costume, however, should be reasonably accurate." Frein also proposed that one could do a Chautauqua presentation by being either strictly in the past time until the question-and-answer portion of the program or strictly in the present time and talking backward as Clay Jenkinson advocated, speaking as if Thomas Jefferson were alive today and not of his day, the eighteenth century.[17]

### The Kansas Chautauqua

Loren Pennington, father and member of the Kansas Chautauqua and writer of the 1985 grant, wrote the *Profiles*, served as the narrator in 1986–1989, and also was known for years for his Chautauqua performances as Alfred M. Landon and Dwight D. Eisenhower.

Pennington noted, in the 1989 Kansas Chautauqua program, "It was at the Chautauqua that the American people heard the issues, considered the alternatives, and made their political and social decisions. This forum of debate was the great legacy of popular as opposed to traditional Chautauqua, and it is this aspect of Chautauqua that the present Kansas Chautauqua seeks to emulate."[18]

The pattern of the Kansas Chautauqua followed the circuit tent Chautauqua tradition. Scholars were hired under a grant from the then called Kansas Committee for the Humanities. These scholars provided the scripted text that was to be approximately given at each site. The Emporia State University's Costume Shop, in the Theater Department, provided their representational look. This was, in part, because all four of the scholars were faculty members. John C. Lehman portrayed Theodore Roosevelt or Frederic Remington. David Matheny portrayed Jeremiah Simpson, Eugene V. Debs, or John R. Brinkley. Lehman and Matheny were part of the Theater Department, while J. Karen Ray was from the English Department. Ray portrayed Katherine Richards O'Hare or Osa Johnson. Loren Pennington, a historian, because he conceptualized the idea of having a Kansas Chautauqua, was grant writer, overall "boss" of the grant, portrayer of Alfred M. Landon, and narrator each night of the Chautauqua. Don Koke, from nearby El Dorado, served as the balladeer, opening each evening's program with songs appropriate to the topic of the era that would be portrayed. As tour manager, Nancy Kelley, the drama teacher at Emporia High School, made sure the stage was set up correctly for the evening and helped Pennington make local arrangements work for the scholars. Other Emporia State University departments and staff members assisted with the design and printing of *Profiles*. This forty-page booklet contained a biography and bibliography written by the scholar who did the portrayal—thus the adult and popular education aspect of the circuit Chautauqua continued in this newer version. Pennington wrote the introduction, "Chautauqua: An American Tradition."[19]

Also, because the original circuit Chautauqua was in town for almost a week before it moved on—this troupe moved on as well. In addition to the evening program that was under the tent, with no sound system and a minimal setting (a chair, a table, and a glass of water), Pennington tried to recreate the older style of Chautauqua.

Also, there were scheduled "meet-the-scholar" events where the locals and scholars informally interacted. Also scheduled were established humanities-style speakers bureau programming, some aimed at adults and others for children.

I toured with the troupe in 1990, serving as moderator, wearing the Chautauquan uniform of a yellow T-shirt with the name on it (think red-shirt role). The balladeer wore his regular 1990-era clothes with his guitar.

Promptly at 7:00 p.m., I was to walk onto the stage, thus signaling the Chautauqua was to begin. I made a short greeting to the audience and explained that there would be three parts of the formal Chautauqua during the evening. First, we would meet [the speaker] and hear them speak about their topic. Then the audience would have a chance to ask questions of the honored speaker of the evening, and later, after all that, they would have a chance to discuss the evening lecture with the evening scholar. This was the protocol that Pennington, "Father of the Kansas Chautauqua," had discovered worked the best. Then I would introduce the balladeer. We would all collectively sing with him a song, such as "Home on the Range," and then we would do a musical monologue about the songs of the era, sing and play a few, for approximately fifteen minutes. At that point, I as moderator was to step onto the stage again and introduce the individual who would speak that night under the tent by giving a brief biography about the speaker and establishing the time era of the evening. I was to again explain the rules and protocol of the Chautauqua. "Wave your Chautauqua fan if you agree. If you did not agree, please save your questions until after the speaker has delivered the speech, and then you will have a chance to ask questions." The Chautauquan speaker would step onto the stage, really only a small riser, in front of folding and lawn chairs.

The Chautauquan would deliver a historical performance of about forty to forty-five minutes of scripted text, footnoted from writings. As the speaker concluded, I as moderator was to step onto the stage, leading the audience in applause, thus allowing the speaker to bow and get a drink of water. I then asked the audience members if they had any questions of the speaker. I would repeat the question loudly so all could hear. This also gave the Chautauquan a bit of time to think about how to answer the question. And, if an audience member asked an anachronistic question or "when did you die?" I was to rephrase the question into one the speaker could answer from the era without making the audience member feel stupid. Over the course of the four-week tour as a moderator, I certainly became a better historian and better yellow T-shirt (aka red-shirt). When I sensed the audience was running out of questions for the scholar or when time was extending too long on this phase, my task shifted again: "Thank you ——— for visiting us here in the ——— [town], good-bye," leading the audience in applause again. The Chautauquan would walk to the other side of the small stage and usually pick up her or his glasses from the table as I would shift the audience to 1990. I would say, "And now I would like you to meet Dr. ———, from Emporia State University, here in Kansas. Do you have any questions for the scholar behind the evening's presentation? Such as about research or . . . well, anything you might want to discuss?"[20]

I was also a Chautauqua performer in Boulder City, Nevada's, 1998 "Shaping American Myths," along with Buffalo Bill/Eric Sorg, P. T. Barnum/Dug Misner, and Calamity Jane. Both Amelia Earhart/Ann Birney and Calamity Jane/myself were the Chautauqua for Fort Casper, Wyoming, and will be there again in the summer of 2009.

Because of this in-depth experience, we were tapped to create a Youth Chautauqua model that we have now used in Kansas, Nevada, and Wyoming. This is discussed in the next chapter.

## NOTES

1. National Women's History Project, "Women's History Performers," at http://www.nwhp.org/whm/performers.php.

2. A quick brush-up on your history: the Kansas-Nebraska Act was significant not only because it created Kansas Territory but also because it stated that territorial residents would determine whether Kansas would come into the Union as a free or slave state. The tensions of "Bleeding Kansas" led directly into the Civil War.

3. Diane Eickhoff, *Revolutionary Heart: The Life of Clarina Nichols and the Pioneering Crusade for Women's Rights* (Kansas City: Quindaro Press, 2006).

4. Everett Albers, "Reflections on Doing Chautauqua," handout at Kansas Humanities Council History Alive! scholar training session, 1993, p. 1. In author's possession.

5. *Digging for Slavery: The Excavation of American Slave Sites*, BBC Films for the Humanities and Sciences, 1989.

6. Research notes, from Deadwood.

7. Doris Day, *Calamity Jane*, DVD (Burbank, Calif.: Warner Bros., 1953); Larry McMurtry, *Buffalo Girls*, DVD (Los Angeles: Hallmark, 1995).

8. Chuck LeCount, "Travel and Animal Programs," *ALHFAM Bulletin* 38, no. 3 (Fall 2008): 1.

9. Barbara Corson, "Disaster Prevention: Planning a Livestock Event for Maximum Safety," *ALHFAM Bulletin* 38, no. 3 (Fall 2008): 22.

10. Corson, "Disaster Prevention," 23.

11. Charlotte M. Canning, *The Most American Thing in America: Circuit Chautauqua as Performance* (Iowa City: University of Iowa Press, 2005).

12. Loren Pennington, *The Kansas Chautauqua: Understanding America: Land, Peoples, and Culture: Profiles* (Emporia: Kansas Committee for the Humanities and Affiliates, 1989).

13. Clay Jenkinson, "Chautauqua," http://www.dakotaskyeducation.com/Chautauqua .htm, accessed July 4, 2009.

14. Doug Watson, conversation with the author, June 28, 2009.

15. *Chautauqua on the Great Plains* ([Bismarck, N.Dak.]: Great Plains Chautauqua Society, 1992), 4.

16. North Dakota Humanities Council, "Chautauqua on the Great Plains."

17. George H. Frein, "Historical Characterization: Some Ideas for Scholars," handout from a Chautauqua training session. I received this handout from him in the early 1990s as part of a training session for Chautauquans. In author's possession.

18. Pennington, *The Kansas Chautauqua . . . Profiles.*

19. Pennington, *The Kansas Chautauqua . . . Profiles.*

20. Nancy Kelley's tour notebooks and my moderator notes are all are in my possession.

# 8

# Dreams and Plans

MY vision for historical performance is that it is entertaining, believable, and historically accurate; has learners at every stage of their development; and is highly prized and universally recognized. I want every historical performance to inspire me to suspend my disbelief. Performances, both the look and the script, will link audience members' existing knowledge with stimulating new information. Compelling stories, well told, will reach people of all ages and be told by people of all ages. Every historical performance will be followed by scintillating discussion. Aspiring historical performers of all ages across this country will be researching in archives, gathering oral histories, and learning their performance craft. Historical performance will take place in venues ranging from airports to zoos, from historical site visitor centers to school auditoriums. This is the vision. Now for the plan.

The plan to make historical performance the best it can be involves museum and historic site staff members and volunteers, public history students and faculty members, schoolteachers, and everyone who wants to do historical performance. I know that the plan that follows is achievable because Ride into History has already implemented much of it on a small scale (even having performed at several airports and one zoo). It is all possible—it is just a matter of identifying even more people with the passion for taking history's stories to the people, training us all to the highest of standards, and providing opportunities to share with the public the stories that we learn. Because our lives are the result of decisions made over time by others, everyone deserves history's inspirations and cautionary tales, and our audiences deserve the best we can deliver. To that end, here is what you and I need to do:

1. Establish historical performance standards, and identify performers who meet those standards.
2. Provide opportunities for initial training and ongoing learning for people of all ages and backgrounds.
3. Create opportunities for people to see historical performances.
4. Create a structure to support the above.

Let's consider each in order.

### ESTABLISH HISTORICAL PERFORMANCE STANDARDS, AND IDENTIFY PERFORMERS WHO MEET THOSE STANDARDS

As discussed in the last chapter, there are many fine *non*juried directories of performers. How, though, do organizations that would like to present historical performance know that the performers are as good as their marketing? The most useful rosters are juried and include each historical performer's credentials as a historian and as a performer, including education, training, research, and a performance history with contact information for references. Performers should also include an artist statement about their motivation and their preferred audiences and venues. The standards used for jurying should be clear and readily accessible to the prospective presenter. If a historical performer is on such a roster it is an assurance to presenting organizations that she or he meets the stated standards. The keepers of the roster should do their best to see that they provide presenters with as deep a list of historical performers as possible, one that crosses eras and experiences, containing both real and composite characters performed by diverse scholar-performers.

What will the standards be? Broadly, those iterated throughout this book: historical accuracy in look and script, enough knowledge of historical context to be able to answer questions outside the text of the performance, and the artistic abilities to structure a monologue and tell the story compellingly. As a professional, the performer should demonstrate that they have

- developed a thirty- to fifty-minute first-person narrative of a historic figure or composite historic character;
- provided historical accuracy in their monologue, including their look;
- written a compelling narrative;
- learned to tell their narrative convincingly in first person;

- enough knowledge to take questions in character and as the scholar;
- a familiarity with primary and secondary resources about the individual and the historical context;
- drafted a contract and invoice for their program;
- set a fee and calculated travel costs for a program;
- created at least one marketing piece (brochure/flyer/video);
- made themselves accessible via telephone number and e-mail;
- developed at least one resource list, curriculum guide, or other educational material; and
- indicated their next goal in their professional development as a historical performer.

Historical performers who successfully demonstrate the above to a jury of scholar-performers have made a commitment to the profession and to their audiences.

As historical performers we have obligations. Obligations to the future as well as to the past, to the audience, and to the people we represent on stage. We owe the audience our sincere attempt at authenticity: authenticity in the representation of the personality of the historic figure, authenticity in the look, and authenticity in the content of the script. And we owe the audience an attempt at the elusive objectivity.

Anthropologists have a cautionary term called "going native," which happens when researchers practicing participant observation go beyond being involved in the setting they are studying to identifying so completely with the culture that they cannot see the larger picture. Occasionally, someone leaves their research identity permanently to join the culture they see as more desirable. Historical performers owe their audience a detachment from their historic figure, an objectivity, that will enable them to discuss flaws and the extent to which outside events determined the figure's decision making.

Fred Krebs portrays, among many others, early twentieth-century Louisiana governor, senator, and dealmaker Huey Long. During his monologue as Long he speaks ardently of sharing the wealth, of "Every Man a King," and paints a rosy picture of what will happen if the audience supports his reelection. "Long" also defends his position as people ask him questions. But I remember in the 2008 Kansas-Nebraska Chautauqua when narrator and master of ceremonies Doug Watson stopped being Will Rogers, and introduced Fred, who took off his straw hat, leaving Long behind. An audience member demanded to know if Fred really believed all that. Fred said simply, "No," and went on to say how truly outlandish Long was and what else was happening in Louisiana during and after the setting of the performance. Fred had been convincing. He had to be to be true to Long. But then as the scholar he had to be as objective as he could be in placing Long within historical context.

On the other hand, the intricate web of obligations includes honoring the person we are choosing to "become." We need to always keep in mind that we are honoring someone else's life stories. Keeping these concepts of honor before us at all times as historical performers helps us remember that we do indeed have deep obligations to that person and what they did. It is our duty to honor the truth by seeking it among the mythic persona but also to understand how the myths came to be created and why our mythic figures have been important to our cultures. And then it comes back to honoring the audience by letting them in on the debate as you step out of character. Discuss fact and myth. They will appreciate this type of dialogue. Sometimes, the people we chose did x and y; or maybe one or the other; or did nothing at all like that. Sometimes, one historian will say they did x, and another historian will argue they did quite the opposite. The historical performer's task is to take a side and tell why you chose that explanation. History, after all, is not only the story of the decisions we have made but also the story of how we as a people, as cultures, and as scholars have chosen to explain those decisions. Our concept of obligations and honoring sets historical performers apart from other interpretive modes that have their own encoded sets of obligations.

Our commitment to authenticity is why historical performers try to provide clothing and props that possess the attributes of the real thing. Unless it is relevant to our script, the clothing that we wear on stage is worn, not crisp and new like a Halloween costume just out of the box. We let the audience know afterward if we are using or wearing a reproduction and how it is similar to and different than the "real" thing. We welcome questions about our clothing and props because they help tell the story not only of our historic figure but also of the choices that we have made based on our research and resources. Audiences appreciate both my vintage saddles and my handcrafted reproductions, but, let's face it, the vintage tack has more stories. Fakes are faux flags for the public. Likewise, language should respect the audience's desire for authenticity by using words and slang contemporary to the era you are portraying in your narrative and avoiding words and phrases unique to other times. Historical performers would no more give spurious or unvalidated information than we would use counterfeit or "fakey" items. We as historical performers have an obligation to seek authenticity, to create a setting free of dishonesty in which audiences can respond honestly, both cognitively and emotionally.

Speaking of emotion, honest passion for what we are doing is the key for doing really good historical performance. If you enjoy what you are doing the audience will be able to tell and will appreciate it. Many, many times I have had audience members comment afterward on the fact that they can tell that I really enjoy what I do. Passion is what hooks the audience. It is difficult to sustain a pretense of passion. Wendy Jones of the Minnesota Historical Society says that one of their challenges is that the actors they hire for museum theater are not loyal to the job. In a theater-rich community like Minneapolis-St. Paul, while there are never *enough* opportunities for actors, there are many plays and events. She understands a young actor wanting to leave the museum to take a role in a more professionally challenging play, one that might lead to yet another step up the ladder.

The problem is that, while the players may enjoy their job, it is not their passion. What if the center hired history majors who also had theater backgrounds or were interested in performance? What if they hired people who liked history and kids but did not want to be in a classroom nine months of the year? What if "actor" was dropped from the job requirement/description in favor of requiring a demonstration video of historical performance, storytelling, or speech giving? What if they had a crew so passionate about their work that they did not want to look elsewhere but only wanted to do more of the same, better, and for more audiences?

## PROVIDE OPPORTUNITIES FOR INITIAL TRAINING AND ONGOING LEARNING FOR PEOPLE OF ALL AGES AND BACKGROUNDS

A plan for growing historical performance must include training new historical performers and providing passionate performers the opportunity to continue to develop their knowledge and skills. This will include independent historical performers and organizations who want to grow their own troupes, including schools as well as communities, museums, and historic sites.

We have a model for introductory training. Twice a year beginning in 2002, and a few times before that, Ride into History has offered weekend historical performance workshops to the public. Typically, workshops draw people who know who they want to interpret, but we also have those who have seen us or someone else perform and want to, as we like to joke, "run away and join the circus" with us. In those cases we match them with a historic figure who fits their interests. By the afternoon of the second day everyone performs.[1] They know by then if they want to take it further at the time. In addition, we have trained volunteers at over twenty museums, historic sites, and communities.

But this general training in historical performance is not enough. Fledgling historical performers need to be part of a larger network that will encourage them to go beyond a basic knowledge of their figures to develop (1) a deeper specialized historical knowledge of their character's era and the environment that led to the decisions that changed history; (2) a broader historical context; (3) hands-on skills such as how to ride a horse, fly a plane, or start a fire with flint and steel; and (4) technical or academic knowledge such as Rachel Carson's understanding of oceanography.

Actors memorize a script, usually one that someone else has written. Historical performers, on the other hand, not only research, write, and learn a script but also must be ready to "be" their historic figure outside of the script. Historical performers do not just study for a test but also go beyond to become experts on their subject. They assume the mantle of authority. If they do not do so, they are not meeting the standards—they may pretend to have the mantle of authority, but eventually they are exposed as an emperor without clothes. Ever-increasing knowledge acquired with hands, body, and mind will provide not only more detail and greater accuracy but also greater confidence in answering questions.

The other side of this is that there is a need to encourage people with specialized knowledge to become historical performers. Every field, every endeavor, and every profession has its stories, and who better to learn the history and tell the stories than practitioners in those fields, endeavors, and professions? Steve Brosemer, for example, has a surveying company and is active in his professional association. When his national association met in Kansas, he decided he wanted to brag on his state while educating his peers by performing as John Calhoun, who not only hired young Abraham Lincoln but also surveyed Kansas Territory. Since then he has shared his performance with several groups, including youngsters.

Steve "John Calhoun" Brosemer has created his own venues. We know that organizations and sites need programming as much as performers need audiences. Potential presenting organizations planning for specific events or wanting to attract the public over the long run will want to develop troupes, whether they are hired or trained locally.

Creating troupes increases synergy and flexibility. As discussed in the last chapter, troupes increase programming possibilities. Individuals can be members of more than one troupe, such as a thematic troupe. Most Chautauquas are organized around a theme, such as the Boulder City, Nevada, "Shaping American Myth" 1998 Chautauqua that included P. T. Barnum, Buffalo Bill Cody, and Calamity Jane. Or the "Bright Dreams, Hard Times: America in the

Thirties" theme of the 2008–2010 Kansas-Nebraska Chautauqua. These use independent historical performers. Specific events can be celebrated with Chautauquas, such as Junction City, Kansas', sesquicentennial Youth Chautauqua that celebrated local history. Individual sites can have a troupe that reflects their history or collection.

I promised, beginning in the introduction, to address the need to involve young people in historical performance. It amazes me that more has not been done. Museum programming literature refers to youngsters as audiences for historical performance, or participants in living history demonstrations, not as historians in their own right. And too often children are described as a necessary evil with which the staff must cope (we need the numbers). There is a presumption that one must have special affective qualities to even lead a group of children through a museum. "No one should ever be assigned to conduct a school group who does not have a genuine love for children"[2] is far too limiting. In other words, must one have a "genuine love" for all adults to interpret for an adult group? Would "respect" not be a far better quality to seek in those who work with either or both children and adults?

Unfortunately, museums, like libraries, have in the past often been staffed by people who are lovers of things—artifacts and books—but not those who enjoyed sharing those "things" with groups of people. I am convinced, though, that adults can be trained to overcome their reluctance to work with youngsters and to actually enjoy sharing their knowledge and, more to the point, helping youngsters become experts.

Involving youngsters as researchers and interpreters of history brings new audiences to historic sites and museums, illuminates the participation of children in shaping and witnessing history throughout time, and inspires a sense of museum (and history!) ownership among the young. Involving youth in a deep way also provides opportunities to learn new skills and inspires increased interest in classroom history. It is great for youngsters and for historical organizations.

Ride into History has trained historical performers through arts camps and Youth Chautauqua Camps in conjunction with humanities-council-sponsored Chautauquas. We have also trained young docents in artifact-based programs, including one intergenerational program. The goal of these programs has been to take young people through the basic steps of the processes described in chapters 2 through 5 of this book: choosing a character, researching, creating a script, and putting together the "look" and performance. They do one performance for a scheduled event, and then the community can invite them to speak individually or in groups for future programs. I am also passionate about involving young people as historical performers.

Ride into History's youth programs began as Ann and I discussed how much we had learned through historical performance about ourselves as well as about history and our characters' roles in history. We kept going back to my experience as a youngster struggling with school, learning in different ways than my teachers had been taught to teach. And we talked about young adolescents and the struggle for identity. Would it not be powerful for youngsters—all youngsters, not just those who are chosen for the school play—to be given permission to be someone else, someone respected, someone maybe who struggled with similar issues but made decisions that led to being mentioned in history books? At the time it felt like a daring vision. We decided to make it happen.

We decided to teach teachers how to teach their youngsters to do what we do. To be both credible and confident that we knew what we were doing, we had to have a classroom experience. Ann had been on the Emporia State University (ESU) library school faculty where the average age of her students was thirty-six. My ESU students were as young as seventeen, but that was not going to give us the creds we needed. I did have one link with youngsters and the teachers college: I had recently taught a lab course that involved teachers teaching gifted students. And I stuffed as much educational theory into our minds and our proposal as we could absorb, and when we approached the ESU lab school, requesting that they contract with us to teach a ten-day intersession class, it went through without a hitch. We had eight girls, grades 3 through 6, with a wide range of interests and abilities, for thirty hours—ten half days. We gave them the scenario that they had been hired by a museum to entice more people to the museum with a historical performance program. They named their troupe, created a logo, and began helping each other find a historic figure and research.

Part of the exercise, because we did have all girls and this was the nineties, was a technology empowerment component. They created their scripts using laptops provided by the school (no Internet, though), and they videotaped each others' performances, everyone taking a turn at the camera. On the last day they performed for families and friends and handed out a program they had constructed themselves. It was very successful. We kept in touch with several of the girls who became involved in high school and college dramatics. Even Amy, who came in saying that she hated history but loved to act, was successful and continued to read and learn about Sacagawea. They gave us the confidence to continue. If our theories worked with them, they would work with other youngsters. The quickest way to impact youngsters was, we reasoned, through teacher workshops.

For about three years we gave teacher in-service workshops and conference presentations at every opportunity. We presented at teachers' social studies conferences, language arts conferences, middle school conferences, and even a conference for math teachers. We discussed, described, and, usually, modeled. We distributed several pages of handouts with the steps involved to incorporate historical performance in the classroom. The teachers loved it and gave us good evaluations, but few, we found when talking with them afterward, could imagine themselves stepping out of the role of teacher to model a first-person narrative for their students. Much as they wanted this experience for their students they were more concerned about maintaining authority. It just felt too risky for the students to see them in any role other than "teacher."

About this time we were juried onto the Kansas Arts Commission's roster and found that they would support school workshops. We evaluated my university teaching schedule and decided that, while we could not go to a school for a week, we could go for four Fridays. We worked with the language arts and social studies sixth through eighth grade in a rural school with kindergarten through eighth grades. Here the goal was to have each youngster perform for a class in the lower grades. There was some resistance from at least one of the teachers, who told us later that she had taught all of these middle school kids and could not imagine what they would have to offer her students. She admitted that she had been wrong. She was impressed with their ability to be in character, their confidence, and above all their knowledge—every one of them had knowledge. One of the middle schoolers spoke very rarely, having grown up letting her twin speak for her. But in character as Olympic gymnast Nadia Comaneci she had a lot to say. And there was an Albert Einstein who had me convinced, for a short time, that I could understand the theory of relativity. But my personal favorite was the girl who did Jackie Kennedy Onassis. She wanted to be Jackie Kennedy decorating the White House and looking glamorous. But we told her she had to do more research and learn about the historical context. That weekend she went with her grandparents to an antique store where they bought a box of 1960s news magazines. She became the school's expert on the Bay of Pigs. Throughout high school and college she continued to develop this interest, even majoring in political science. The reason we are telling you these stories is because the vision works. Self-esteem goes up. Children learn. No Child Left Behind has scuttled many such programs, leaving no time for children to develop expertise on subjects of their own choosing.

At another school, one student who was labeled as "slow" internalized enough about John Brown that whenever the abolitionist's name came up, all eyes went to this boy. He had the mantle of authority and shared his knowledge willingly.

In Pinedale, Wyoming, we worked with fourth-, sixth-, seventh-, and eighth-grade youngsters. We saw 186 students a day for five days. One of the most impressive results was when a severely learning disabled student became Confucius. His paraprofessional assistant worked with him, someone loaned him a kimono, and he walked on and delivered a tight, three-minute performance that he ticked off on his fingers. And he knew even more than he delivered just then, and more than the teachers knew he knew. He was one who was not expected to actually be able to present in front of a group. We watched his pride and, not coincidentally, his status among his peers, grow. Would that everyone had these experiences.

In fact, this was the school that we had first visited in the summer for a Calamity Jane performance at Museum of the Mountain Man and been asked to do an impromptu workshop for their environmental camp (see trail story 6.12). What impressed the science teacher was that we treated all of the youngsters alike (of course, we did not know them) and had the same expectations of them all. So when we worked patiently and persistently with the girl whose learning was challenged by fetal alcohol syndrome, and she triumphantly gave a short presentation based on her learning, as did all of the youngsters that afternoon, we were brought back the next school year. That child not only participated in the school workshop, but also she and her father were front and center at our evening performance.

When they find out that some of their heroes survived great challenges when young, it seems to help them through their own lives.

In addition to one-week residencies, we have also done two-month residencies involving four or five Fridays. We conduct a workshop with the youngsters, and the teachers help students work on their research or writing in between our meetings. Spread-out residencies encourage gradual learning, but sometimes there is dramatic change. I like to challenge students to behave physically as their person would behave—and throughout the day to think, "How would she have brushed her teeth, or would she?" "How would he get to work?" "What would she eat, where, and how?" One principal was amazed because the tenor of the lunchroom altered totally the day I challenged them to walk, talk, and eat as their person would. "They were so mature!" she said. We always hope that our model is adopted and adapted after we leave. One middle school social studies teacher has for many years now built her student assessments around historical performance instead of the dreaded term paper.

Usually we have children portraying adults, but we have been rethinking that, especially in museums and at historic sites. It is important that young people understand that people their ages have always been part of history, and that people of all ages are making history now with their decisions and actions.

Gaynor Kavanagh critiques open-air museums for staffing with younger adults only, "portray[ing] a life without children, old-age and the continuity of skills and working practices."[3] Children do, indeed, have a role to play in museum and historic site interpretation in more ways than one. They have energy and insights to offer, and, hopefully, a lifetime of commitment ahead of them. Conner Prairie involves youngsters age ten and up who "interact with the public in modern clothes, portray costumed characters, do behind the scenes work, [and] attend training sessions." They commit to work 120 hours between March and October, pass tests, and keep up their grades. At age sixteen they have the opportunity to graduate to paid employment.[4] Most organizations have not developed Conner Prairie's resources, but they can do a great deal with a small staff.

Our response has been "Night at the Museum" tours. Curators identify artifacts for which there is provenance, and young docents select one of the artifacts to make their own. They research the object and decide the best perspective from which to tell its story. We help them identify a child of about their own age if that is possible. At the Santa Fe Trail Center Museum in Larned, Kansas, two of the youngsters were adults, but the other eight were young people. The public signed up for tours, and in Larned we were sold out for all but the first tour, word of mouth working its magic. A "night watchman" greeted groups at the door and told them that the museum was closed but was overruled by a "vintage docent," one of the regular adult volunteers. She, while hoping to have the tour group all night to tell them everything she knew, was constantly interrupted by mannequins coming to life or children in period dress running up to the group to regale them about an object in the display. Everyone had a splendid time and expressed the desire for an ongoing program. We met our objectives of enhancing the experience of museum visitors, increasing youth involvement in the Trail Center, and bringing in new local visitors, especially young families.

We conducted a similar cross-generational camp in one community that involved simultaneous tours and two small museums. Flexibility is always the watchword, and, as at Larned, we handed the audience evaluations and found that almost everyone was surprised at how well the docents (of all ages in this case) did, that they learned about methodology as well as about artifacts (docents answered questions formally after the tours), and that they would return for another such tour.

Most of our youth camps have been sponsored by humanities councils. Sponsorship by the Kansas Arts Commission, however, let us do something a little bit differently with two camps. As usual the youngsters researched local people and prepared performances that were presented sequentially, but we grouped the performances thematically and had younger children as a chorus between the performances. The tiny community of Courtland had a thriving arts center. The theme for the entire event was, very loosely, transportation over the county's history. The surveyor had written about encountering herds of buffalo, so "buffalo" stampeded over the stage before he arrived and commented on them. Then there were horses pulling a stagecoach, a train, a plane, and, to tell you the truth, I do not remember what else, but it was a great deal of fun for all concerned, and the little ones looked forward to one day being able to do a "solo."

When the Kansas Humanities Council approached us about programming for the 2004 "Bleeding Kansas: Where the Civil War Began" sesquicentennial Chautauqua, we initially discussed something that would work for all middle school–aged children, something that would last for several days but could be attended by drop-ins. While we all got quite creative, everything was for, not by and with, the youngsters, and we went back to versions of what we knew best: the model of children choosing a local figure to portray, having adult help to research that person, and then presenting their findings as a first-person narrative. We were very pleased that they were able to present on the Chautauqua stage just before the adult Chautauquans. It was so successful that we have done Youth Chautauqua Camps every summer since in conjunction with Great Plains Chautauqua in Kansas (2005–2007), Great Plains Chautauqua in Nebraska (2007), or the Kansas-Nebraska Chautauqua (2008–2010).

In 2005, Fort Caspar Museum and Historic Site had us conduct a weeklong workshop with youngsters (see trail story 8.1). We met at Casper College because the museum did not yet have a classroom; meeting in adult space tells young people that what they are doing is important, and we had ready access to college librarian/archivist Kevin Anderson, who enthralled the young people with stories about exploding photo negatives and had newsprint crumble before their eyes. They felt very professional when they donned white gloves to examine documents and photos, which played into our issuing them pencils (not pens) to use with their historians' toolkits. The youngsters performed on the last day, and we performed afterward. It was a different take on the museum's annual "Chautauqua Festival" tradition. We are scheduled to return soon, adding an artifact component.

> ## A Trail Story
>
> ### 8.1. TRUST THE PROCESS
>
> Fort Caspar Museum and Historic Site's young historians were in dress rehearsal shortly before they would cross the stage for an audience. Local television staff members wanted to tape one of us and two of the youngsters. Ann had to handle this because I was clipping microphones to youngsters. She told me that she was really in a panic: which youngsters should she pick? Those at the first of the alphabet had been our more consistently strong performers, and we knew they would sing the program's praises to the media, but they were either onstage or in the wings. Logistically, it made sense to select the last two youngsters, but one of them had had a complete "I can't do this" meltdown only a few days before. Ann and his older sister had really had to work to calm him down. What would he say if asked if he had enjoyed the workshop? And then she thought how on day one we had discussed how we were all colleagues, working together on this project, and how all of these youngsters had claimed the title of historian/researcher/scriptwriter/actor. All had worked hard to be ready to share history's stories. It should, therefore, make no difference which ones were interviewed. Any part could represent the whole and do just fine. And so it was. Just fine.

We distribute a printed program the evening of the youth performance. In addition to having a color photo of the group in the front, and a list of the young performers and whose stories they are telling, we ask that the community do two things: first, continue to connect the young researchers with information about their historic figures, and, second, use them as a resource—ask them as small groups or individuals to share what they have learned with civic and other organizations. The response to this last is usually surprise (this isn't the end, their final product?) followed by delight—I can see the wheels turning in the minds of program chairs. And, indeed, we have heard about both happening. One girl wrote to us, ecstatic because she found out that her great-grandmother had known the person she portrayed, that they had shared a rowboat ride across a river. This made her progenitor suddenly as alive to her as her historic figure. And children have presented at a wide variety of meetings, which keeps them connected as well as learning.

Historical performers combine historical knowledge and artistic skills. Can the skills be learned? As much as to one's ability. If anyone had told me twenty years ago that I would become an award-winning artist, I would have laughed. I could not imagine "artist" as part of my identity. Of course, my understanding of art was pretty narrow at the time. Aside from Charlie Russell,[5] it just wasn't something I had thought about. I just thought about history and getting history's overlooked stories to people.

Who determines ability? When we talked about Pinedale's young people, we mentioned that with high expectations everyone succeeded, but this is also true of adults. In August of 2008, Ann Birney and I met for the first two of four days with Leavenworth County, Kansas, people who were willing to at least consider telling local stories, in character, at the county courthouse open house four months thence. Introductions involved their names and whom they thought they might portray. Lovella Martin told a moving story. She really wanted to become Viola Hannah, the first black teacher to teach in a white school as Leavenworth prepared for integration. Lovella said, however, that she had had brain surgery and had several learning disabilities. Memorization was difficult. Her presentation style was painful to watch: she looked deep into her mind to find her thought, translate it into language, and then go back for the next thought. Several people who were close to her had told her she could not do it, that theater was too demanding for her abilities. I told her, though, that we would work with her as long as she felt good about her accomplishments. She participated in all of the activities. A colleague (Mary Ward/Mother Xavier Ross, mentioned earlier) took Martin under her wing during the months between the workshop and the dress rehearsal. They interviewed Ms. Hannah together, wrote the script, and practiced. There was more than one person who was very nervous the afternoon and evening of the three series of performances. Lovella Martin, though, used her focus points and had enough confidence that when her clip-on microphone fell to the ground, she handled even that with aplomb, speaking without it and then picking it up on her way off the stage—to great applause by an appreciative audience, one member of which Ann heard say, "It's about time people heard about that." The audience was patient, in part because many of them remembered Ms. Hannah, and they appreciated Lovella Martin for telling them the untold story of triumph against personal and institutional racism.

Know yourself—how badly do you want to do historical performance? Why? What are your skills? Can you find someone to portray with whom you share some basic characteristics? Are you bringing a local story that no one else is telling, and will people be willing to overlook distractions inherent to your performance in order to hear that story? As Amelia Earhart said, "Never do things others will do if there are things that others will not or cannot do."

## CREATE OPPORTUNITIES FOR PEOPLE TO SEE HISTORICAL PERFORMANCES

There are endless possibilities for historical performance events. Showcases are the traditional means for performers to introduce their product to presenters, and we would benefit from more opportunities for presenters to "shop" for historical performers. Typically, showcases last about two hours with a sample performance lasting about fifteen minutes. The Kansas Alliance of Professional Historical Performers has partnered with the Kansas Sampler Foundation to create an unusual showcase. Alliance members take turns showcasing for most of two days during the annual festival, which is designed to introduce visitors to Kansas sights and products.

---

**A Trail Story**

### 8.2. OUR SHORTEST WORKSHOP EVER

In chapter 6 I cautioned historical performers to think twice before turning down a booking just because it is something you have never done before. Topeka-Shawnee County Public Library challenged us to create a one hour and ten minute workshop and present it twice as one of the choices for their staff in-service day. We did it and it was great fun. We also distributed the two-day workshop schedule: who knows, maybe someone will want more! Here's what we did:

5 min. Introduction (model)
4 min. How to Choose a Character
3 min. Go Find Yourself Using the Y.A. Collection
1 min. Cacophony: Introduce Yourself in Character to the Group
13 min. Fill Out "One-Day First-Person Narrative"
5 min. Tell Someone about Yourself (Dyads)
10 min. Acting Exercise—Doing It without Words
30 min. Perform What You Learned
4 min. Where from Here?
Fond Farewells!

Traditionally, historical performances have been seen at annual meetings and special events at museums, historic sites, libraries, and even soil conservation districts and Flying Farmers. And, of course, historical performers are featured in theaters and auditoriums. But what about historical performance as the anchor for a tourism campaign, a direct contribution to economic development outside major history organizations? As cultural organizations are scrambling to prove their financial value to governmental entities, it is important to be able to demonstrate a direct correlation between history and dollars. A statewide or regional project involving partnerships between museums and historic sites, convention and visitor bureaus, and professional historical performers would advertise that every day, all day, of a designated week (realistically from Saturday through the next Sunday during the summer), museums across the state or region (such as the Freedoms Frontier National Heritage Area) will have costumed performed history interpretation, including not only historical performance but also reenactments, living history demonstrations, and museum theater. In Kansas, the project could be called History Comes Alive in Kansas! Week.

Preparation for the event would help museums and historic sites incorporate history performance into their programming on an ongoing basis, taking even small museums to the next level, that of active rather than static interpretation. One week every year smaller museums would focus their efforts on outside visitors. Visitors could come to a region during the designated week and visit a large number of sites in the period, knowing that they did not have to worry about a detailed schedule—they could go from delightful site to fascinating museum, and they would encounter during that week a rich diversity of costumed interpretation: historical performance, living history, reenactments, and museum theater (see figure 1.1).

Transforming Chautauqua is another possibility for providing more opportunities for performers and audiences to find each other. Reconsidering Chautauqua might seem like a strange request, coming so soon after a chapter in which I extolled the possibilities of Chautauqua. What is now called Chautauqua ideally adopts all of the principles and best practices of historical performance—authenticity of the look and a stringent standard for storytelling being in some cases the last frontiers. However, much as I love Chautauqua, I have come to the realization that we need to reconsider the use of the word "Chautauqua."

Chautauqua as a brand has had very limited success. It is a fine word, but, let's face it, it does not encourage sightreading, nor does it cognitively resonate with anyone who has not had direct experience with a Chautauqua. They may picnic in a Chautauqua Park, but they do not know the origins of the name. Even among denizens of Chautauqua County, Kansas, nay, even among those who live in the town of Chautauqua in Chautauqua County, Kansas, there are few who know the origins of the name.

As mentioned in trail story 1.3, some people, ironically, associate "secular humanities" Chautauquas with religious tent revivals because the image of the revival is, if not ubiquitous, much more common than that of Chautauqua. A quick search of the Internet provides the names of companies that make tents specifically for religious revivals. In fact, the Wikipedia article on "tent revival" (defined as "a gathering of Christian worshipers in a tent erected specifically for revival meetings, healing crusades, and church rallies") includes "Chautauqua" as its only link. While this might be because of Chautauqua's beginnings as a church institution, the association emphasizes the confusion inherent with today's Chautauqua.

The bottom line is that while it never occurred to me that the two might be confused, this association with religious revivals explains not only the man in trail story 1.3 but also why communities have presumed that the Kansas Humanities Council Chautauqua would want religious music as the pre-Chautauqua entertainment. One very small community had four churches, and each took a night of the Chautauqua to "entertain." This built the audience but sent a confusing message. Damage control was attempted by stipulating that the music not be overtly denominational and there be no preaching or testimonials, which is a challenge for some folks. It's like saying, sing your heart out, but don't get worked up about it.

In very small towns the churches often have the only meeting rooms other than schools, so shoulder programming such as the lectures usually given by Chautauquans in the mornings and afternoons might be associated with specific denominations. The 2008–2010 Kansas-Nebraska Chautauqua includes radio evangelist Aimee Semple McPherson, portrayed by scholar Tonia Compton, which makes great sense for the 1930s theme, but is another reason for people in communities who are familiar with tent revivals to be confused when they are told that it is not about religion—just the idea of religion.[6] I have not conducted a formal poll, but it seems that more people know of tent revivals than Chautauquas, even if it is from such popular culture classics as the Elmer Gantry film.

It is a grand cause, to "revive" Chautauqua and provide opportunities for communities to set aside a block of time to discuss important ideas. But maybe we are discouraging attendance by using a word with which people are not familiar and an image that people associate with an altogether different activity.

We have to do a lot of education before we can even get them under the tent. Some communities often stage or bring in Chautauquas, so for them the opportunity to educate about Chautauqua is ongoing. That seems, however, to be the exception.

I humbly suggest, therefore, that we ditch the word Chautauqua. I prefer the term History Alive! Festival. We could use Chautauqua in the subtitle, for instance, "History Comes Alive in the Park: A Chautauqua About the Dirty Thirties," or "History under the Big Tent: Chautauqua for Everyone." But then we lose the opportunity to be more descriptive about content. We are taking up time, space, and attention with a long, albeit beautiful, empty-to-most-people word. Leave "Chautauqua" for particular places, the institute at Chautauqua Lake in New York, for instance. Reframing Chautauqua under a different name and expecting accuracy in all aspects of the presentation, including the look, will invigorate a venerable institution created by passionate individuals.

Another opportunity that we will have is in the schools. Educators have been lamenting that, under the federal No Child Left Behind program, testing has gobbled up time that used to be available for the arts. Historical performers should be ready to offer No School Left Behind programs, including curriculum material that correlates with standards.

## CREATE A STRUCTURE TO SUPPORT THE ABOVE

To ensure the recognition of standards, to provide a wide variety of training opportunities, and to encourage the widespread availability of historical performance, we will need to organize. We will need a strong Internet presence, partnerships with other cultural and educational organizations, and physical space in which to provide workshops and showcase historical performance. In short, we will need an organization, a Center for Historical Performance.

The Center for Historical Performance will identify, create, and communicate opportunities for historical performers to learn—and to perform. In addition, it will evaluate programming for both efficacy and efficiency, and disseminate its findings to performers, trainers, and presenters.

We have done the conceptual work, identifying the characteristics that make historical performance unique among the various forms of performed history interpretation. We have determined that best practices for historical performance include accurate text and look, knowledge far beyond that required for a monologue, and the ability to hold an audience by sharing that knowledge in a compelling manner. Now we need a Center for Historical Performance, or perhaps several regional organizations, to sustain all that we have done and all that we can do. And do you know what? We can do it!

---

## A PLAN FOR DEVELOPING
## HISTORICAL PERFORMANCE

- Create a deep, juried roster of historical performers
- Identify standards of professional historical performance
- Provide ongoing training
- Identify learning opportunities for historical performers
- Grow historical performers through youth troupes
- Encourage people to develop specialized knowledge
- Encourage people with specialized knowledge
- Celebrate abilities and passions
- Create troupes for specific events and individual sites
- Create showcases for historical performance
- Create a "No School Left Unserved" program
- Model a tourism event that saturates a geographic area
- Transform "Chautauqua" to History Alive! Festivals
- Create and maintain a space for workshops and showcases
- Have a strong Internet presence
- Network with cultural and educational organizations
- Encourage dreams
- Establish the Center for Historical Performance, Inc., to coordinate the above
- Provide for the sustainability of the above

---

I know that we can do it because Ride into History, Ride into History Cultural and Educational Project, Inc., and the Kansas Alliance of Professional Historical Performers have a start on much of what I have outlined here. We have formed organizations. We have a workshop/studio space in Admire. We are taking customized workshops to sites as well as providing workshops for the public. Thanks to a Kansas Department of Commerce grant we have a website, at http://www.historicperformance.com/, which describes many of the standards for professional performers outlined here and provides a juried roster. You and I are able to share our vision with others, individuals and foundations. We can create the compelling narratives that will help them imagine being part of this dream of ours, this dream to make historical performance available to more audiences. Imagine the support, long-term and committed, that can be gained for cultural organizations if more people were doing and viewing historical performance!

Yes, we can do this. Together, we can tell history's stories to the world.

## NOTES

1. Workshop schedules that outline activities are at http://www.historicperform ance.com/.

2. William T. Alderson and Shirley Payne Low, *Interpretation of Historic Sites*, 2nd rev. ed. (Walnut Creek, Calif.: AltaMira Press, 1996), 113.

3. Gaynor Kavanagh, *History Curatorship* (Washington, D.C.: Smithsonian Institution Press, 1990), 147.

4. Informal discussion with interpreters, Conner Prairie, August 9, 2007; Conner Prairie Interactive History Park, "Youth Volunteers," at http://www.connerprairie .org/join-and-support/volunteer.aspx (accessed February 9, 2009).

5. There may be one or two of you who don't know that Charlie Russell is probably the number one Western artist ever, although I am also passionate about nineteenth-century Swiss artist/visitor Karl Bodmer for his portraits of tribal people. The Joslyn Art Museum copublished its phenomenal collection of Bodmer's watercolors in Karl Bodmer, David C. Hunt, and Marsha V. Gallagher, *Karl Bodmer's America* (Lincoln: University of Nebraska Press, 1984).

6. Disclosure: Ride into History has a contract with the three-year National Endowment for the Humanities–funded Kansas-Nebraska Chautauqua.

# Appendix A

## *How to Create a First-Person Narrative*

- Decide on your time period or theme.
- Find someone you will enjoy who lived an interesting life.
- Make a commitment to perform on a given date.
- While you work, wear an article of clothing that you will wear in character.
- Surround yourself with pictures of your character and setting.
- Allow time to revise and to rehearse.
- Look for both primary and secondary sources.
- Write (take notes, scribble thoughts) as you research.
- Write in first person, using active voice.
- Ask questions of your sources.
- Keep a list of where you found your information.
- Keep a list of questions for which you have not found answers.
- Have someone interview you in character to find out what you don't know.
- Select stories based on her or his relationship to national, regional, and local events.
- Choose stories that tell what your character is best known for.
- Tell stories with conflicts that illustrate personality, and help explain motivation for decision making.

- Think constantly about how your character felt.
- Write and talk about sights, sounds, tastes, and smells.
- Use language appropriate for the time but that your audience will understand.
- Listen to people talk: how stories are not always linear, how people raise and lower their voices with emotion, and how people use their bodies, their hands, and their faces while talking.
- Write your audience into your script.

# Appendix B

## *Structuring the First-Person Narrative Script*

| Narrative Section | Example from Amelia Earhart Script |
|---|---|
| Entrance | Runs in, "late" |
| Introduction—establishes setting, audience's role | "I'm Amelia Earhart, and it's April 14, 1937, so this is [town], so I am at the right place at the right time . . ." |
| Transition to first story | "Everyone asks about my first flight . . ." |
| First story | Sled story—AE as risk-taker, conflict with gendered rules for behavior |
| Transition to second story | "But, of course, that flight had nothing to do with aeroplanes . . ." |
| Second Story | Toronto, the war, "That plane spoke to me" passion, altruism |
| Transition to third story | "It wasn't until after the war . . ." |
| Third story | First flight, learning to fly, focus, aesthetics |
| Transition to fourth story | ". . . Mother and Pidge and I moved to Boston" |
| Fourth story | First woman to fly across the Atlantic Organized, sense of humor |

| Transition to fifth story | "I promised myself that one day I would fly by myself across that ocean . . ." |
| --- | --- |
| Fifth story | Solo across the Atlantic; it all comes together here |
| Wrap-up, transition to discussion | "I feel I have one last record-setting flight left in me . . ." "But I promised to take your questions . . ." |
| Questions in character | "Who has a question for me?" |
| Questions as scholar | [take off jacket] "My name really is . . ." |
| Exit | "I see coffee at the back of the room. I want to thank the _____ for inviting me. I will be glad to talk with anyone who wants to explore this further." |

© Ann Birney, Ride into History, 2002

# Appendix C
## *Setting and Clothing*

Your historic figure's occupation(s):

Year from which you will be speaking:

Context/physical location from which you will be speaking (a picnic, an encampment before a battle, a press conference, concerned friends at home?):

| Categories of Clothing Items | Description | Source |
|---|---|---|
| Head covering | | |
| Shirt/blouse/ waist/dress | | |
| Vest/apron | | |
| Jacket | | |
| Suspenders/belt | | |
| Jewelry/necktie | | |
| Pants/skirt | | |
| Socks | | |
| Shoes/boots/ foot covering | | |

# Appendix D
## *Sample Contract*

The parties to the Agreement are [troupe] (hereinafter Producer) and [organization] (hereinafter Presenter).

For good and valuable consideration, the parties hereto agree:

1. The Presenter hires the Producer to provide one performance of [title] in [specific location and city, state] at [performance and setup times] on [date].
2. The performance responsibilities shall be:
   • [troupe] will provide [performer] as [title role] and [publicity material, transportation, add-ons].
   • [organization name] will provide [performance space, seating for audience, sound, lodging, transportation].
3. The Producer will receive compensation of [total fee] (travel expense included) payable immediately following the performance.
4. The Producer shall use their best efforts and their entire time to fulfill the job responsibilities as listed above.
5. In the event of cancellation the canceling party will pay the other party half of the total fee.
6. Performances may be photographed and portions video- or audiotaped but not recorded in their entirety.
7. These services will be available to all persons without regard to age, ancestry, color, creed, disability, national origin, race, religion, sex, or sexual orientation.

8. In the event that either party must violate any particulars of this Agreement, then, at the option of the other party, this Agreement shall be terminated and a new agreement negotiated.

Executed as a sealed document this _____ day of _____, 20__ .

Presenter _____
(Authorized Representative)
Producer _____

Please sign, make a copy, and return this contract to: [your name and address]

Presenter's Representative: [presenter's name and address]

# Appendix E
## *Sample Invoice*

Invoice # [start with 101]
Invoice Date: [when you send contract]

Contracted by: [presenting organization]

For: [performance]
Date of Program:

Amount: $_____
Due: immediately following the program

Pay to: [troupe name]
FEIN: [federal employer identification number followed by how you are registered with the IRS if your troupe uses a doing-business-as-name—we are Birney-Thierer Partnership dba Ride into History]
CCR DUNS # [if you want to work for the federal government, this is helpful and free]

Thank you!
[and put your contact information here or on your letterhead]

# Appendix F
## *Youth Registration Forms*

Youth Registration Forms should include a space for

- [ ] Child's name
- [ ] Date of birth
- [ ] School attending
- [ ] Current grade level
- [ ] Parent/guardian name(s)
- [ ] Address
- [ ] Home phone, mobile phone, work phone
- [ ] E-mail address
- [ ] Emergency contact name and telephones
- [ ] Physician's name and telephone
- [ ] Food and medical allergies and other medical information of which the staff should be aware
- [ ] Building/information access concerns
- [ ] T-shirt size (indicate if size is child or adult)
- [ ] Permit to transport to research sites
- [ ] Permit for organization to use child's photograph in media releases, websites, videos
- [ ] Instructions for child to wait or walk after workshop, who will pick up
- [ ] Signature and date
- [ ] Where to send/take registration form
- [ ] Information on days, dates, and times
- [ ] How to get more information about the event

# Appendix G
## *Local Arrangements for Workshops*

**THE IDEAL LOCATION**
- Near/in library or museum (easy access to local history primary sources)
- Large meeting room with breakout space
- Tables (about three feet per participant; not a school desk)
- Blackboard, whiteboard, or flip charts and tape
- Noise tolerant
- Little ambient noise (no whines from ballasts going out on fluorescent lights, no roller coasters outside the door)

**IDENTIFY LOCAL HISTORY SOURCES**
- County history books
- Newspapers (on microfilm?)
- Archives
- Photographs
- Built environment
- Artifacts
- Elders who have good stories
- Youngsters who have heard stories from elders
- Whose—which individuals, what groups of people—stories haven't been told and should be told?

# Appendix H

## *Ride into History's Historical Performance Definitions*

**Artifacts.** Individual material culture objects from the past.

**Character.** A person portrayed in a play or first-person narrative.

**Composite character.** A fictional person created to represent many different people.

**Farb.** Derogatory term used by reenactors to describe someone whose garb and gear are not completely accurate.

**First-person narrative.** A story told from the perspective of an individual other than the storyteller/writer/performer (first person means the use of "I" or "we").

**Great wo/man history.** Tells the stories of leaders of large groups of people and suggests that the better characteristics of that individual are shared by his or her followers.

**Historical anachronism.** A "glitch" when something from a future time ("chron") is superimposed on an earlier time—an impossible ("ana") combination of ideas or objects.

**Historical context.** Other events that were happening at the same time as the event at which we are looking.

**Historical mindedness.** An awareness of what happened when, which enables us to avoid historical anachronisms.

**Historical performance.** Direct-address first-person narrative in correct clothing followed by taking questions in character and as the scholar.

**Historic figure.** A particular person who lived in the past.

**History.** The story of the decisions we have made over time, and the story of how we have explained those decisions.

**Living history.** Carrying out and usually demonstrating daily activities as closely as possible to the manner in which they were pursued at a designated time and place in the past.

**Material culture.** Physical objects surrounding us that are made or shaped by humans.

**Monologue.** A one-person performance (first-person narratives are a type of monologue).

**Persona.** The identity, whether real or fictional, assumed by an individual participating in a reenactment.

**Popular culture.** Entertainment (music, art, video, etc.) consumed by large groups of people.

**Primary source.** Information coded (written, photographed, or recorded in some way) at the time of a particular event or later by someone who was a participant in the event.

**Props (properties).** Items of material culture used in a play or other dramatic performance.

**Reenacting.** "Play acting" a particular recorded event in history such as a battle, the signing of an important document, or a fur traders' rendezvous.

**Secondary source.** Information recorded during or after an event by someone who was not a witness to the event.

**Social history.** The daily life of categories, or groups, of people.

# Bibliography

**BOOKS AND ARTICLES**

[Advertisement] *Architectural Digest* 66, no. 2 (February 2009): [29].

Aikman, Duncan. "Life and Adventures of Calamity Jane, by Herself." In *Calamity Jane and the Lady Wildcats*, 351–62. Lincoln: University of Nebraska Press, 1987.

Albers, Everett. "Reflections on Doing Chautauqua." Handout at Kansas Humanities Council History Alive! scholar training session, 1993.

Alderson, William T., and Shirley Payne Low. *Interpretation of Historic Sites*. 2nd rev. ed. Walnut Creek, Calif.: AltaMira Press, 1996.

American Dental Association. "Provider Taxonomy Codes," at http://www.ada.org/prof/resources/topics/topics_npi_taxonomy.pdf (accessed January 23, 2009).

Anderson, Jay. *A Living History Reader: Museums*. Vols. 1 and 2. Nashville: American Association for State and Local History, 1991.

———. *Time Machines: The World of Living History*. Nashville: American Association for State and Local History, 1984.

Becker, Carl. "Everyman His Own Historian." *American Historical Review* 37, no. 2 (January 1932): 221–36.

Begley, Sharon. "Living Hand to Mouth." *Newsweek*, November 2, 1998, 89.

Biles, Jan. "Going with Life's Flips and Turns: Auburn Woman Nannied for Builder of Lindbergh's The Spirit of St. Louis." *Topeka Capital-Journal*, December 26, 2006, at http://www.cjonline.com/stories/122606/kan_burger.shtml (accessed April 17, 2009).

Blanton, De Anne, and Lauren M. Cook. *They Fought Like Demons: Women Soldiers in the Civil War*. Baton Rouge: Louisiana State University Press, 2002.

Blum, Stella, ed. *Everyday Fashions of the Thirties: As Pictured in Sears and Other Catalogs*. New York: Dover Publications, 1986.

———. *Everyday Fashions of the Twenties: As Pictured in Sears and Other Catalogs*. New York: Dover Publications, 1981.

Bodmer, Karl, David C. Hunt, and Marsha V. Gallagher. *Karl Bodmer's America*. Lincoln: University of Nebraska Press, 1984.

Bridal, Tessa. *Exploring Museum Theatre*. Walnut Creek, Calif.: AltaMira Press, 2004.

Canning, Charlotte M. *The Most American Thing in America: Circuit Chautauqua as Performance*. Iowa City: University of Iowa Press, 2005.

Cather, Willa. *My Antonia*. Boston: Houghton Mifflin, 1926.

———. *O Pioneers!* Boston: Houghton Mifflin, 1933.

*Chautauqua on the Great Plains*. [Bismarck, N.Dak.]: Great Plains Chautauqua Society, 1992.

Clark, Barbara. *Optimizing Learning: The Integrative Education Model in the Classroom*. Columbus, Ohio: Merrill, 1986.

Compton, Ralph. Western series. New York: Signet, 1992–.

Conner Prairie Interactive History Park. "Youth Volunteers," at http://www .connerprairie.org/join-and-support/volunteer.aspx (accessed February 9, 2009).

Corson, Barbara. "Disaster Prevention: Planning a Livestock Event for Maximum Safety." *ALHFAM Bulletin* 38, no. 3 (Fall 2008).

Davol, Ralph. *A Handbook of American Pageantry*. Taunton, Mass.: Davol Publishing, 1914.

Druesedow, Jean L., ed. *Men's Fashion Illustrations from the Turn of the Century, by Jno. J. Mitchell Company*. New York: Dover Publications, 1990.

Eickhoff, Diane. *Revolutionary Heart: The Life of Clarina Nichols and the Pioneering Crusade for Women's Rights*. Kansas City: Quindaro Press, 2006.

Fletchall, Ann. "The Spectacle of the Festival." Unpublished paper in author's possession, acquired January 26, 2009.

Frein, George H. "Historical Characterization: Some Ideas for Scholars." Handout from a Chautauqua training session.

———. "Reflections on Doing Chautauqua." Handout from a Chautauqua training session.

Fry, Steve. "Topeka Teens Chalk Up Wins at History Contest." *Topeka Capital-Journal*, June 15, 2001, at http://www.cjonline.com/stories/061501/com_history.shtml (accessed February 9, 2009).

Gardner, Howard. *Multiple Intelligences: New Horizons*. Rev. ed. New York: Basic Books, 2006.

Garrison, Webb, with Cheryl Garrison. *The Encyclopedia of Civil War Usage: An Illustrated Compendium of the Everyday Language of Soldiers and Civilians.* Nashville: Cumberland House, 2001.

Gergen, Mary McCanney, ed. *Feminist Thought and the Structure of Knowledge.* New York: New York University Press, 1988.

Goldstein, Jeri. *How to Be Your Own Booking Agent.* Rev. 2nd ed. Charlottesville, Va.: New Music Times, 2006.

Goodwin, Doris Kearns. *Team of Rivals: The Political Genius of Abraham Lincoln.* New York: Simon & Schuster, 2005.

Hadden, R. Lee. *Reliving the Civil War: A Reenactor's Handbook.* Mechanicsburg, Pa.: Stackpole Books, 1996.

Haraway, Donna. "The Biological Enterprise: Sex, Mind, and Profit from Human Engineering to Sociobiology." *Radical History Review* 20 (1979): 206–37.

Harding, Sandra. *The Science Question in Feminism.* Ithaca, N.Y.: Cornell University Press, 1986.

Hickok, Jane Cannary. *Calamity Jane's Letters to Her Daughter.* San Lorenzo, Calif.: Shameless Hussy Press, 1976.

Horwitz, Tony. *Confederates in the Attic: Dispatches from the Unfinished Civil War.* New York: Pantheon Books, 1998.

Hubbard, Ruth. "Some Thoughts about the Masculinity of the Natural Sciences." In *Feminist Thought and the Structure of Knowledge,* ed. Mary McCanney Gergen, 1–15. New York: New York University Press, 1988.

Hughes, Catherine. *Museum Theatre: Communicating with Visitors through Drama.* Portsmouth, N.H.: Heinemann, 1998.

Jenkinson, Clay. "Making Hay while the Sun Shines in Reno," at http://nevada humanities.org/programs/chautauqua/clay-jenkinson-article (accessed February 8, 2009).

———. *The Thomas Jefferson Hour,* at http://www.jeffersonhour.org/ (accessed January 26, 2009).

Jones, Dale. "Theater 101 for Historical Interpretation." *AASLH Technical Leaflet,* no. 227, included in *History News* 59, no. 3 (Summer 2004): 1–8.

Kavanagh, Gaynor. *History Curatorship.* Washington, D.C.: Smithsonian Institution Press, 1990.

Keller, Evelyn Fox. *Reflections on Gender and Society.* New Haven, Conn.: Yale University Press, 1985.

Kornfeld, Eve. "History and the Humanities: The Politics of Objectivity and the Promise of Subjectivity." *New England Journal of History* 51, no. 3 (Winter 1995): 44–55.

LeCount, Chuck. "Travel and Animal Programs." *ALHFAM Bulletin* 38, no. 3 (Fall 2008).

Living History Farms. *Site Manual 1900 Farm.* Urbandale, Iowa [n.d., unpaginated]. Donated by LHF, in author's possession.

Livo, Norma J., and Sandra A. Rietz. *Storytelling: Process and Practice.* Littleton, Colo.: Libraries Unlimited, 1986.

Loewen, James W. *Lies My Teacher Told Me: Everything Your American History Textbook Got Wrong.* New York: New Press, 1995.

Mason, Harriet. *The Power of Storytelling: A Step-by-Step Guide to Dramatic Learning in K–12.* Thousand Oaks, Calif.: Corwin Press, 1996.

McDowell, W. H. *Historical Research: A Guide for Writers of Dissertations, Theses, Articles, and Books.* Upper Saddle River, N.J.: Longman, 2002.

Meyer, Eugene L. "The Soldier Left a Portrait and Her Eyewitness Account." *Smithsonian* 24, no. 10 (January 1994): 96–104.

Morsella, Ezequiel, and Robert M. Krauss. "The Role of Gestures in Spatial Working Memory and Speech." *American Journal of Psychology* 117 (2004): 411–24.

Novick, Peter. *That Noble Dream: The "Objectivity Question" and the American Historical Profession.* Cambridge: Cambridge University Press, 1988.

Olian, JoAnne, ed. *Everyday Fashions: 1909–1920, as Pictured in Sears Catalogs.* New York: Dover Publications, 1995.

———. *Everyday Fashions of the Forties: As Pictured in Sears Catalogs.* New York: Dover Publications, 1992.

Peers, Laura. *Playing Ourselves: Interpreting Native Histories at Historic Reconstructions.* Lanham, Md.: AltaMira Press, 2004.

Pennington, Loren. *The Kansas Chautauqua: Understanding America: Land, Peoples, and Culture: Profiles.* Emporia: Kansas Committee for the Humanities and Affiliates, 1989.

"Plagiarism." *All Things Considered,* National Public Radio, January 10, 2002, at http://www.npr.org/templates/story/story.php?storyId=1136141 (accessed January 23, 2009).

Plotz, David. "The Plagiarist: Why Stephen Ambrose Is a Vampire." *Slate,* January 11, 2002, at http://www.slate.com/toolbar.aspx?action=print&id=2060618 (accessed February 9, 2009).

Rauscher, Frances H., Robert M. Krauss, and Yihsiu Chen. "Gesture, Speech, and Lexical Access: The Role of Lexical Movements in Speech Production." *Psychological Science* 7 (1996): 226–31.

Roach, Joyce Gibson. *The Cowgirls.* Denton: University of North Texas Press, 1977.

Robertshaw, Andrew. "From Houses into Homes: One Approach to Live Interpretation." *Social History in Museums* 19 (1992): 14–20, at http://www.hrw.ndo.co.uk/index1.htm (accessed January 31, 2009).

Roth, Stacy F. *Past into Present: Effective Techniques for First-Person Historical Interpretation.* Chapel Hill: University of North Carolina Press, 1998.

Sachatello-Sawyer, Bonnie, et al. *Adult Museum Programs: Designing Meaningful Experiences.* Walnut Creek, Calif.: AltaMira Press, 2002.

"Samuel Taylor Coleridge: Biographia Literaria (1817)," chapter XIV, at http://www .english.upenn.edu/~mgamer/Extexts/biographia.html (accessed February 8, 2009).

Scott, Joan Wallach. *Gender and the Politics of History.* New York: Columbia University Press, 1988.

Severa, Joan L. *Dressed for the Photographer: Ordinary Americans and Fashion, 1840–1900.* Kent, Ohio: Kent State University Press, 1997.

Shagan, Rena. *Booking and Tour Management for the Performing Arts.* New York: Allworth Press, 1996.

Smith, Randy D. "The Historical Dramatic Monologue: Creating the One-Character Reenactment Presentation." *Muzzleloader* (May/June 2002): 71–74.

Sorg, Eric. *Buffalo Bill: Myth and Reality.* Santa Fe, N.Mex.: Ancient City Press, 1998.

Steingold, Fred S. *Legal Guide for Starting and Running a Small Business.* Berkeley, Calif.: Nolo Press, 2009.

Swaim, Don. Interview with Fanny Flagg. CBS Radio Station, New York, October 6, 1987, at http://wiredforbooks.org/fannieflagg/index.htm (accessed February 9, 2009).

Thompson, Jenny. *War Games: Inside the World of 20th-Century War Reenactors.* Washington, D.C.: Smithsonian Books, 2004.

Tilden, Freeman. *Interpreting Our Heritage.* 3rd ed. Chapel Hill: University of North Carolina Press, 1977.

Turan, Kenneth. "French Thriller 'Tell No One' Gains Momentum in U.S." *Morning Edition* [audio], August 12, 2008, at http://www.npr.org/templates/story/story .php?storyId=93522536.

Wilhelm, Bob. "Fort Hays: Graveside Conversations." [News release], October 27, 2007.

Wilkening, Susie, and Erica Donnis. "Authenticity? It Means Everything." *History News* 63, no. 4 (Autumn 2008): 18–23.

Willett, C., and Phillis Cunnington. *The History of Underclothes.* New York: Dover Publications, 1992.

Wishart, David J. *Encyclopedia of the Great Plains.* Lincoln: University of Nebraska Press, 2004.

## OTHER MEDIA

### DVD/CD

*Buffalo Girls.* DVD. Los Angeles: Hallmark, 1995.

*Calamity Jane.* DVD. Burbank, Calif.: Warner Bros., 1953.

*Opening Doors to Great Guest Experiences.* DVD/CD. Fishers, Ind.: Conner Prairie, [n.d.].

**VHS/Video**

*Digging for Slavery: The Excavation of American Slave Sites.* BBC Films for the Humanities and Sciences, 1989.

**Websites**

American Frontier Reenactment Guild, at http://www.wheelerjobin.com/clients/afrg (accessed January 31, 2009).

"Chautaqua" at http://www.dakotaskyeducation.com/Chautauqua.htm (accessed July 4, 2009).

Chautauqua Institution, at http://www.ciweb.org/ (accessed January 31, 2009).

*Godey's Lady's Book,* at http://www.iath.virginia.edu/utc/sentimnt/gallgodyf.html (accessed April 21, 2009).

Kansas Alliance of Professional Historic Performers, at http://www.historic performance.com.

National Association for Interpretation. "Definitions Project," at http://www .definitionsproject.com/definitions/index.cfm (accessed February 9, 2009).

National Women's History Project. "Women's History Performers," at http://www .nwhp.org/whm/performers.php.

**Interviews**

Adams, Mike. Informal conversation with the author, Concordia, Kans., May 3, 2008.

Bubp, Ken. Interview at Conner Prairie, August 9, 2007, notes in author's possession.

Ellis, Rex. Interview at Colonial Williamsburg, 1993.

Fort Snelling, Minn. Informal discussions with interpreters, notes in author's possession.

Jones, Wendy. Interview at the Minnesota Historical Society, May 4, 2007, notes in author's possession.

Kansas Alliance of Professional Historic Performers. E-mail poll, July 2008, member website at http://www.historicperformance.com/.

Kelley, Nancy. Interview in Lawrence, Kans., December 20, 2008.

Pennington, Loren. Interview in Emporia, Kans., December 18, 2008.

Thatcher, Anna Marie, and Graham Thatcher of Periaktos Productions, 1998, notes from conference in author's possession; e-mail to author, August 9, 2008; see also http://www.periaktos.com/.

Watson, Doug. Conversation with the author, Plattsmouth, Neb., June 28, 2009.

# Index

# About the Author

Joyce M. Thierer has been on the Kansas Humanities Council's History Alive! roster since 1992 and on the Oklahoma and Nebraska humanities council rosters, all as Calamity Jane. She is the founding (1989) partner of the Ride into History historical performance touring troupe. Providing entertainment as well as the sound scholarship required by humanities councils, Ride into History has been repeatedly juried onto the Kansas Arts Commission's touring program and Mid-America Arts Alliance rosters.

Dr. Thierer's other programs include composite figures ranging from a farmer of the earth lodge peoples from about 1800 to a veteran of Bleeding Kansas and the Civil War. She has provided workshops for adults and children in a wide variety of settings, including weekend intensives for adults, daylong teacher in-services, and weeklong Youth Chautauqua Camps in conjunction with Chautauquas in Kansas, Wyoming, and Nebraska. She was recipient of a grant from the Kansas Department of Commerce's Travel and Tourism Division to enhance historic destinations through historical performance. She has made presentations concerning historical performance at National Council for Public History, Mountain Plains Museums Association, and Kansas Museums Association conferences.

Joyce Thierer also teaches public history (as well as American history, Kansas history, women of the West, and agricultural history) and supervises museum internships at Emporia [Kansas] State University. Her doctorate in American history is from Kansas State University.